A HISTORIE

—OF—

LONDON

AND

LONDONERS

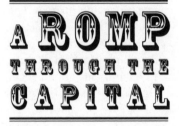

SEAN BORU

I dedicate this book to someone who has been very special to me for 29 years,
my wife Lesley Ann.
Lesley has been my pillar, and has looked after me in good times and bad, in sick-
ness and in health. Without her I would have gone under many times. We have a
unique relationship in the respect that not only are we man and wife, but we are
good soulmates as well. So, I dedicate this book to her.

First published 2009

The History Press
The Mill, Brimscombe Port
Stroud, Gloucestershire, GL5 2QG
www.thehistorypress.co.uk

© Sean Boru, 2009

The right of Sean Boru to be identified as the Author of this work has
been asserted in accordance with the Copyrights, Designs and Patents
Act 1988.

British Library Cataloguing in Publication Data.
A catalogue record for this book is available from the British Library.

ISBN 978 07524 4861 9

Typesetting and origination by The History Press
Printed in Great Britain

Cover illustration: St Paul's Cathedral in the nineteenth century.
(Illustrated London News)

CONTENTS

ACKNOWLEDGEMENTS

I would like to thank Jimmy White, who has been a wonderful friend, for his foreword. Special recognition should also be given to Peter Deacon who gave me my first job as a tour guide in 1997, when I started working for London Pride Tours. Peter was not only a great boss, but also a great teacher who gave me so much information and encouragement. Lastly I would like thank all the people I have worked with over the years in the tour business; there are far too many to mention individually but they know who they are.

FOREWORD

by Londoner Jimmy White MBE

I have always had a love for London: the past, the present and the London of the future. Being able to call myself a Londoner is a great honour and privilege. London stands for all that is British and is a wonderfully diverse city, a melting pot of culture, ambition and comradeship that has been forged over centuries by many nationalities. It is very exciting for me to be in a position whereby I can now inspire people from around the world, through snooker, to visit London and support this great capital.

This book about the history of London and its people is a wonderfully interesting one, in that it not only tells us about the way London and the people developed, it teaches us very subtly how to read the history for ourselves as we walk around. Who would have given Garlic Hill or Friday Street a second thought? Sean Boru has a wonderful manner about him as he tells us the answers to all the questions we have asked ourselves over the years, as we travel around London. When I next venture into Eastcheape I will quietly smile as I see the street names, and imagine the activity that went on there in the past; buying a chicken in Poultry, shoes in Leather Lane and cures for aliments in Apothecary Street. I will know in future that Shoe Lane is named after a shoe-shaped field and that Piccadilly is named after lavender-picking. Sean's stories about the evolution of the capital are wonderful, as are his amusing and anecdotal paragraphs on the sewage system, the law-makers and the English language.

Sean Boru was once a guide in London, and the capital lost a great advocator when he turned to writing instead of the spoken word. However, if his written tour is as fascinating as his spoken tour, London's loss is very much our gain. I support anyone who wants to carry the word of the greatness of London to the world, and so I support Sean in this wonderful book. London welcomes all those who want to come here and support us, or to just come here and enjoy the result of many centuries of hard work.

Enjoy the book and please come to London and visit us, even if you have been before. If you live in London, then I hope you will visit the wonderfully entertaining aspects your city has to offer on your own doorstep, from attractions to shops, restaurants, museums, exhibitions, street entertainers, theatres, snooker at Wembley or even an afternoon watching parliament in session.

www.jimmywhirlwindwhite.com

INTRODUCTION

The city of London has evolved into a bustling capital today, despite the riots, fires, corruption, treason, civil wars and royal intrigue. Most tour guides will talk to you about the Civil War in 1642, but there were many civil wars; they will talk about the Great Fire of London in 1666, but there have been many great fires of London; they will talk about the Peasants' Revolt in 1381, but there have been many peasants' revolts. Throughout its tempestuous history the city has grown, been destroyed, then raised again like a phoenix from the fire. Many great men and women have lived and worked in the city, and their presence has left its mark. The city is an entity unto itself, and has outlived and outfought those who have entered its boundaries to destroy it. There have also been many major events which happened elsewhere, but at the time had a significant effect on the city of London. These events have often taken the city off on a tangent and helped it, for better or worse, to develop into one of the most beautiful and busiest, as well as one of the most historic places in the world.

A day out in London is a wonderful experience today; it is one of the few cities in the world where you will find the past, the present and the future, and often next to each other. The history of London is very diverse and that's what makes it so exciting. You still see the Roman influence and indeed some of their original roads and boundaries. You will come across Anglo-Saxons in the form of place names. The Normans who invaded in 1066 are still heavily represented in London in their castles and churches. Kings and queens from over a thousand years ago are remembered in their magnificent tombs. You can walk the worn-out paths of monks, royals, traitors and heroes. They are all still in London and accessible to everybody. This book was designed to give you information on the history of London, but you may also use it as a reference book and a guide book as you wander around the capital. Revealed within the pages of this book are the original sites of many famous and infamous buildings, on whose remains stand other edifices which a thousand years from now may well be historical in their own right.

Enjoy the book, and the city, and don't forget to come back and visit us again.

THEY CAME, THEY SAW, THEY STAYED A WHILE!

The Roman Period
(AD 43–410)

AD 43

The Romans invaded the Tin Isles and settled near Dover before moving up country. They came to a tidal river which they named Thamesis, meaning 'dark river'. They looked at the swampy area and decided to build an encampment on a high bank. At low tide this point of the river was only three inches deep and easy to cross. Later, the encampment became a barracks.

The Roman governor Paulinus set about building permanent stone buildings and temples further upriver. The streets were paved around the new settlement called Londinium, which means 'new town'.

AD 55

The Romans built a wooden link from the south of the river to the north side. Around the area, they established docks for their merchant ships, bringing supplies from all over the empire as well as some civility to Londinium. The south works were set up to extract gravel from the islands on the south side of the river. They were eventually joined up to form one land mass now called Southwark. The bridge they built was the first London Bridge.

AD 60

Britons began rioting in protest at the Roman rule of law. The Iceni and other tribes led by Queen Boudicca attacked the Roman garrisons in Camulodunum (Colchester), Verulamium (St Albans) and London. The temporary governor of London, Catus Decianus, fled to France with his personal bodyguards. The remaining Roman troops were outnumbered by 10 to 1 and lost the battle and the town, which was then destroyed by fire. The wooden London Bridge was destroyed for the first time and 5,000 reinforcements from the Leicester garrison were ambushed and slaughtered. The Roman governor Suetonius Paulinus was busy in Wales breaking the Druids' grip on the country. Suetonius returned to Londinium to battle with the rebellious Britons. When he arrived, the rabble army of Boudicca was in control. He was forced to back away from London as he only had cavalry with him. He waited until his main army finished off the Druids, and returned to reinforce him near London.

The final battle took place in the Chiltern Hills; the well-disciplined and organised Romans beat the rabble army into retreat. The Britons had brought hundreds of wagons laden with women and children. These blocked their retreat and trapped the rebels in the open. The Roman archers slew thousands before the main band of troops and cavalry moved in to finish them off. They slaughtered thousands more of the Britons, including the women and children, using their short swords. The Britons' long swords were useless in confined battle. Boudicca initially escaped, but was soon captured. She committed suicide with her two daughters by consuming a hidden bottle of hemlock poison. The Britons' rebellious traits succumbed to Roman supremacy and the Romans continued to build more towns around Britain made of stone and marble.

AD 80

After nearly twenty years of neglect, the Romans decided Londinium was to be their new capital. Elaborate buildings started to spring up in the wake of the old burnt-out town. They built temples, houses and trading buildings, as well as commercial areas for traders to buy and sell goods from all over the empire.

AD 85

London was given orders from Rome to build new wharves and warehouses to facilitate the increasing trade that it had encouraged. Every day ships arrived in the capital to bring goods from all over the empire. Many traders now looked to London to buy luxuries to be exported around the known world.

AD 90

London got public bath houses and stone houses as the old wooden buildings were replaced with Roman-designed buildings. Londoners were now literally romanised and liked all that Rome had to offer. Rich British families were now dressing like Romans and even spoke Latin.

AD 100

Gladiators were performing in London for the first time. Londoners didn't quite know what to make of it all but they supported their rulers' liking for bloodsports. Bear-baiting and dog-baiting were also making a mark in the new capital.

AD 125

The Roman army were convinced they had completely entranced all Britons into their culture. In London they set up schools to train soldiers for the empire, and Britons were encouraged to join and become part of the Roman future.

AD 165

London was declared the most successful city in the country for self-government and expansion. In the previous twenty years, the military overlords of London had slowly handed down their powers to civilian rulers. London was a self-sufficient city in its dealings with the rest of the empire. New technology in agriculture and wine-making needed a trading centre where goods could be bought and sold, without the need to bring all the goods to market. The first British guilds grew out of the success London had as a trading centre.

AD 180

The wealth of the country was being reflected in the elaborate designs of mosaics and fittings for houses in London. Huge properties were decorated by the élite of the Roman designers and the best materials were plentiful in the capital.

AD 195

The Romans had almost finished building a defensive wall around the town of Londinium. It was made from Raglan stone which was cut in the quarries of Kent 70 miles away. There were three main gates which were posted on the roads to Camulodunum (Colchester), Verulamium (St Albans) and Eboracum (York). More gates were added later. The wall was 18ft thick, 40ft high, ran in an arc and completely enclosed the garrison barbican.

AD 208

A Roman Briton was executed in the town of Verulamium after hiding a renegade priest from the authorities. The man named Albanus was discovered disguised as a Christian priest when Roman soldiers, seeking out a fugitive priest, raided his home. His execution in June was a spectacle that inflamed the Christians. It was said that first he made a river dry up so he could walk across it, then the military executioner refused to cut off his head, as he feared him a sorcerer. The soldier was killed by his general who then beheaded Albanus; as his head came off his eyes popped out and this was seen as divine intervention. The town was later named after him (St Albans), when he was canonised. A church was later built on the site of the execution.

AD 230

The Temple of Mithras was built in London to the Persian god of light and truth. The temple was a male-only domain and had about thirty members in line with the rites of Mithras. The rituals were secret and the members broke up into smaller groups, with names such as Raven and Lion. The groups had a ranking and in accordance with your rank you wore a mask. New members were initiated by a ceremony which involved, among other things, lying in a grave next to a fire. They were covered with stone slabs so they could feel the heat of the fire of the netherworld, and the cold of the grave.

AD 277

The Emperor Probus sent a mercenary force of German tribesmen to London to put down a revolt led by the Gauls. The attempted coup followed an earlier failed coup by Bonosis, who was the Roman commander of the Rhine fleet.

AD 288

There was another military coup in London, this time successful. The Roman commander of the Imperial fleet, Mausaeus Carausius, seized the city, and set himself up as an independent Roman governor of London and the south-east.

AD 290

Mausaeus set up his own mint to produce silver and bronze coins for his new kingdom. The booming economy in London, which was still trading with the rest of the empire, needed to have its own money market.

AD 293

Mausaeus was killed by Ellectus who had by now taken control of the independent empire. In 296, Constantius Chlorus killed Ellectus in battle restoring the capital back to Roman rule, to the delight of Londoners. Britain was now split into four provinces, each overseen by a Vicarius (vicar) in London, who reported to the Emperor via the Prefect in France.

The textile industry in Britain was faring very well, trading throughout the empire.

AD 401

News from Rome was bad. The Eternal City and the Roman Empire were slowly being destroyed by Goth invaders from the east. The Roman garrisons were ordered to send troops back home. Each year, more and more troops were sent back.

AD 410

The last of the Roman army left Britannia and went back to Rome in a vain attempt to save the empire. Britain was now left to a few inexperienced and incompetent Roman officials who had their own private armies. The provinces of Britain grew further apart and, as a divided country, it was much easier to raid and pillage. European tribes who watched the Romans leave Britain's shores and head home, saw this period as an opportunity to raid the country and take what the Romans had left behind.

2

FROM ANGLE-LAND... TO ENGLAND!

The Anglo-Saxon Period (410–1066)

411–90

For nearly eighty years Britain was invaded by many tribes from Europe. England wasn't united enough and with only a few thousand Romans in the whole country, the people were soon overrun by Jutes, Danes, Vikings, Angles and Saxons. The two latter tribes, from the area known as North Germany, amalgamated and took control of vast areas of the country, expelling the Danes and Vikings. The Angles formed East Anglia in the south east; the Saxons formed Sussex in the far south, with the Jutes forming Kent and Suffolk. Londinium was abandoned during this period; the town stopped trading with the rest of Europe, as the ships coming up the Thames were constantly attacked.

491

Chieftain Aelle of the South Saxons put down a rebellion by the local Britons. He arrived in Britain in 476, and waged a pogrom on the Britons of Sussex and the Weald. Many hundreds were slaughtered, but the tribes had recovered and held up in a fort that Aelle had built to protect his coastline. With his son Cissa, he besieged and slaughtered most of the rebels; the rest again fled into the Weald.

520

A new settlement was established about 2 miles upstream from the original Roman town. It had no name as such and was referred to as Lundunewic, a Saxon word meaning a town market or a port town. As the town had no established landing wharves, it was mainly used as a village and a market for country folk to trade their meat and vegetables. No London Bridge existed at this time.

580

The Briton king of Kent, Athelbert, married the daughter of the Frankish King Charibert. The union reaffirmed the long-standing peace the two kings had enjoyed. Athelbert was Jute by birth and the Kent area of England was one of the richest of the old Germanic tribes. Trade between the Franks and the Jutes had been in force for decades, the most profitable being the slave trade. There was a condition from the Franks that Bertha was allowed to continue her Christianity, and to make sure Bishop Liudhard was sent over to be a personal religious advisor. Athelbert granted him an old Roman church in Canterbury, and Luidhard renovated it as a Christian centre of knowledge.

594

Abbot Augustine (later St Augustine) landed in Ebbsfleet near Canterbury, Kent, as the first Christian emissary from Pope Gregory the Great. He converted King Aethelbert to Christianity in 597 and founded the first English Christian church. The king's wife, Queen Bertha, daughter of the King of Paris, was already a Christian. Bertha received a message from Augustine telling of his arrival. She persuaded Aethelbert to meet with him and his monks on the Isle of Thanet, Kent. Aethelbert was not convinced immediately, but gave the monks permission to take over the old Roman church ruins of St Martin's in Canterbury. The monks used the church as a base to heal the sick, and converted them to Christianity. Being an archbishop, Augustine became the spiritual head of the new Christian faith. He was the first Archbishop of Canterbury and so therefore the spiritual head of the church. In 601 Augustine was granted certain rights in London to provide his office with an income. However, he decided to keep St Martin's as his headquarters, with a vision to build a cathedral there at some point.

604

Archbishop Augustine ordained the first Bishop of London, Bishop Mellitus, and he built a small wooden church on the east hill of London named after St Paul.

616

The East Saxon Prince Seigeberht, who was converted to Christianity while in exile in France, had a dream in which St Peter told him to build a church to the Christ at Thorny Island. The site of the church was west of the township of Lundunewic. He became king in 631 and built his church in 634 which he named St Peter's. Then he abdicated to become a monk.

660

The Anglo-Saxons passed laws giving equal rights to women of nobility and the higher classes. They could own land in their own right, divorce and remarry. A widow was allowed to keep at least one-third of her husband's estate. They were allowed to keep the whole of it, provided they had children and remained unmarried. The dowry, better known as the wed, remained hers for life. Women could also buy, sell and set slaves free under the new law.

663

A plague struck England and wiped out many of the monks in the Christian monasteries. A pagan revival then occurred. King Wulfhere of Mercia sent Bishop Jaruman to the countryside around London to reconvert the people.

675

Monks from the Saxon abbey of Barking founded the church of All Hallows. The church was their first in the City of London and stood near the old Roman wall to the east.

740

London was the most populated city in England. After years of decline and depopulation, it was thriving with so much commerce that there were now many markets, trading with the hundreds of ships that visited each month, coming from all over the known world.

764

A fire struck in London and wiped out a large area of wooden buildings. The Romans used stone as a building material and their houses were less susceptible to fire. The recent population increase had resulted in a need for quicker construction. While wood was much cheaper and easier to fabricate, it had now proved to have its disadvantages.

792

King Offa, who ruled Mercia, ordered a new coinage system in his kingdom. The new coin was to be known as a penny after the great Mercian King Penda, who founded the Mercian dynasty. The new coins were struck from one pound of pure silver, which gave it value, and mixed with other metals. Offa had decided to mint 240 pennies from the pound of silver. Henceforth, the new system would mean that there were to be 240 pennies to a pound.

878

London was invaded by the Vikings, and the reigning King Alfred fled to the southern marshes.

886

King Alfred and King Athelred took London back from the Norsemen. Athelred was installed as king with Alfred's blessing. Wessex, the domain of Alfred, was provided with more forts along the coast to help prevent any future attacks. He also started regular naval patrols, effectively founding the first coastguard.

893

King Alfred passed the first new laws since King Ine 200 years earlier. It was now a capital offence to plot against the crown or any lord. Theft was punishable by a huge fine, and legislation was passed on compensation for committing acts of negligence against your neighbours. The Vikings were continuing to break the treaty not to attack the kingdom. Alfred commissioned the *Anglo-Saxon Chronicles* which was the first book chronicling the history of England, from the Romans to Anglo-Saxon times.

899

King Alfred of Wessex died on 26 October. He left behind a vastly successful region, and a navy of ships that protected the coastline. He was succeeded by his son Edward.

900

A witch was drowned in the Thames near London Bridge for putting a curse on her neighbour. All her property was passed onto the family of her victim in accordance with King Alfred's law.

924

King Edward of Wessex died in Nottingham on 17 July. He was succeeded by his son Alfward. However, Edwards's illegitimate son, Athelstan, became king in August after the sudden death of Alfward.

960

Abbot Dunstan (later St Dunstan) visited the Thorny Island monastic school and the church of St Peter. He set about constructing a bigger building to house the monks, with a school and a new library. The building was called The Minster and because it was west of the City of London, the area was renamed Westminster. The new college of theology was revered as the best school in the kingdom. Abbot Dunstan was made Archbishop of Canterbury for his efforts.

984

London Bridge was used for the first time as a place of execution. Having been found guilty of witchcraft, a widow was tied up and thrown off the bridge to her certain death in the river below. Her son was burnt alive at the stake at the place of the nine elms. They were convicted by a church court of causing harm to a neighbour. They had made a wax doll of the man and pushed metal pins into it to cause him injury.

988

Archbishop Dunstan died on 19 May. The former abbot, who founded Westminster, had held the office of Bishop of Worcester and London before he was appointed the Archbishop of Canterbury.

1013

London was invaded by the Danes again. King Sweyn of Denmark, known as 'Forkbeard', had also taken control of most of the country and was effectively the new ruler of England. Londoners fought bravely to repel the invaders with many pitched battles taking place on London Bridge, but eventually the forces of the Saxons were beaten, and the city was pillaged.

1014

Sweyn died and his son Harald inherited the Danish throne. He was the brother of Cnut, who was now ruling England in Sweyn's place. The Witan, a group of clerics, nobles and royal advisors, asked Ethelred to return as king, now that Sweyn was dead. He accepted. Cnut was in the north with a large army primed to attack London. He delayed while he negotiated with the Witan. Ethelred and his ally, King Olaf of Norway, sneaked up on the Danes at night and tied ropes round the piles that held London Bridge up. As the tide turned they sailed under the bridge and, using the current, they pulled the bridge down. Many Danes were drowned. The city was recaptured after a fierce battle. The incident is said to have inspired the song 'London Bridge is Falling Down'.

1016

Ethelred died and his son Edmund Ironside succeeded him. Cnut was furious and attacked London several times without success. Finally, Edmund and Cnut met in Essex at Ashingdon, but the ensuing battle, though won by Cnut, settled nothing. Both sides agreed to peace talks and the country was divided between them. Edmund took East Anglia, Wessex and London, Cnut took the north. Within months Edmund was murdered at a party, with a poisoned wine chalice given to him by Edric Streona. Edric was renowned for changing sides in battle to whoever was winning.

Cnut was asked by the Witan to become king of all England in an effort to attain peace, and one of his first acts was to execute the treacherous Streona. Cnut did, however, show mercy on Edmund's children. Instead of killing them to ensure his own line, he sent them to Denmark to live and be educated. Cnut also put aside his wife and married the widow of Ethelred, named Emma. This gave him a claim to the Dukedom of Normandy. There were conditions, though. Emma was older and wiser and made Cnut agree to ban any of their previous children from having any claim to the throne of England. Only children from their own union were to follow in line. Her children with Ethelred went to live in Normandy.

1018

Cnut became King of Denmark and conquered Norway and Sweden. He passed the first known charter of liberties in England. The act was so famous it was known as Cnut's law.

1031

Cnut conquered Scotland and forced King Malcolm to recognise him as overlord of all England. King Malcolm's nephew, Duncan, also paid him homage, as did a Lord Maelboethe, both of whom were later immortalised by Shakespeare's *Macbeth*.

While on a visit to Southampton, it is said Cnut was acclaimed king of all the land and the seas. He called the title an insult to God, and to make his point he placed a chair on the seashore. He then ordered the sea to retreat as it was coming in. The sea of course didn't retreat and so Cnut proved his point that no man could rule the seas. The story was corrupted throughout history, and the reverse is often told where he tried to show that he was so powerful, he could command the tides.

1035

Cnut died aged only forty years old on 12 November at Winchester. He was succeeded by his illegitimate son, and not his son with Emma. King Harald, the son of Cnut and Cnut's common-law wife, Aelfgifu, was crowned king after a long fight to claim the throne from the other contender, Harthacnut.

1040

Harald died on 17 March and Harthacnut was crowned king. King Harthacnut died on 8 June in mysterious circumstances at a celebration in Lambeth. It was often suspected he was poisoned. Edward, his half brother, handed him the alleged poisoned wine chalice and he was now the new king. Edward was the son of Ethelred II who was Cnut's predecessor. Edward became known as the Confessor and was so pious that he took a vow of celibacy. His wife, Edith, who was fifteen years his junior, was said to have taken many lovers because of it. They never produced any children. They lived in a large mansion near the Westminster originally built by Cnut. Edward increased the mansion in size, and it became a palace called the Palace of Westminster.

1065

King Edward the Confessor opened the new abbey at the site of the Westminster on 27 December and named it the Westminster Abbey. It was built on the site of the old St Peter's church.

1066

Edward died on 5 January and Harold Godwinson took the throne when he was crowned three days later in the abbey. On 25 September Harold defeated Tostig, his exiled brother, who with Harald Haardraade III the King of Norway, invaded England. King Harold turned south to meet with the forces of the Duke of Normandy who was also seeking a claim to the throne. William of Normandy defeated Harold at Hastings on 14 October and took London days later, after burning Southwark. Harold died in the battle and William was crowned King of all England on Christmas Day outside the abbey. The cheering crowd made such a noise that William's guards mistakenly thought a riot was taking place. They attacked some of the crowd and the rest dispersed into nearby buildings. The troops set them on fire, killing some of the monks. William later paid the church compensation for the mistake, and promised to improve the abbey, honouring Edward the Confessor.

London became a major trading centre, as William encouraged the wine trade.

3

THEY CAME, THEY FOUGHT, THEY CONQUERED!

The Norman Period (1066–1154)

1070

King William I commissioned an abbey to be built on the site where he defeated King Harold four years earlier. Battle Abbey, as it was to be known, was a memorial to his victory and the thousands who died at the now famous Battle of Hastings which was depicted in the Bayeux Tapestry.

1072

King William was worried about fires breaking out through the carelessness of the people after another fire destroyed part of London. He introduced a new law saying that no fire should be sustained in a house or yard after dark. The law was known as '*couvre feu*' which means cover the fire. From this law we got the word curfew.

1075

William I put the Norman mark on his reign, and on the conquered Saxons of Britain. He ousted many of the Saxon barons and landowners who opposed him. Loyalty was the dish of the day; land was confiscated and given to the new friends of the Normans. The church and the judiciary were also reformed. The old Saxon rule of law was based on a perpetrator compensating his victim; the new laws were punishment bound and the rule of law was enforced by the Moot Courts, held in villages and towns and overseen by the barons, lords and the church. The hierarchy of the church was replaced with imported Norman clergymen, many of whom were builders, and William allowed them to raise their own taxes to build new churches. Archbishop Lanfranc declared that in future all clergy must refrain from sexual activity. Existing clergy with genuine wives would be allowed to keep them; when they tried to enforce this rule in France, the bishops were stoned by their own clergy.

1077

King William was immortalised in a huge tapestry known as the Bayeux Tapestry, made on the orders of William's half-brother, Odo the Bishop of Bayeux. The undertaking was completed by the nuns and novices of St Augustine's Abbey in Canterbury, Kent. It is 230ft long and 20in wide; it was first displayed in Bayeux Cathedral, hence the name.

1078

William laid the foundation stone for the White Tower. This tower now formed the centrepiece of the Tower of London. It was white-washed to protect it from the elements and to make it look even bigger. It was 107ft by 118ft with four turrets, three square and one round. The tower was designed by a monk named Gundulf who was born in Rouen, France, in 1024. Gundulf was a clerk to Bishop Lanfranc. He became a monk after surviving a ship wreck on his return from a pilgrimage to Jerusalem. Lanfranc brought him to England after William made him Archbishop of Canterbury. Gundulf was accredited with designing many French churches and abbeys. While supervising the building work, he lodged with a very powerful and rich man named Eadmer Anhoende. In 1077 Gundulf was appointed Bishop of Rochester. He died at the age of eighty-four, and was buried in a lavish tomb at Rochester Cathedral.

1086

William ordered the first public census of England. The book became known as the Domesday Book, and was a recording of all the lands and chattels in the kingdom, who owned what and their worth. This was calculated at a paltry £10,000 – not even a king's ransom in those days.

1087

William the Conqueror died in France after his horse threw him in battle. He was suffering from internal injuries for three days and died on 9 September having united the English and French as one nation. His funeral, however, was a series of disasters. As the monks at St Stephens's monastery in Caen started the procession, a fire broke out. Then a man named Iselin claimed that the king had no right to be buried there, as the land was his and had been stolen by William. The monks bribed him to go away. The stone sarcophagus was then found to be too small. As the decomposing body was manhandled into it, the body split open and the awful smell brought a quick end to the ceremony.

English history started to number its monarchs. He became William I. William Rufus succeeded as King William II, and was crowned on 26 September. He was the third monarch to be anointed at Westminster Abbey.

1097

The White Tower was completed. The tower, started by William I in 1078, was the biggest castle in the land and the most prominent building in London. It rose some 85ft from the foundations of the old Roman wall, which was dismantled in places to provide much of the material for the construction. It was the intention of William II to add some more battlements.

1099

The new hall at Westminster Palace was now completed. William II added the hall to the original palace built by Edward the Confessor and now called the Palace of Westminster. The new hall was built to last a millennium with twelve bays lit by natural light through opaque glass windows. The entire building was 240ft long and 62ft wide

1100

William Rufus was killed in a hunting accident in the New Forest on 2 August, though it was alleged to have been murder. The assailant was a French knight named Sir Walter Tyrel who escaped to Holland, and was never tried. The king's brother and the Conqueror's youngest son, Henry William, claimed the throne and was crowned in the abbey on 5 August. He immediately invited the exiled Archbishop of Canterbury, Anselm, back to England. The archbishop had been exiled for protesting about the high taxes and the effeminate court of William II, who was accused by Anselm of being gay.

1101

The first recorded prisoner was imprisoned in the Tower of London. He was the Bishop of Durham, Rannulf Flambard, and stood accused of corruption and theft of church money. Rannulf was a rich man and so King Henry allowed him to keep his status while in the White Tower. Rannulf had wine and the best of food sent in daily. One day a rope was hidden in a barrel of wine and he got his guards drunk; then he escaped by climbing down the steep walls. Now he was famous for not only being the first prisoner, but also for being the first escapee.

1106

The monks at St Mary Overie, who had a priory near Southwark Minster church, established a small hospice for themselves and the poor of the borough. The hospice was named St Thomas after the apostle. The priory of St Mary was founded by Marie Overs, the only child of a skinflint ferryman named John Overs who owned the ferry rights next to the wooden London Bridge. He was beaten to death by his servants one day when he faked his own death. He did it to save money as when a corpse lay in a house, no one was permitted to consume any food for twenty-four hours. The servants, however, rejoiced at his passing by raiding the larders and wine vaults to stage a party. Overs suddenly sat up in his coffin and they thought he was a ghost, so beat him to death. His distraught daughter sent for her lover with a message saying, 'Come with haste, you are the new master of the house.' He rode so fast his horse tripped and he broke his neck. The distraught Marie used her father's fortune to found the Priory of St Mary Overie.

1110

The king's minister and treasurer Bishop Roger le Poer of Salisbury (the chancellor of the treasury), designed a unique system for counting the king's taxes from the sheriffs of the counties. The system consisted of an oak table 10ft by 5ft, covered with a large cloth divided into black and white squares. Counters (chequers) were used to determine the incomings and outgoings of each county. Because the cloth was chequered the new system became known as the Exchequer. The sheriffs met twice a year. Bishop Roger was now called the Chancellor of the Exchequer. After each sheriff paid the taxes due, he was given a coloured chequer as a receipt. From this we got the word cheque, which was a receipt for an amount of money.

1117

Matilda, Henry I's queen, founded the first London leper hospital at St Giles near Holborn village. The queen was very passionate about helping the poor and intended the hospital to be the first of many. Matilda, known affectionately to the people as Maud, was born Edith and was the daughter of King Malcolm III of Scotland. She died on 1 May 1118 having also established the Augustine Priory of Holy Trinity at Aldgate, which was the first such religious house in the city.

1120

King Henry's royal boat, *The White Ship*, tragically sank in storms off the French coast on 26 November. All were lost except a French cook. The crew and pilot were seen getting merry and were thought to be very drunk when they put to sea. The king was sailing ahead of them and therefore survived. However, three of his children were drowned, including heir to the throne, Prince William, who died when a group tried to board his lifeboat and it capsized.

1123

A new hospital and priory were built in the city, at Smithfield. The hospital was the idea of Canon Rahere who, on a visit to Rome, became ill with malaria. He promised that he would establish a hospital in London after St Bartholomew appeared to him in a dream, and told him to build one at Smithfield in return for a full recovery. The canon, a former jester at King Henry's court, had therefore decided to dedicate it to the saint. The sick of London would be cared for by eight Augustine monks and four nuns.

The king granted lands to the governor of London Bridge, the rents of which were to be used to maintain the bridge in good order.

1129

Jousting on the Thames became popular. The jousters stood in boats and the oarsmen rowed towards each other; many knights were drowned when they fell into the river and were dragged under by the heavy weight of their armour.

1135

King Henry died of food poisoning at his estate in Rouen in France after eating lampreys (eels) on 1 December. He was succeeded by his daughter Matilda. The problem was that Matilda was married to Geoffrey Plantagenet of Anjou, who was an enemy of the Normans and therefore not welcome in

England (Plantagenet comes from the family coat of arms, which bears a sprig of broom which in Latin is *Planta Genesta*). King Henry had tried to reconcile Matilda with the church and barons, but failed to secure an agreement. Henry's nephew, Stephen of Blois, dashed across the Channel to London to get support from the church and Bishop Roger le Poer, who controlled the crown after Henry's death.

On 22 December, King Stephen was crowned in the abbey after a knight named Hugh Bigod swore that he witnessed Henry on his deathbed declare Stephen his heir. Stephen later gave the bishops possession of all the churches in gratitude.

1136

Another fire broke out in the city. It started on Boxing Day at the house of a man named Ailward who lived in the parish of Candlewick. The fire destroyed most of the west of the city; to the east it destroyed the buildings around London Bridge and then damaged the bridge itself. It finished at St Clement Danes church. Hundreds perished in the two-day fire, trapped in overcrowded houses and overcome by the thick palls of smoke.

Since the Romans left, more buildings had been made of wood as the brick and tile style was deemed too expensive and took too long to build. The wooden bridge was rebuilt with forced labour.

1141

Henry's daughter, the Empress Matilda, who was the widow of Holy Roman Emperor Henry V before marrying Geoffrey Plantagenet, contested King Stephen's claim to the throne. Civil war broke out in February when Stephen gave the county of Cumberland to Henry, the son of King David of Scotland. The king fell out with Earl Ranulf of Chester over the gift and while a battle was in full force, Robert, Earl of Gloucester took Stephen prisoner after a servant knocked him out. Robert's forces included Empress Matilda's own army. Matilda arrived in London with the support of the populace and made arrangements to be crowned queen.

Within weeks Londoners become angered by her attitude towards them and the introduction of new taxes. They revolted when they saw her army camped on the south bank. The protesters stormed a banquet being held before the coronation and Matilda fled London uncrowned. Empress Matilda met with her half-brother Robert of Gloucester on 14 September and they besieged the castle of Bishop Henry of Blois, King Stephen's brother.

Stephen's wife, also called Matilda, had meanwhile sent an army under the leadership of the mercenary William of Ypres to assist Henry. The army surprised Empress Matilda and Robert and then quickly took the city of Winchester back. Robert was captured at Stockbridge but Empress Matilda escaped. In December 1142 King Stephen was finally released from captivity in a prisoner exchange. He returned to London to be re-crowned king. Empress Matilda was under siege at Oxford, but escaped over the frozen Thames.

1148

The civil war continued as Empress Matilda returned to her husband, Geoffrey Plantagenet, in France. The empress had finally given up her claim to the throne after her biggest supporter, half-brother Robert, Earl of Gloucester, died. However she supported her fifteen-year-old son Henry Plantagenet's claim to the throne, so the civil war continued.

1153

On 6 November King Stephen met with Duke Henry of Normandy, the son of Empress Matilda and Geoffrey Plantagenet, who was claiming his right to the English crown. The treaty of Winchester was drawn up and signed by both parties; this document gave Henry Plantagenet the right in succession to the throne after King Stephen died and effectively ended the civil war. Duke Henry initially came to England in the summer to continue the civil war started by his mother. His efforts were not too successful, and he lost many battles before the treaty was brokered by Archbishop Theobald and Stephen's brother, Bishop Henry.

1154

King Stephen died on 25 October and was succeeded by Henry Plantagenet, the grandson of Henry I, whom Stephen himself had succeeded. Henry was besieging a castle in Normandy when he heard the news; he immediately settled the battle and set out for England with his wife, the thirty-two-year-old Eleanor of Aquitaine. The twenty-one-year-old arrived in England on 7 December and was crowned the first Plantagenet king on 19 December, becoming Henry II. He vowed to make England a united country again and struck deals with the church and the barons. He needed both on his side if he was to avert another civil war.

4

A TWIG BY ANY OTHER NAME, PLANTA GENESTA!

The Plantagenet Period (1154–1485)

1155

Thomas of London was appointed chancellor by King Henry II. Thomas A' Becket was also Archdeacon of Canterbury under Archbishop Theobald. A' Becket supported a new proposed act of the king to end arranged marriages. Since Roman times women had been treated like chattels to be given away by their fathers to whomever they pleased. A' Becket and a band of bishops supported the rights of women to refuse to consummate forced marriages. The recent case of annulment brought by Christina of Markyate had strengthened their argument.

1162

Thomas A' Becket, the rich and influential chancellor, was anointed as Archbishop of Canterbury by King Henry II on 23 June. A' Becket's riches were flaunted in public and this disturbed the king. They started to argue over minor issues.

1163

Henry and A' Becket fell out over the king's insistence that the church pay tribute to the crown. The king also proposed that the clergy be tried by courts other than the clerical ones, for all offences. This was the start of a feud that lasted for years. Henry was also jealous of A' Becket's influence in France.

1164

On 14 October, fearing that the king would imprison him and strip him of wealth and office, Thomas A' Becket fled to France where he was welcomed and kept safe. The king had finally lost his temper with A' Becket, who had been jealously guarding the wealth and power of the Church against the wishes of the monarchy.

1166

Law reforms were implemented by Henry II. Juries were introduced in criminal law and every hundred hectares of land would have its own court system run by sheriffs appointed by the king only. The barons, who had previously run the legal system, would lose their powers. In future all convicted felons would lose their lands and property to the lord of the manor. All moveable goods would be sold with the revenue going to the crown.

1170

The Archbishop of Canterbury, Thomas A' Becket, was murdered by four knights of Henry II on 29 December while he was taking evening mass at Canterbury Cathedral. It was well known that the king and Thomas were constantly arguing about religion. Thomas had spent six years in exile in France, and returned to England in July to make amends with the king who then reinstated him as archbishop. One of his first acts was to punish the bishops who abused his office while he had been in exile. This angered the king who was in France at the time and he lashed out by saying, 'What pack of fools and cowards have I nourished in my household, that not one of them will avenge me of this turbulent priest.'

Four knights of the king heard this and, to show their loyalty, they set out for Canterbury to arrest Thomas. The knights, William de Tracy, Richard le Breton, Reginald FitzUrse and Hugh de Murville left France and sailed to the south coast of England, landing late in the night. They stayed overnight with Thomas's enemies, the De Broc family. The next day they rode to the cathedral where they argued with Thomas, his advisors intervened and the knights left. They went to a nearby garden and armed themselves, then returned to find him. They caught up with him in the cathedral, and as they tried to arrest him a struggle broke out. A' Becket was struck with a sword taking off the crown of his head, killing him instantly. He was later buried just feet away. The knights fled back to the house of the De Broc family who had supported them with an army of trained soldiers, though they were never needed.

The aftermath of what they had done shook the entire civilised world, though many close to A' Becket were secretly relieved. While preparing him for burial it was discovered that he had been wearing an undershirt made of human hair for many years, without taking it off. It was heavily infested with lice. This act made many of his former enemies look at him with awe and it made him more pious, famous and worshipped. For many years it was believed that the murderous knights later hid in a castle near Leeds for ten months, before committing suicide. This wasn't true. De Broc was ostracised by the Pope, but later forgiven and ordered to build a shrine to A' Becket in his biggest house. The king was ordered to go to Canterbury walking the last mile barefoot, then prostrate himself at the new shrine to A' Becket while the monks beat him with sticks for his sin. The four knights were ordered by Rome to return to the crusades, and within five years all of them had been killed in battle.

1171

The population of London was calculated at being about 300,000 and huge houses were being built for the rich merchants of the bustling city. A riverside public toilet was put up to assist the health problem. It had 128 closets, 64 for men and 64 for women. The toilet, sited near the stock exchange, was flushed by the Thames as the tide came in and out. A public cook house was also opened on the embankment to feed the populace with fish and game. St Bartholomew's priory and hospice expanded as the rich gave money to support it. There was also a large Jewish quarter in the city with ten synagogues to serve the Jews, the only people licensed in England as moneylenders. One of the most popular areas of Cheapside for the moneylenders to operate from was called Old Jewry. It was off the thoroughfare called Poultry.

1173

In Southwark, just over London Bridge, there was a thriving hospital serving the community situated next to St Mary Overie. The hospital was originally named St Thomas after the apostle. The monks, in consultation with the king, had now dedicated the hospital to the newly canonised St Thomas A' Becket.

1174

Canterbury Cathedral was rebuilt after a fire. The original building, designed by the first Norman Archbishop, Lanfranc, was to be replaced with a Gothic design which was popular in Europe. Henry II decided to honour Thomas A' Becket with a new shrine to be included for pilgrims. The pilgrims took two days to get to Canterbury from London. Their horses were paced at a rhythmic speed now called a 'canter'. In 1176 the people of London decided to commemorate Thomas A' Becket and proposed a new bridge over the Thames in his honour. The bridge was never built.

King Louis VII of France became the first reigning French monarch to set foot on English soil when he went to Canterbury to visit the shrine of St Thomas A' Becket. Louis stayed with Henry II while in London.

1176

The wooden structure of London Bridge was so weak that large carts and sledges were now banned from crossing it. The strength of the river constantly threatened to wash it away. A priest named Peter, of the parish of Colchurch, was chosen to design and build a new stone bridge. The Normans encouraged priests to build bridges and many French religious orders had the word 'pont', meaning bridge, in their name. The king imposed a tax on the wool trade to pay for the bridge, and chantries were set up to sing at funerals with the payment going to the upkeep fund. Many people set aside dowries in their wills at the behest of the royal household to support the maintenance of London Bridge

The proposed new bridge, in honour of Thomas A' Becket, was cancelled, and the saint was instead remembered in a chapel on London Bridge. A lottery was also run in London to fund the stonemasonry. The bridge would now have some twenty arches, and a drawbridge as a defence in times of civil unrest or invasion. On completion, the many arches caused the river to slow down so much that the level of the river was some 4ft higher on one side than the other. In harsh weather this caused the river to freeze over so deeply that fairs were held on the ice.

1189

King Henry II died in France on 6 July and was succeeded by his son Richard of Aquitaine, Richard the Lionheart. Richard's mother, Eleanor of Aquitaine was released from her prison. Henry II had had his wife imprisoned when he fell out with young Richard and she sided with their son. Richard was crowned on 3 September and freed all those imprisoned on Henry II's orders; he needed as much support as he could muster. At the coronation, a delegation of Jewish moneylenders turned up to honour the king and get his assurance that they would be protected from persecution. This angered Richard as it had been declared that no Jew should attend a coronation. The delegation was ushered out, but argued with the guards who struck out, killing some of them. This started a riot and the Jewish population were purged within the city. Richard was concerned enough to have the three leaders of the riot arrested, tried and hanged as he needed the moneylenders to provide him with ready cash to fund his crusades. The incident caused a lot of problems for the Jews of England after Richard left the country in 1190 to fight the crusades. The problems boiled over to York where over 160 Jews committed suicide or were butchered by rioters, demanding their conversion to Christianity.

Richard declared the office of the Lord Mayor of London and appointed the first Lord Mayor, Henry Fitzailwyn, who served for twenty-three years.

1192

King Richard was taken hostage by Duke Leopold V of Austria. Richard and his followers were returning from the Holy Land. He sailed from Cyprus with only four knights, disguised as Templars, but was shipwrecked and forced to carry on overland. At a tavern he was discovered when a knight loyal to Leopold spotted his ring. He was held on the charge of murder and ransomed to England for 150,000 marks. His brother John offered 80,000 marks to the duke to hold him for longer. However, his mother Eleanor of Aquitaine raised the full amount and he was set free on 4 February 1194. He returned to England and made up his differences with John.

1196

The first recorded public hanging at Tyburn took place in 1196. The victim was the leader of rioters protesting against the unfair implementation of taxes. He was a soldier named William FitzOsbert and had managed to gather a following of some 50,000 supporters. The city guards tried to arrest him outside St Paul's church where he was addressing a large crowd; he escaped on foot after the crowd closed ranks. He ran down the road and hid in the church of St Mary le Bow. The guards threw lighted bales of hay inside to flush him out and grabbed him. FitzOsbert was a former soldier of fortune who considered himself a protector of the poor. He was charged and found guilty of sedition. His body hung on the Tyburn tree for many months as a deterrent to others.

1199

On 25 March King Richard was struck by a stray crossbow arrow in Limousin, France. He was walking around the castle perimeter at Chalus-Chabrol without his armour on; someone fired an arrow from the battlements and it struck his shoulder. The surgeon made a hash of the wound and it became gangrenous. It turned out the fatal arrow was fired in revenge by a boy who accused Richard of killing his father and two brothers. Richard forgave the boy and set him free with 100s. The king died of blood poisoning in his mother's arms on Tuesday 6 April. He named John his heir. The boy was later tracked down by a Captain Mercadier who skinned him alive in a barbarous ceremony, then hanged the corpse in public. On 27 May, John was crowned king against the wishes of Walter Hubert, who had ruled England in Richard the Lionheart's absence.

1202

The first known charity fair took place in London. It was to raise money for St Bartholomew's Hospital. The event was a cloth fair which had replaced the old horse fairs. The Lord Mayor opened it by cutting the cloth for the first purchaser. After this it became traditional to cut a ribbon when opening fairs or new buildings.

1205

Peter De Colchurch died and was buried beneath the floor of the chapel of A' Becket on London Bridge. King John commanded that buildings be erected on the bridge and taxes raised to maintain it. London Bridge was finally completed in 1209.

1212

An early Great Fire of London damaged the capital. It started in Southwark at the church of St Mary Overie. It soon spread along Borough High Street to the bridge, and then it crossed over and destroyed 40 per cent of the city, killing 3,000 people. The incident also destroyed the hospital of St Thomas; the monks vowed to build a new one opposite the burned-out site. The land was donated by the Bishop of Winchester who was in control of Southwark, and owned most of the land there. Although the fire crossed London Bridge, it didn't destroy it. The buildings on the bridge helped the fire cross but the main structure remained intact. Also in 1212, the second Lord Mayor was elected by the merchants of the City of London. Henry Fitzalan served for three years.

1215

King John was forced to sign the Magna Carta (great charter) at Runnymede, west of London, on 15 June. The document gave justice to all and was the basis of future civil law in England and Wales. The third Lord Mayor was appointed by the merchants, one Serlo Le Mercer. After King John signed the Magna Carta he appointed his own man to the office of Lord Mayor. The new Lord Mayor, William Hardel, had to swear allegiance to the king and not the merchants.

1216

France invaded England. In May the successful French army walked over London Bridge unopposed, and took the capital. The French forces, led by Louis Capet, were backed by English barons who had fallen out with King John over his failure to implement the Magna Carta. Louis claimed his right to the English throne through his wife Blanche, who was the granddaughter of Henry II. The French controlled the city and most of the south coast. Louis's supply lines were cut by Hubert de Burgh, the king's deputy, who sank most of the French supply ships in the channel. King John took back Windsor Castle from the French and secured Dover, thereby stopping further supplies reaching Louis in London.

King John set out in October to visit the Bishop of Lincoln at Newark Castle. The journey was beset with bad omens and the king contracted dysentery at Lynn in Norfolk, which changed its name to King's Lynn soon afterwards.

While crossing The Wash, his heavily laden train was bogged down and many of the horses were swept away. Most of the royal treasury and jewels were lost for eternity. John rested at Sleaford before proceeding to Newark where he died of dysentery on 18 October.

His son and heir was hurriedly crowned Henry III by the Bishop of Chichester at Gloucester Abbey Church on 28 October; he was just nine years old. The coronation was so rushed that they used the queen's bracelet as the crown and improvised the robes; the ceremony took place at Gloucester because it was far too dangerous to take the boy king to London. William Marshall was appointed joint regent with Hubert De Burgh by the barons. They were eager to see a lasting peace in England and stop all further attempts by Louis Capet to claim the throne.

1217

Louis Capet lost much of his support in his claim for the throne, suffering many setbacks. Louis's forces were held up in Lincoln Castle awaiting reinforcements. The castle was stormed by William Marshall and after many street by street battles, he managed to rout the rebels and retake the castle. Louis was in Dover and decided to retreat back to London where he intended to make a stand. He was holed up in the White Tower. In August his supply ships were again sunk by forces led by Hubert de Burgh; Louis was forced to sue for peace after his supplies dried up and his army was left starving. After signing the Treaty of Lambeth on 12 September, Louis was allowed to leave London with his remaining army, which was now in tatters.

1218

The fifth Lord Mayor was appointed. Serlo Le Mercer, who had served under King John for just eight months, served a term of four years, and officiated at the opening of Newgate Prison.

1220

On 17 May the Archbishop of Canterbury re-crowned King Henry at Westminster Abbey. The archbishop had been away in Rome when the king's father died.

1227

King Henry III, who was now twenty years old, finally took full control of England. The country was prosperous and peaceful due to William Marshall and Hubert De Burgh making peace with the barons, and turning around the bankrupt coffers of the treasury. William Marshall died at the grand old age of seventy-five in 1225.

1234

The third Earl of Pembroke, Richard Marshall, son of the king's former advisor and friend William Marshall, led a rebellion in Wales and Ireland against the throne. Richard had become incensed with the French influence at court. Hubert De Burgh had been a prisoner of the crown since losing influence at court, which was due to the French Bishop of Winchester, Peter Des Roches, who had persuaded the king that De Burgh was plotting against him. Richard Marshall was killed in battle, but the barons had appointed the Archbishop of Canterbury, Edmund Rich, to persuade the king to take control of administrative matters and banish all the French from court. He did so and the new advisors were all Englishmen. Hubert De Burgh successfully challenged his imprisonment at court under the Magna Carta, and he and the king were reunited.

1236

The king was married to Eleanor, one of the four daughters of the Countess of Provence. The new queen was said to have a beauty beyond imagination. The marriage took place in Canterbury Cathedral on 14 January. Eleanor was crowned queen in Westminster Abbey on 30 January. Henry had substantially renovated Westminster Palace with glass windows, bigger fireplaces and plumbing so the queen would feel more at home.

1238

A fierce rebellion had broken out between King Henry and his brother Richard. It had festered over the marriage of their sister and widow of the second Earl of Pembroke, Eleanor, to Simon De Montford which Henry had sanctioned.

Richard met with the barons at Kingston in Surrey to discuss his demands with the king. Richard was apparently jealous of De Montfort's influence with the crown. He was also angry at Eleanor for breaking her promise to her husband on his deathbed to remain chaste.

1239

Queen Eleanor bore the king a son, whom Henry named Edward after his favourite saint, Edward the Confessor. This was a significant move by the king to put down talk at court about his French wife's influence over the English throne.

1245

King Henry commissioned the great French architect Henry of Reyns, who had built the magnificent gothic cathedral there, to build a new Westminster Abbey. The king paid for it himself as a tribute to Edward the Confessor, who had established the first abbey. Work began on 6 June and it was built in the modern French style.

1247

Richard, Earl of Cornwall, and the king's brother, had reformed the coinage of England and made vast profits for the crown on the deal, of which it was rumoured he received half. Reforming the coinage of the realm was common among kings who wished to top up their treasury.

1252

The Bishop of Winchester was appointed the new patron of the expanding and well run hospital of St Thomas. The hospital, which was run by Augustinian canons in Borough High Street, was the most modern and well-funded in Southwark. Many people crossed London Bridge each day to seek treatment there.

1254

Henry III called the barons to London to sit as his councillors in the first parliament, so called after the French word for discussion, '*parlement*'. In October, Prince Edward, the king's son, was married to Eleanor of Castile in Spain forming an alliance between the two great kingdoms.

1256

Henry III built a large barn at the White Tower to house London's first menagerie. The barn was home to many exotic animals including elephants from the east. The king started his collection of exotic animals in 1237 when he acquired two leopards. In 1252 he was given a polar bear, which delighted Londoners as it entertained them by catching salmon from the Thames for the royal household. The king lost a crocodile while walking along the banks of the Thames; the creature bit through its leash and slipped into the river. Londoners were on the look-out for this dangerous man-eater, and the king offered a reward for its safe return. The crocodile was found weeks later wandering around the graveyard of a church in Essex. The local lord, Sir Thomas Tyrel, a descendent of Walter Tyrel, the man accused of murdering King William Rufus in 1100, tackled the creature and was bitten before he managed to kill the crocodile with his sword. His wound festered and he died of blood poisoning within weeks. His son William returned from abroad and went to see the crocodile's rotting carcass in the church yard, with Thomas's sword still in the head. William removed the sword and kicked the carcass in temper; his foot went through the creature's mouth, and its teeth ripped his boot open, gashing his foot. The wound turned septic and he also died within weeks.

The menagerie was the forerunner of the present London Zoo, now situated in Regent's Park.

1258

A coup forced King Henry to agree a new constitution. He was also forced to banish his French relatives, the Lusignans, from England.

The Great Seal of England was held by the barons who had sought a new council at parliament with twelve members elected by the king, and another 12 members to sit with the peers of the realm.

No taxes would be levied on the clergy and a new Justiciar (chief legal officer) took up office at the Tower of London. He was Hugh Bigod. The king also agreed to three parliaments a year where any matters of state could be discussed by the king and the members, who were mostly barons.

1264

Civil war broke out between Simon De Montfort and King Henry. Henry was in France discussing an agreement with Louis IX when De Montfort gathered the barons to his side. Richard, the Earl of Cornwall, dashed back to England to prepare for the king's return in February. The north fully supported the king, and bridges over the Severn had been destroyed to prevent an invasion by armies under the control of De Montfort's sons. The armies of De Montfort and the crown met at Lewes, Sussex, on 14 May. De Montfort fooled Henry into thinking he was off the battlefield in a brightly decorated wagon. Henry and Edward attacked the wagon and while they were away from the main body of their army, De Montfort destroyed their cavalry units. The king and his son Edward were then taken prisoner by De Montfort.

1265

While out riding, Henry's son, Prince Edward, escaped from his guards and managed to join up with allies of the crown. Edward met the De Montfort army at Evesham on 4 August, crushed the rebels, and freed the king. The rebel archers were blinded by a sudden heavy fall of rain enabling Edward's men to rout them, and they fled the field. Simon De Montfort, Earl of Leicester and brother-in-law to King Henry was killed and dissected on the battlefield. His head was gifted to the wife of Roger Mortimer, his most bitter enemy. King Henry III took the money for the repair and maintenance of London Bridge to pay his army; the bridge fell into disrepair very quickly.

1269

King Henry III was proclaimed the most pious of kings by the Archbishop of Canterbury, for his work on the abbey at Westminster. The king donated a bejewelled tomb to his favourite saint Edward the Confessor, also known for his piety. The king also promoted the arts in England by encouraging mural painting at the newly refurbished Palace of Westminster. The new marble top for Edward's tomb cost over £5,000 alone. Henry also took an active part in the rebuilding of the abbey, often supervising the stonemasons. Henry founded the country's first university at Oxford with 3 colleges: University, Balliol and Merton. The university was overseen by a chancellor named Roger Grosseteste.

1272

King Henry III died in London on 16 November; his son Edward was now king. Henry was buried in a lavish tomb in Westminster Abbey, which he had rebuilt during his reign of fifty-six years, the longest yet of any English monarch.

Edward was unaware that his father was dead, as since 1270 he had been in the Holy Land fighting the crusades. Edward freed Acre from the Muslims and captured Nazareth during his many battles with Charles of Anjou. It was on his way home, on a stop-over in Sicily, that the news was finally broken to him.

1274

King Edward I was finally crowned in Westminster Abbey, nearly two years after becoming king. The coronation was the most spectacular of any such event, with free wine and food donated to everyone in London, rich and poor. He vowed to take on the Welsh usurpers Llywelyn and Dafydd, and formed an alliance with his brother-in-law, King Alexander III, who married Edward's sister in 1251 at the tender age of ten years old, Queen Margaret being just eleven years old herself at the time. The Scottish king and his wife were special guests at the coronation.

1275

King Edward called his first parliament in April. One of the matters that he discussed was what to do about the Welsh usurpers, who were threatening to disengage themselves from previous agreements signed with King Henry III.

1277

Edward invaded Wales on 29 August, but his army was defeated by Llywelyn ap Gruffydd of Gwynedd. King Edward limped back to London pledging to return and kill Llywelyn.

1278

Llywelyn angered Edward even more by marrying Eleanor De Montfort, who was Edward's cousin.

1283

As London Bridge was literally falling down due to lack of funding, the king ordered alms to be collected countrywide to pay for repairs. Tolls were introduced on the bridge and this caused merchants to voice their disapproval. More land and the rents from the stock market were granted to the new Bridge Wardens; they had to be elected each year to prevent corruption.

1285

King Edward passed a Statute in parliament proclaiming new reforms and clarifying old laws on land rights and criminal offences. He also appointed more Justices of the Peace and more courts to deal with crime. In 1284 he came down hard on criminals and prostitution in London. With his loyal chancellor, Robert Burnell, the new reforms were passed with the consent of parliament, bringing a new enforceable court and justice system to the country.

1290

Eleanor of Castile died in Harby, Nottinghamshire, on 28 November and was buried in Westminster Abbey on 17 December. She and Edward were very much in love, and her death was a blow to the king. For many years he indulged his love of soldiering in Europe, and when the queen was twenty years old she bore him the first of thirteen children, four sons and nine daughters. Prince Edward, heir to the throne, was the only son to survive. Many of the children died in infancy with only five daughters surviving. As the queen of Edward I she is remembered by the twelve carved stone crosses put up at the resting places of her funeral cortège to London. The places were Lincoln, Grantham, Stamford, Geddington, Hardingstone, Stony Stratford, Woburn, Dunstable, St Albans, Waltham Cross, West Cheape and Charing Cross (from Chère Reine, meaning 'beloved queen' in French). Only Hardingstone, Geddington and Waltham Cross crosses survived. There is a replica of one of the elaborate crosses outside Charing Cross railway station in The Strand, London.

In July Edward ordered all Jews to leave the country. In 1275, at his first parliament, he had banned Jews from charging interest on loans. The practice known as usury was already illegal under English law, but only by the church. Edward gave the Jews fifteen years to comply with the law of 1275. They were also ordered to wear yellow bands to distinguish themselves from Christians. All Jews would receive safe passage certificates to ensure their safety to the ports.

1295

The first ever real parliament met at the Palace of Westminster in June. In the past, parliament had met mostly at the whim of the king at wherever he happened to be in the realm. This 'Model Parliament', as it was dubbed, was unique in that it consisted of two knights chosen by the courts of each shire, and two officials chosen by the people of each city or borough. They sat with the barons and the clergy to form the new parliament.

1296

In March at Berwick, the Scots faced the English army and were quickly defeated by the king's highly trained, well-equipped and obedient soldiers. Trouble began when in 1294 John vowed to help Edward against the French king Phillip IV, only to go back on his word, ally with the French and then invade England. In 1295 Edward sent for Scottish King John to discuss the right of English courts to hear appeals of Scottish courts, and to enforce their will on the people. John did visit, but refused to discuss the matter or pay homage to Edward. After the defeat at Berwick in which over 6,000 Scots were killed, the last of the Scottish rabble were routed at Dunbar and King John was captured. In a humiliating ceremony in July he was dethroned and stripped of all his royal regalia in public, before being forced to sign away his right to rule Scotland to his English overlord, Edward. Afterwards he was exiled to England. Edward also seized the Stone of Scone and ordered it to be taken to Westminster Abbey, to ensure no further kings were crowned in Scotland.

1305

The trial took place, in August, of the Scots rebel Sir William Wallace (Braveheart), in the Westminster Hall on the orders of Edward I after Wallace was betrayed by disloyal Scottish knights. Wallace refused to recognise Edward as his regent and was therefore found guilty of sedition and treason. The criminal was to be hung, drawn and quartered in public. The sentence was carried out before a large crowd at Smithfield. Wallace was offered a quick end if he repented and swore allegiance to the crown of England. Instead the Scot made a speech to the crowd damning the king and all who followed him. The crowd was deeply insulted, and shouted for the execution to continue. Wallace died after resisting the pain, but not for some time, to the great delight of the crowd. A plaque on the wall of St Bartholomew's Hospital commemorates the event. The head of Wallace was taken to be displayed on London Bridge, parboiled then dipped in tar to preserve it. This was the first time the head of a traitor was displayed on the bridge. His quartered body was sent around the country to be displayed as a warning to others.

1307

King Edward I died of dysentery on 7 July. Known as the 'Hammer of the Scots' for his wars with them, Edward very reluctantly left the throne to his son, Edward II. This giant of a man, said to stand some 6ft 2in tall, fought many battles and was feared by all his enemies bar one, William Wallace. Edward was also known as Longshanks which means long-legs.

1308

Edward II was crowned at Westminster Abbey on 25 February. The king was accompanied by his wife, the twelve-year-old Isabella of France. The king was suspected by the barons of being gay and having an unnatural relationship with his deputy, Piers Gaveston. The barons threatened to stop the ceremony if Gaveston wasn't banished, and when he later appeared wearing a flowing robe of purple and pearls, the French contingent left the celebrations in disgust.

1312

On 19 June, Piers Gaveston was beheaded on the orders of the barons. He had been banished three times from the court by both Edward I and II. Edward II apparently had given his permission to the barons, though reluctantly, after falling out with his suspected lover.

1321

Edward II banished the Despenser family from court after the barons threatened to revolt once again. The barons were not happy that the king's promise to be rid of evil councillors wasn't being adhered to. The family was led by father and son (both named) Hugh Despenser, who had been increasing their land holdings with favours from the king. The Despensers were later returned to court. The barons and Queen Isabella were concerned with the daily effeminate actions of young Hugh Despenser and the king, who were suspected of being lovers. The queen left England with her son, and headed back to France after Edward refused to give up his lover.

1326

Isabella, the now estranged French wife of the openly gay King Edward II, invaded England with a French-backed army led by her new lover, Roger Mortimer of Wigmore. They landed with the help of many English barons and bishops on the banks of the River Orwell in Suffolk on 15 October. The army then marched on London to depose her husband. Londoners were rioting and looting the city in protest at the king's courtiers, and in support of Isabella. The Archbishop of Canterbury was put in charge of the capital, but was murdered with a butcher's knife in the Tower. Edward, along with the Despensers, was heading to Wales to drum up support.

On 16 November Edward and young Hugh Despenser were captured at Neath Abbey, where they were awaiting a ship to Ireland. Hugh Despenser was executed at Hereford in front of the queen. He was given a crown of nettles to wear and was dragged before a baying crowd. He was then strung up on a high scaffold and castrated for unnatural practices with the king. Then he was disembowelled with his entrails being burnt on a brazier before him. He was finally beheaded and quartered while Isabella sat and watched, taking lunch. A month earlier, Hugh Despenser the senior had been hung, drawn and beheaded in a similar fashion in Bristol. Edward was taken to Kenilworth Castle to await his fate.

1327

In January, Edward III, the eldest son of Isabella and Edward II, became a boy king after parliament deposed his father. The ceremony was witnessed by the barons, bishops and leaders of the London riots. Edward II was sadistically murdered by having a red-hot plumber's smoothing iron pushed up his rectum and into his stomach, through a funnel, so as not to mark the body. The murder was probably committed on the orders of Isabella and Roger Mortimer. Edward III vowed to restore the monarchy to its former glory by becoming one of the most revered warrior kings.

1349

A plague called the Black Death arrived in London and within six months it had killed 20,000 people. Most of the bodies were buried near Clerkenwell by the city wall on 13 acres of land. The disease was known to have killed 12 million people in Europe and originally came to England via Bristol, where it wiped out 40 per cent of the population. The symptoms were horrendous and started with a large white tumour under the armpit; this buboe (from bubonic plague) then developed into a rash, coughing and then chest pains. The last stages were the vomiting of blood, and a sneezing bout before death set in. Just about everything divine was blamed for the outbreak with some zealots even blaming it on the sins of Londoners, and the lining up of the planets.

1351

Edward III passed the Statute of Labourers, an act of parliament that attempted to fix the wages of peasants. Since the plague wiped out so many of them in previous years, the scarcity of labourers had driven up wages. London repopulated due to country folk pouring into the city from the surrounding countryside. Many were former farm labourers seeking their fortune in the wealthy wool trade that London was now famous for.

On 23 April the king created the Order of the Garter of St George, which was to be presented to knights who showed exceptional courage in battle. He invoked the help of a legendary Roman soldier who was beheaded for his Christian beliefs in Lydda, Palestine, in AD 303. The head of the knight named George was interred in a Roman church dedicated to him, and he was later canonised to become St George. Legend has it that St George killed a dragon on Dragon Hill, Uffington, Berkshire, but the story isn't true as George never came to Britain, though in the Middle Ages a dragon was used by zealots to illustrate the devil. The story derived from the crusades and was brought to England by the Knights Templar to encourage patronage. The king declared St George as the patron saint of England, and declared that 23 April be his celebratory day.

1363

Edward III banned all worthless and foolish sports on holy days. Football, stick ball, handball and cock-fighting were to be replaced with archery, so every Englishman would be a master of the bow ready to defend England. Edward also ordered all churches to plant yew trees in their grounds to provide the wood for the bows.

1377

On 27 February parliament approved a new tax; a Poll Tax of four pennies (there were 240 pennies to an imperial pound) would be levied on all persons over the age of fourteen, except beggars. Londoners rioted over the tax, and many influential people left the capital in fear of their lives.

Edward III died on 21 June and his ten-year-old grandson Richard II was crowned in Westminster Abbey on 16 July.

1381

The Peasants' Revolt on 15 June over the poll tax reached London. The riots were inflamed by the preaching of a monk in Kent named John Ball who insisted that all men were equal, and therefore the serfs shouldn't have to pay the poll tax. Ball was arrested by the Archbishop of Canterbury and imprisoned in Maidstone gaol. Wat Tyler (also known as Walter Tyler), a Kent peasant, killed the king's tax collector near the village of Hartdown, and word soon spread that Tyler had an army who were planning to free John Ball. The peasants from miles around swelled Tyler's mob and they stormed the gaol, freeing Ball. They then marched to London for a showdown with the king. The rioters burned down the Savoy Palace on The Strand, the home of John O'Gaunt, one of King Richard's advisors. They then met with other rebels from Essex and Suffolk led by Jack Straw, who struck the ancient Lode Stone in Candlewick Street (now Cannon Street) with his sword and marked it. This was considered to be an unlucky omen by many of the rioters.

The king was secured in the Tower as the rioters killed many lawyers and other officials in the city, before setting fire to buildings in Fleet Street. Richard met with the main band of usurpers at Mile End Field. He agreed to their demands of the abolition of the poll tax, which was now one shilling, along with the laws on serfdom and church reforms. On his return to the Tower, Richard discovered that rioters had broken in and murdered the Archbishop of Canterbury, Simon of Sudbury. They had also killed the king's treasurer, Sir Robert Hales, and several other royal officials. The head of the archbishop was placed on a spike on London Bridge, with his mitre nailed to the skull to identify him. At a further meeting with the 60,000 rioters at Smithfield, the Lord Mayor of London, William of Walworth, rode forward and struck the ringleader Tyler dead with his sword. Tyler had felt insulted by the presence of the lords and had drawn his dagger threatenly. The rioters turned on King Richard and pointed their drawn bows at him. He bravely rode towards them saying,

'Sirs, will you shoot your King? I am your captain, follow me.'

The crowds dispersed after Richard promised them all a pardon. Wat Tyler's head replaced that of the archbishop on London Bridge, along with the heads of Jack Straw and John Ball. Months later, Richard reneged on his promise and toured the country, hanging the ringleaders as he passed through villages that had supported the rioters.

1382

John of London, the Mayor of London, enacted a statute forbidding any member of the Victualler's Guild from holding any judicial office.

1385

A clampdown on prostitutes was ordered by the mayor after Elizabeth Moring, the wife of Alderman Henry Moring, was found guilty of running a brothel for leading churchmen. Elizabeth was sentenced to three years' exile. The city's prostitutes fled beyond the judicial boundaries to Southwark, where they were to become known as Winchester Geese after they were licensed by the Archbishop of Winchester. He was in control of Southwark, and quite happy for the brothels to exist.

1388

The barons seized control of the kingdom from Richard II. Parliament found the Earls of Oxford and Suffolk, the Archbishop of York and Sir Nicholas Brembre guilty of treason. They were the king's friends and advisors, so the barons removed them to take control of the boy king's realm.

1389

Richard came of age and seized back his kingdom. At a meeting of summoned councillors on 3 May he demanded, and was given back, the seals of his office. He appointed a new chancellor, William of Wykeham, the Bishop of Winchester, who now held the Privy Seal. A royal declaration was sent to all the sheriffs in the kingdom to inform them of the situation and to demand their loyalty.

1390

A joust took place on London Bridge between the English ambassador to Scotland, Lord John Welles, and the Scottish knight Sir David de Lindesay. It started as a jovial conversation at a banquet in Scotland but after becoming a heated exchange, Lord Welles challenged Sir David to the joust, to find out who had the better knights. Sir David chose the date, 23 April being the saint's day of St George patron of soldiers. Lord Welles chose the venue. Thousands, including the king and queen, turned out to see it. The knights passed twice, but neither was thrown from their horse. On the third pass Lord Welles was caught by Sir David and fell heavily from his horse. His injuries were life-threatening and so Sir David took him home and nursed him back to health, such was the chivalry among knights.

1397

On 25 September Richard II exacted revenge on the Duke of Gloucester and the Earls of Arundel and Warwick; he found them guilty of treason for executing his councillors nine years earlier to take control of the kingdom. The trial took place at Westminster in a large marquee. Arundel was executed in the Tower immediately after being convicted, while Warwick had his sentence commuted to banishment to the Isle of Man for life. Warwick apparently confessed the guilt of all three, thereby justifying the king's sentences on the other two. Gloucester was taken to Calais and smothered with a mattress by the king's men. Richard raised taxes and the aldermen of the City of London protested.

A mercer named Richard Whittington sided with the king and helped to quell the situation. When the Lord Mayor suddenly died on 1 September, the king appointed Whittington as mayor in his place. Whittington was already supplying the royal household with the finest of cloth, and was re-elected as mayor the following year. He served four terms in total during his lifetime.

1398

King Richard II took all the power away from parliament, and handed all decision-making to a new committee of eighteen of his most trusted followers. The king now had autonomous power over the kingdom. By doing so he alienated himself from his most powerful barons.

1399

John O'Gaunt died and Richard II seized all his property. O'Gaunt's son, Henry Bolingbroke, demanded the king return all the seized land. Civil war broke out and Henry was triumphant after Richard was tricked by Percy and Thomas Arundel, brothers of the executed earl, into thinking that he could remain king if he returned to London. After leaving their castle he was arrested. Henry Bolingbroke was crowned king and became King Henry IV.

1412

Richard Whittington, the Lord Mayor of London, made a magnificent gesture after visiting the hospital of St Thomas's in Southwark. He donated sufficient funds to build a new wing. It was for the young women of the borough who went amiss; the ward had eight beds.

1413

King Henry IV fainted at the tomb of Edward the Confessor on 20 March and died shortly afterwards; he was succeeded by his son Henry V.

1415

After his victory at Agincourt on 25 October, the king was granted all custom revenue as a reward by parliament. Londoners started a new trend of sticking up two fingers as an insult, mainly to the French. The insult came about because of the French tradition of lopping off the bow fingers of captured English archers; the archers at Agincourt raised their two arrow fingers at the French to dare them to take them off. It was the archers who were accredited with bringing victory to the king by gaining the advantage over the French foot soldiers.

1422

Henry V died of dysentery in France on 31 August; he was succeeded by his one-year-old son Henry. Before journeying to France, Henry V put his brother, Humphrey, the Duke of Gloucester, in charge of young Henry's upbringing and also appointed Thomas Beaufort to assist. Effectively, Humphrey now ruled in the boy king's place. Humphrey and the Beauforts fell out over Henry, and civil war loomed for control of London and the country. The City of London was divided and it culminated in a confrontation on London Bridge. Londoners supporting each faction lined up on opposite banks of the river. After days of throwing insults and threats, the crowds dispersed and the battle never took place. Humphrey came out triumphant.

1429

The eight-year-old Henry VI was crowned in Westminster Abbey on 6 November. He was given his favourite meal of jelly and roast meat fritters at a celebration afterwards. He found the crown very heavy and the ceremony so tiring, that he fell asleep half way through.

1432

Henry VI was crowned King of France. The boy king was now considered the most powerful monarch in the world. On his return to London he was greeted with a great pageant, and free wine flowed from a conduit in Cheapside for the people to celebrate.

1437

Catherine, the king's mother, died in London on 3 January and was buried with her first husband, Henry V. It was revealed that the queen had secretly remarried in 1430 to Owain Tudor. The marriage did not have the king's permission and was therefore considered invalid. Owain was now in danger of being arrested for the crime of marrying a dowager without a licence. Up till now the marriage had been tolerated, as the queen was looking after her son, the boy king.

1450

On 4 July rioters seized the City of London; it was in revenge for the murder of the Earl of Suffolk on the orders of Henry VI after an attempted coup. Suffolk was beheaded at sea after he was tricked into thinking he was being exiled to France and boarded a boat with the king's men. His body was found dumped on the beach at Dover. William Crowner, the sheriff of Kent, and his father-in-law Lord Saye, the royal household's Lord Chamberlain, were both killed, and had their heads placed on pikestaffs. The crowd cheered when the heads were made to kiss each other. The rioters' leader, a soldier named John Cade, led the forces that Henry tried to put down with his own soldiers. However the king's men mostly deserted to the other side and Henry fled London, alone, to Kenilworth Castle in the Midlands. After three days of rioting, the king's wife, Queen Margaret of Anjou, who had remained in London, routed the rebels with an army of loyal Londoners and the tower garrison. After a bloody all-night battle, the queen persuaded most of the rebels to lay down their arms for a royal pardon. John Cade refused and took a small contingent with him back to Kent to make a last stand. He was killed with his remaining men at a battle days later. His head ended up on a spike on London Bridge, which he had set on fire during the riots.

1455

Richard, Duke of York, contested the validity of Henry VI's claim to the throne of England, and so civil war broke out once more, this time between the houses of York and Lancaster. Both houses had a rose as their symbol, white for York and red for Lancaster. The wars were known as the Wars of the Roses. Richard defeated the king's men at a pitched battle in St Albans on 22 May and was planning to march on London to seize the throne. In November, parliament and Londoners opposed Richard and his army after refusing to back them; the Yorkist leaders were condemned as traitors. Richard fled to Ireland.

1460

Richard of York was killed in a battle along with his son, Edmund, on 30 December. His army was scattered by Lord John Clifford who caught Edmund as he attempted to flee. As he struck the fatal blow, Clifford exclaimed, 'By God's blood, thy father slew mine; and so will I do thee, and all your kin.'

1461

Just seven weeks after routing the Yorkist traitors, the Lancastrian army was plundering and burning its way to London; the troops had been given permission to punish any town which previously gave support to the Yorkists, such as Stamford.

On 17 February Queen Margaret's army won a pitched battle at St Albans in Hertfordshire. Richard Neville, the Earl of Warwick, was wounded and his army slaughtered. The queen also freed her husband Henry VI, who had been brought to witness the battle by Richard. The civil war had cost so many barons and knights their lives that the armies were now at the command of much younger men. The Yorkists marched on London to install Edward IV as king, and he was crowned in the abbey. Queen Margaret decided to march north after the victory at St Albans, but on

29 March, at Towton near Leeds, her army was beaten by the Yorkist supporters of the newly crowned Edward IV. Margaret and Henry VI fled to the safety of Scotland with their son Edward.

1465

On 13 July, while out riding with two clergy and a servant, the former King Henry IV, who had been in hiding since 1461, was captured. He was taken to the Tower of London to await his fate. Queen Margaret and their son Edward had been in France since 1463 after they lost the protection of Mary of Guelders, the Scottish Queen Dowager, when she died.

1469

Richard Neville, Earl of Warwick, declared his opposition to Edward IV. With his supporters, who included the Duke of Clarence, King Edward's brother, he intended to oust Edward from the throne.

1471

Edward had been in hiding in the Midlands for months while Richard Neville was searching the country for him. Edward returned to London on 9 April. On 14 April, in a battle north of London, Neville and Clarence were defeated by Edward's loyal Yorkists. Both Neville and his brother John were killed. Edward had spared the bodies being dismembered as they were once allies, and the brothers were entombed in St Paul's. The nearly bankrupt Edward seized all of their property to replenish his treasury. George, the Duke of Clarence, had been spared the death penalty, reconciled with his brother, King Edward IV, and returned to his estates. On 5 May King Edward defeated the army of Queen Margaret of Anjou. Her son, Edward, the Prince of Wales, was killed during the battle. She was now a prisoner of King Edward. Henry VI was murdered in the Tower on 24 May; it is thought that the ruthless Duke of Gloucester did the dirty deed. His body was displayed to the public. Edward's brother, Richard, Duke of Gloucester arrested the Duke of Bedford and his brother John, and then cut their heads off for supporting Henry VI and Margaret.

1478

A most unusual royal wedding took place at Westminster on 15 January. The betrothed couple were five-year-old Richard, Edward VI's son, and the four-year-old Anne Mowbray who was the heiress to the estates of the late John Mowbray, Duke of Norfolk. The arranged marriage was the idea of the Duchess of Norfolk and the king. The wedding took place at the Palace of Westminster in St Stephen's Chapel. If Anne died then Richard would inherit all her estates. Richard, Duke of Gloucester officiated at the celebrations while his other brother George, Duke of Clarence, lay in a cell at the tower, charged by King Edward with treason.

After falling out with his brother again, George, Duke of Clarence was murdered in the Tower of London. It is believed that he was drowned in a vat of wine on his brother's orders, to save him a public execution for treason. They had fallen out again after a servant of George drew up an astrologer's chart telling of the downfall of King Edward. The servant was executed and when George spoke up for him he too was arrested, and then charged with treason.

William Caxton set up a printing shop at the Chapter House near Westminster Abbey. Caxton had been in Cologne, Germany, for many years learning the new trade from the inventor of the printing press, Johannes Guttenberg. Guttenberg thought up the idea as a child when a wooden letter used to teach reading fell into a tin of purple paint. He left it on a piece of paper to dry and when he removed it he discovered it had left a print.

Guttenberg printed the first bible and now the art of printing was causing a revolution in the world of learning. It was now possible to print in minutes what it had previously taken weeks to hand write, with the reproduction getting better every year. Caxton first set up shop in Bruges, Belgium, where he printed his first book *The History of Troye*. The first book printed in England is said to have been Chaucer's *Canterbury Tales*.

1479

Another outbreak of the plague hit England, London in particular. Though the outbreak was sporadic in London, it killed about 4,000 people and lasted until the winter when it mysteriously disappeared again. The cause of the outbreak is still a mystery.

1483

Edward IV died of a stroke on 9 April and was succeeded by his son, Edward V. Edward IV had been worried that the twelve-year-old boy would be the subject of some controversy between the barons and the church; on his death-bed he urged that the boy be crowned as soon as possible.

A coronation date was set for 4 May. Meanwhile, the new king and his younger brother, Richard, Duke of York, were staying with the Woodville family, who were related through the marriage of Elizabeth Woodville to Edward IV in 1464; Elizabeth was Edward V's mother. Another relative was his paternal uncle Richard, Duke of Gloucester, an extremely dangerous and ambitious man. Anthony Woodville, the king's uncle and brother of his mother, was charged with accompanying the king to London for the ceremony. They started out on 30 April with Richard planning to meet them at Stony Stratford to complete the journey to the Tower of London, where the king would stay until his coronation.

The royal party stopped at an inn in Northampton for the night, where they were to be met by Richard and his ally Henry Stafford, the Duke of Buckingham. After a night of drinking, Anthony Woodville awoke to find his door locked and himself under arrest for conspiracy to assassinate Richard. The Duke of Gloucester had by now disappeared with the young king and was on his way to London. The boy king was imprisoned in the Tower of London. The king's mother fled with his younger brother Richard to Westminster Abbey and sought sanctuary, but the Duke of Gloucester persuaded her to part with her son, who also ended up in the Tower. On 26 June Richard, Duke of Gloucester, was crowned Richard III on a petition passed by parliament. Richard had put a good case to parliament claiming that Edward IV was not entitled to marry Elizabeth Woodville, as he was already betrothed to another. Therefore his offspring were bastards and not entitled to the throne.

Richard was the brother of Edward IV, thereby the next legitimate successor to the throne and parliament agreed. Earl Edward, the son of the Duke of Clarence, also made a plea to parliament claiming his father was the next in line and so he, Edward, must now be entitled to the crown. Richard argued that George, Duke of Clarence was convicted of treason and so forfeited his son's claim. On 2 November Richard's ally in the affair, the Duke of Buckingham, was executed for turning against Richard and siding with Henry Tudor, a Welsh Lancastrian, now living in Brittany. Henry's troops were unable to land for an invasion, so they returned to France leaving Buckingham alone to face the bigger army of Richard III. In October the two princes in the tower disappeared; it was feared they were murdered by James Tyrrell and other followers of Richard. The Tyrrells had an awesome reputation for being involved in the murder of English kings. Tyrrell was later convicted of the murders then executed. Richard denied any involvement and he blamed his enemies, who he claimed had kidnapped the boys to make him look bad. The bodies were never found, although in the 1600s two small skeletons were discovered under a stairwell when repairs were being made to the White Tower. The bones are thought to be those of the murdered princes, and were interred at Innocents' Corner in the chapel of Henry VII at Westminster Abbey.

1484

On 2 March, Richard III opened the new College of Arms after he donated a large house he owned in Thames Street as the headquarters. Since Henry I had knighted Geoffrey Plantagenet in 1127 and gave him a shield bearing three golden lions, all knights had designed their own coat of arms to represent the family name through their deeds. The college still exists today at Coldharbour House on Thames Street, where there is a register for all coats of arms of English, Norman and Anglo-Saxon descendants.

1485

William Caxton printed the first illustrated book, a new version of Chaucer's *Canterbury Tales*. Caxton, who had a shop in Fleet Street, was busy translating French books as well. He was soon to print the *Tales of King Arthur* by Sir Thomas Malory.

King Richard III suffered a new blow to his life, when on 16 March his twenty-nine-year-old wife died. He had already lost his only son and heir, Prince Edward, the previous year. Anne, Duchess of Gloucester was once married to King Henry VI and was the daughter of Richard Neville, Earl of Warwick. She had married Richard after Henry was killed at the Battle of Tewkesbury in 1471. It was a most unusual match considering Richard had a hand in the demise and deaths of her father, father-in-law and husband. In August, Richard's luck took another turn for the worse when Henry Tudor, the Lancastrian who escaped after Henry VI was defeated at Tewkesbury, returned to Wales with an army to take the throne.

Landing at Milford Haven in Wales, Henry mustered up a band of some 2,000 Welshmen to add to his own army of nearly 3,000. The armies met at Bosworth Hill near Leicester. Although outnumbered by seasoned troops, Henry managed to cut Richard off from his main throng of men when Richard charged Henry's position and killed his standard-bearer. The Stanley family deserted Richard when they refused to charge on Henry at the crucial point of the battle. Sir William Stanley ordered his cavalry to join

Henry. Henry then attacked Richard and the two fought a pitched battle to the death, winner taking all. Henry slew Richard with a broadsword. Then Richard's bodyguards surrendered and the cry went up that the king was dead. Henry tore off Richard's armour and displayed him through the bloodied field on horseback for all to see. Richard III was the last of the warring Plantagenets. The crown of England was retrieved from under a bush and Sir William Stanley personally crowned Henry. The new house to serve the throne would be the House of Tudor.

5

THE ORIGINAL 'HOORAY HENRYS'!

The Tudor Period (1485–1603)

1486

Henry VII had promised to bring the warring houses of Lancaster and York together by marrying Elizabeth of York if he won the crown, and on 18 January he did just that at Westminster Abbey.

1493

Reports reached London that an Italian sailor named Cristobal Columbe (Christopher Columbus) had found a new route to India and the east. After sailing for ten weeks from Portugal across the Atlantic Ocean, a sailor on watch named Rodrigo Bernajo spotted an island. On landing Columbe discovered two tribes of natives living there, the Arawaks and the Caribs. As he thought at first that he was in the area of India, he called them Indians. On sailing further north, Columbe discovered that he had not in fact found a new route to the east, but new lands between Asia and Europe. The discovery was received with great joy in London and there were plans afoot to trade with the New World. The voyage of Columbe also disputed the belief that the world was flat.

1496

John Cabot, a navigator from Genoa, was financed by Henry VII to take a ship to the New World discovered by Columbus. He landed at New Scotland (Nova Scotia), and planted the Tudor flag. On his return in 1497, he told King Henry that the New World was teeming with fish and had plentiful resources that would make the king rich beyond his wildest dreams. The City of London petitioned the king for trading rights in the New World.

1497

Another peasants' revolt arose after a rise in taxes. This time the revolt was started in Cornwall and an army of angry rebels arrived in London on 17 June. Lord Daubeney met them at Blackheath and slaughtered some 2,000 rebels, including the ringleaders who were also supporting the Earl of Warwick and Perkin Warbeck in their claims to the throne.

1499

The two claimants to the throne of England were executed at the Tower of London on 28 November. Edward, Earl of Warwick and Perkin Warbeck were in league to overthrow the crown, but both were caught plotting to escape. Perkin had insisted that he was in fact Richard, the Duke of York, who was believed to have been murdered in the Tower in 1483. Perkin had since withdrawn his claim. Henry solved his problem by ridding himself of them once and for all. Warwick was beheaded and Perkin was hanged in the tower after being pilloried outside Westminster Abbey.

1500

The Tudor era brought prosperity and peace to England. In London, businesses were booming and new buildings were going up in a grand new style of architecture, large wooden-framed houses with lathe and plaster walls. Henry started off the fashion when he built a new palace to replace the burnt out Palace of Sheen, whose ruins lay just west of the City of London. The palace was to be called Richmond Palace after Henry's former title, Richmond. The wool trade was bringing great prosperity to the countryside, and a London merchant built a large grandiose country mansion at Coggeshall, Essex, in the new design. Many other merchants around the country were emulating the king's new designers.

1501

Henry's eldest son, Arthur, married Catherine of Aragon at a lavish ceremony at Westminster Abbey on 14 November. Prince Henry, Arthur's younger brother was said to be pleased for him. The marriage showed that the House of Tudor was well established.

1502

Henry VII received some devastating news; his sixteen-year-old son Arthur died suddenly on 4 April. Henry and his wife Elizabeth were shattered by the news, which came on top of the loss of their third son, Edward, two years earlier at the age of sixteen months. Prince Henry, just ten years old, was now heir to the English throne. The king had to deal with not only his grief but what to do with Arthur's widow, the sixteen-year-old Catherine. The royal couple also had two daughters, Margaret and Mary.

In May Sir James Tyrrell and other Yorkists were executed at the Tower of London for plotting to overthrow the crown. Tyrrell also confessed to the murders of the princes in the Tower on the orders of Richard III. Some sceptics however, dismissed the confession as a plot by Henry to exonerate himself from any blame in the affair.

1503

In February Elizabeth died and left Henry a widower. Prince Henry was betrothed to his brother's widow, Catherine of Aragon; the twelve-year-old boy would marry Catherine three years later. Henry VII had considered marrying her himself, and had even applied for a dispensation from Rome to allow the marriage, as the couple were related. In August, Princess Margaret was married to King James Stewart IV of Scotland, and Henry signed the Treaty of Perpetual Peace that effectively ended 200 years of war with Scotland.

1509

King Henry VII died on 21 April of tuberculosis after a long illness. He was succeeded by his son Henry. Henry was now married to his brother's widow, Catherine of Aragon. They were crowned king and queen on 24 June, having married in Greenwich on 11 June. The wedding ceremony was very lavish, and it was seen as a sign that the new king was a lover of all things extravagant.

1511

On 1 January the Queen gave birth to their first son, also named Henry, who was given the Dukedom of Cornwall. The baby boy died seven weeks later, causing a rift between the royal couple.

The Holy Roman Emperor sent Henry a magnificent suit of German-made armour, to honour the king's support and love of jousting. The suit was so well made it prompted Henry to found an armour factory in Southwark. The suit is now on display in the Tower of London armoury rooms.

1512

The Palace of Westminster burnt down. The only part saved was the Great Hall. Henry moved into the home of the Archbishop of York, which was just 500 yards away. The king had to save some money so he paid his royal guards at the Tower of London part of their wages in beef, earning them the nickname Beefeaters.

1514

On 13 June, King Henry VIII launched the biggest warship in naval history. Larger than the *Mary Rose*, it was called the *Henri Grâce à Dieu* and had acquired the nickname 'The Great Harry' as all kings of England named Henry were traditionally called Harry. The five-tiered ship was the pride of the British Navy which, like his father, Henry intended to support.

1515

The Florentine sculptor Pietro Torrigiano, who served under Michelangelo, completed his work in the new chapel of Henry VII at Westminster Abbey. The lavish tomb that would house the bodies of Henry VII and his devout wife, Elizabeth of York, was made of marble and was the most magnificent ever seen. In September the Archbishop of York, Thomas Wolsey, the king's chief minister, was made a cardinal by the Pope.

1516

On 20 February the queen gave birth to a daughter, and the child named Mary seemed fit and healthy. The royal couple had been plagued with bad luck over their efforts to produce a male heir. Their first born, a girl, was stillborn in 1510 and then a son, Henry, died after seven weeks in 1511. In 1513 another son died within hours of being born, and in 1514 yet another son was stillborn.

1517

Race riots broke out in the capital on 2 May, when a Dominican monk stirred up a crowd in the parish of St Martin's. The Flemish community was the target, and it was only when a large troop of soldiers and several lords appeared at the request of the Mayor, that the crowd dispersed.

1518

King Henry VIII was petitioned by a physician named Thomas Linacre to put an end to the practice of unqualified doctors. The king proclaimed a royal seal of approval to be set on a new college, which would be known as The Royal College of Physicians. The college had the power to arrest and fine or imprison any doctor who wasn't a member, or practiced medicine without a licence.

1519

The king was overjoyed to learn that his mistress, Elizabeth Blount, had given birth to a healthy son named Henry Fitzroy. So far the king's efforts to produce a male heir had been thwarted. The child had no claim to the throne, but it proved to Henry that he was still capable of fatherhood, whereas the queen was fast reaching an age where she would not be able to conceive.

Henry fell out with the Bishop of York and seized his property. He gave York House to his friend, Cardinal Wolsey, who turned it into a palace with a magnificent whitewashed hall. The palace became known as White Hall and the thoroughfare on which it stood was named Whitehall after it.

1521

On 17 May the Duke of Buckingham was executed at Tower Green for plotting to overthrow the king. The notorious Buckingham family has had many traitors throughout their history. The Duke planned to fool the king into letting him raise an army on the pretext of collecting rents from rebellious tenants in Wales. His servants secretly wrote to the king telling him of the plot. Buckingham was ordered to appear before the king to discuss the matter, and was arrested as he rode through the streets of London on 8 April. He was convicted and carried upriver with the axeman to face his fate in front of a huge crowd.

The Pope received a copy of a book written by Henry VIII, with help from his most trusted clerics. The book was called *The Assertion of the Seven Sacraments*, in which Henry condemned Luther for his views. The Pope was delighted with the work and imposed on Henry the title of Defender of the Faith, a title that still lives on. Henry also promised a crackdown on Lutherans in England. On 12 May Cardinal Wolsey burnt many books on the subject in the grounds of St Paul's before a crowd of some 30,000. The situation was getting dire in England with many attempts to undermine the Church's authority and establish a Bible in English. John Wycliff and his Dutch friends, known as Lollards, were behind the plot to free the people from the stranglehold of the church.

1526

A new era had begun in England – one that would not go away or be suppressed. An English scholar and Protestant had printed the Bible in English, and successfully distributed many in England. The Bibles were printed abroad and smuggled into the country through a network of supporters for the new cause. The main protagonist, William Tyndale, was captured, and it was ordered after a short trial that he be strangled and burnt at the stake for being a heretic. His ideals, however, guaranteed him martyrdom and many said the church would live to regret it. The book was later to have far-reaching consequences.

1529

After much falling out and continued arguing, it seemed the relationship between Wolsey and Henry was over. With the influence of his young lover, Anne Boleyn, the king charged Wolsey with the offence of Praemunire, which since 1353 had been the crime of usurping the king's authority within the realm. Wolsey was stripped of all his personal wealth and office. He pleaded guilty to the charges on the understanding that he could keep his estates as Archbishop of York. He had already given the king York House and Hampton Court. Sir Thomas Moore replaced him.

1532

King Henry personally interceded on a case of murder and proclaimed an unusual death for the assailant. The man concerned was Richard Rosse, who was the cook for the Bishop of Rochester, one of the king's favourites. Rosse apparently put poisonous herbs into a stew, and it resulted in seventeen people becoming ill with two dying. Rosse was boiled alive in a big stew pot, a punishment that Henry felt was fitting. The irony of it all was that it took place at Smithfield Market in London, where meat was sold.

1533

On 25 January, just an hour before dawn, King Henry defied Rome and married his mistress, Anne Boleyn. The ceremony took place in the Palace of Whitehall and was held in some secrecy. The priest was an Augustinian Friar named George Brown who upon asking the king if he had a licence to marry, was told the king did have one. This wasn't true and Henry hoped the Pope would eventually accept the marriage. In May, Thomas Cranmer,

Archbishop of Canterbury annulled Henry's marriage to Catherine of Aragon which infuriated the Pope. On 1 June, Anne was crowned Queen of England at Westminster Abbey. On 7 September, Anne gave birth to a baby girl, much to Henry's disappointment. Anne named the child Elizabeth. Henry was excommunicated by the Pope.

1534

Elizabeth Barton was hanged at Tyburn for prophesising that King Henry would die a villain's death for marrying Anne Boleyn. Barton, known as the Holy Maid of Kent, along with Dr Edward Bocking and three others, was hanged for stirring up riots against the king with a booklet called *The Nun's Book*. In August the Act of Supremacy was passed to ensure the clergy recognised Henry as the supreme head of the Church of England, and as such they had to obey his rulings and ignore Rome.

Henry VIII declared himself the head of the Church of England at Westminster on 28 November. Through an act of parliament he now had more power than the Pope. Pope Clement VII called Henry and his supporters Protestants, as they seemed to be protesting at Rome's decisions regarding his marriage to Catherine of Aragon. Henry had the royal Princess Mary declared illegitimate. Should the eighteen-year-old princess ever become queen, Rome had promised to restore her legitimacy if she followed the Catholic faith and restored the country to the teachings of Rome.

1535

Bishop John Fisher was made a cardinal by Pope Paul III, and then arrested on the orders of Thomas Cromwell for refusing to swear the oath of supremacy. He was held in the Tower of London. On 22 June he was executed for heresy. Fourteen days later Sir Thomas Moore was also beheaded in the Tower for heresy.

1536

Catherine of Aragon died on 7 January after two years of house arrest at Kimbolton. In March, Thomas Cromwell seized the wealth of the smaller religious houses to bolster the royal treasury. On 2 May, Anne Boleyn was arrested and imprisoned in the Tower for adultery. After a trial which she didn't attend, Anne was found guilty and executed on 19 May, within the Tower walls. On 30 May Henry married his third wife, Jane Seymour.

1537

Jane Seymour gave birth on 12 October to a weak son who she named Edward. The queen delighted Henry who was happy at last to have an heir to the throne. Jane had a difficult birth and became very ill. She died twelve days later and Henry was greatly saddened.

1538

Henry was taken ill when a blood clot moved from his leg to his throat, leaving him incapacitated.

Cromwell stripped the shrine of Thomas A' Becket and took all the gold and silver plate into the royal treasury. The Pope finalised Henry's excommunication, so Cromwell and Henry retaliated by stripping the monasteries of all their wealth, then passing acts to make the Church of England supreme over Rome. From then on every church had to have Bibles written in English. This was a complete about-turn by Henry who earlier had Wycliffe burnt at the stake for attempting to promote this very practice. Hans Holbein, the royal painter, was sent abroad to paint the portraits of potential future wives for Henry.

1540

The Statute of Wills was passed by parliament. This allowed landowners to now pass on two-thirds of their land to their heirs by will. The crown got the other third. In 1536 Henry VIII had passed the Statute of Uses which limited the passing on of land. He relented by passing this act under pressure from the barons and lords.

Henry VIII married Anne of Cleves on 6 January after nearly cancelling the marriage. The new queen was only thirty-four years old, she was part of an agreement Henry signed with her father, Duke Williams of Cleves, in September 1539. Anne didn't speak any English.

Thomas Cromwell was arrested for treason and heresy. He was held in the Tower of London. Cromwell was accused of usurping his powers and blamed by the royal court for the failed marriage of Anne and Henry who, by June, were living separate lives. Cromwell was executed on 28 July still professing his innocence. Catherine Howard, the king's new love, was said to have persuaded Henry that Cromwell was plotting against them. Cromwell was credited with making sure that every church in the land now had an English language bible, so the people could read the scriptures for themselves. Henry VIII married Catherine Howard, niece of the Duke of Norfolk, just hours after Cromwell's death sentence was carried out.

The Guild of Surgeons joined with the Barbers Company (formed in 1461) to form a new association, the College of Surgeons and Barbers, in London. The new college would give surgeons more status in the community. Until this time they had been regarded as little more than assistants to physicians, who unlike surgeons had to have a university education.

1542

Catherine Howard, the fifth wife of Henry VIII, was finally executed at the Tower for treason, after being found guilty of adultery with Thomas Culpepper and Francis Dereham. They were both executed in December 1541. Catherine was arrested in November 1541 and held in the Tower. She was just twenty-two years old. Her uncle, the Duke of Norfolk, was said to be most distressed, this being his second niece to have married Henry and been beheaded. His other niece was Anne Boleyn, who the Duke also introduced to the king in order to gain influence at court. Catherine was beheaded on 13 February.

1543

On 12 July Henry VIII married Catherine Parr, his sixth wife. Catherine was thirty-one years old, and already twice-widowed.

1546

The brothels of London's South Bankside were ordered to cease trading by order of the king. Known as Stews, these houses of ill-repute had been a necessary evil for the people of London. Now, along with the gambling houses, they were no more, though it was thought that it wouldn't be for long. Religious radicals were also being persecuted in London. A woman of means and influence named Anne Askew was tortured and burned alive at Smithfields, on the orders of Richard Rich and Thomas Wriothesley, two senior judges.

1547

On 28 January, King Henry VIII died in his sleep. Henry's untimely death at the age of fifty-five was a godsend to Lord Howard the Duke of Norfolk, who was to have been executed that very morning; the death sentence was suspended. Henry was survived by three children; Edward aged nine who would now be the king, and two daughters, Elizabeth and Mary. Henry willed all his power to Edward Seymour, Earl of Hertford. Seymour ordered the king's death to be kept secret until he could secure all the royal treasures and the seal of England, in order that he may rule as regent for young Edward.

Seymour plotted with Sir William Paget to make himself the Duke of Somerset, and by doing so had now persuaded the Regency Council, set up by Henry VIII, to accept both men as protectors of the boy king.

Henry's death was officially announced on 31 January. Edward VI was crowned in the abbey on 19 February. In July, Catherine Parr married the young king's uncle and Edward Seymour's brother, Thomas Seymour (his sister had been Jane Seymour, Henry's third wife and the king's mother). The marriage caused rumours at court about Thomas Seymour and his philandering with both princesses, Mary and Elizabeth.

On 19 December, parliament passed a law to deal with vagrants. The problem had become increasingly worse since the first acts were passed in 1535 and stemmed from the enclosure acts which threw thousands of peasants out of work. Since then, vagrants had hampered hygiene and social reforms in large towns and cities. The new penalties were severe, but the death penalty for persistent offenders was removed. In future, vagrants would be whipped then ordered to return to their place of birth. On second or subsequent offences they were to be whipped in public and branded with the letter V. The law was needed to distinguish the difference between those who were genuinely in need, and those who chose to live off the goodwill of others.

1549

Thomas Seymour, King Edward VI's uncle, was executed on 20 March for high treason. There was much speculation at court about the true reason for his untimely death. Officially, Seymour was executed for amassing a private army and arms stores at his estate in Sudeley in Gloucestershire. Rumours abounded that he was also philandering with the Princess Elizabeth in the hope of marrying her and one day becoming king. His reputation as a womaniser at court was legendary and it was even rumoured that he had fathered a child with Elizabeth. His wife, the widow of the late King Henry VIII, had died in childbirth on 7 September 1548.

The House of Lords finally passed the Act of Uniformity making it illegal to hold Catholic Mass; they also introduced the Book of Common Prayer, which was written by Bishop Thomas Cranmer. Five Bishops who refused to comply with the order were imprisoned, and rebellious factions in the north and west of the country threatened civil war. The reforms, which were the brainchild of Henry VIII, were being strictly enforced by the Duke of Somerset, Edward Seymour, who colluded in them with the late king. Seymour hired German mercenaries to put down the rioters. They marched to Norwich to quell a series of riots instigated by a tannery owner named Robert Ket, and some 3,000 peasants were killed in the ensuing clashes. The rioters were also enraged at the newly enforced agricultural reforms enclosing the fields system and putting many out of work. Seymour and many other landowners were profiting heavily from the new system.

On 13 October Edward Seymour was imprisoned in the Tower; his arrest came about after his influence at court dwindled. First, his brother Thomas plotted against him and was executed and then it became public knowledge that he was making vast sums of money from land seizures in the West Country. His old adversary, the Earl of Warwick, was the main instigator of the treason charges against Seymour, who had now fallen out with his ward Edward VI.

1552

Things were going from bad to worse for young King Edward. The country was almost bankrupt and inflation so rife that it was running at 50 per cent. The churches were plundered under the guise of religious reform, with most of the plate and gold being confiscated and used to prop up the treasury. The army hadn't been paid for months, and dissent was looming in the ranks as France threatened to seize Calais. In 1550, John Dudley the Earl of Warwick, who was now the Duke of Northumberland, had overseen the surrender of Boulogne by King Henry II of France after an unsuccessful attempt to retake the city from the English. Dudley knew the country couldn't finance another long war with France. As France was now also allied with Scotland, it was expected that a treaty of independence would follow with the Scots.

King Edward was taken very ill with smallpox. Despite his illness, the young king became worried about the increasing population of London, mostly country peasants forced into the city because of the huge unemployment problem caused by the land reform acts. It was the coldest winter for many decades, and many were sleeping on the streets with the hospitals at overflow. Edward managed to found a new school in Newgate Street for over 700 pupils, who would be taught to read and write, as well as spinning and weaving. The distinctive uniform of the school gave it a new name, the Blue Coat School. The guardians of the children (most of whom were orphans), started to soak their long socks in saffron to keep the rats from biting them as they studied. Yellow socks were now officially part of the uniform. The school survived and the building still stands today, although closed, in Victoria. In the king's absence from court, the Duke of Northumberland, John Dudley took control of matters of state and effectively ruled the country.

1553

With the king on his deathbed, Dudley was panicking at the thought of the Catholic Princess Mary becoming queen, and set out to bar her and her sister Elizabeth from the line of succession. Dudley married off his son, Guildford Dudley, to Lady Jane Grey, his theory being that as Lady Jane was descended from King Henry VIII's sister Mary, she had precedence over the royal princesses to the throne of England. It was a thinly supported claim, but a valid one just the same. Edward VI was staunchly Protestant and determined to keep his father's wish to bar Catholics from ruling England. The first beneficiary of the will was Lady Jane, and so a new line would allow her male heirs to inherit the throne. However, a fly in the ointment seemed to be Frances, Mary's elder daughter, so the will was written in such a way as to exclude her as well. Many at court felt it would not be valid and that after the king died, Dudley would become a resident in the Tower. On 6 July Edward breathed his last. He died leaving a country at loggerheads with his religious reforms, with bloody riots taking place and a possible coup lying ahead.

On 10 July, in accordance with the will of Edward VI, the Privy Council declared Lady Jane Grey the new ruler of England, but on 15 July in Suffolk, Princess Mary declared herself queen. John Dudley, eager to protect his position, amassed an army and marched to Framlingham Castle to arrest Mary. His protégée, Lady Jane, refused to declare Dudley's son as king and his army broke up and deserted when the news reached the main body. Dudley fled back to London where he was greeted by an angry mob. The council met again to discuss the matter, and were forced to reverse their previous decision by overwhelming support in favour of the Catholic Princess Mary. While both the late kings Henry VIII and Edward VI had been busy reforming the church to convert to Protestantism, they had failed to realise that the majority of the people were quite happy to remain Catholic. Their fervour to revert back to Rome was the main reason they favoured Mary. On 19 July, Lady Jane Grey was confined to the Tower of London. Meanwhile, Princess Mary was proclaimed queen by the council, and prepared to return triumphantly to London.

On Mary's return to the capital she permitted a Protestant funeral for her brother Edward, albeit a simple one, and proceeded to matters of state. Having been welcomed by the populace and with much support at court, Mary ordered the council to deal with the treacherous John Dudley. Just nineteen days after her return to London, Dudley was executed at Tower Hill. Mary was crowned queen on 1 October and then announced her intention to marry the Catholic Philip of Spain, thereby bringing a powerful ally to her house in the form of the Holy Roman Emperor Charles V, the father of Philip. Mary also announced her decree to return England to Catholicism, by force if necessary.

By mid-September Mary was implementing her will. Bishops and high-ranking clergy officials were rounded up and imprisoned. One of the first to be arrested was Nicholas Ridley who had spoken out in support of Lady Jane Grey, who was still in the Tower awaiting her fate. Thomas Cranmer, the Archbishop of Canterbury and author of the Protestant Book of Common Prayer, was joined in the Tower by Bishop John Hooper and Hugh Latimer, another notorious Protestant speaker. All were expected to be executed soon after. The Princess Elizabeth was also questioned about her relationship with Cranmer. Mary suspected that there may be a plot to put the Protestant sympathiser Elizabeth on the throne; Mary ordered Elizabeth to be confined at Greenwich, where she was to study the Bible according to Rome. In December, Mary called a parliament and managed to get approval on the validity of her parents' marriage, thereby freeing the way to marry Philip of Spain, which parliament also conceded to. The Pope was declared the head of the Church of Rome and England. All Henry VIII and Edward VI's religious reforms were repealed.

1554

In January, a plot was uncovered by Queen Mary's network of busy spies to dethrone her and declare Elizabeth queen, so the country could return to Protestantism. The leader of the plot, Sir Thomas Wyatt, was sent to the Tower. Princess Elizabeth was now in mortal danger and questioned about her involvement in the plot. On 12 February, the sixteen-year-old Lady Jane Grey and her husband Guildford Dudley were executed at Tower Green. Elizabeth was still confined to Greenwich, but in March she was taken to the Tower and confined in a dark cell while she underwent more interrogation. Torture was ruled out for Elizabeth, so her inquisitors used more subtle methods of putting fear into the princess.

On 11 April, Wyatt was executed at Tower Hill. Despite much torture to himself and his fellow conspirators, Wyatt wouldn't confess to the duplicity of Elizabeth and the princess was freed. She was taken to Woodstock where she recovered from her ordeal, before returning to London. On 25 July, Philip of Spain married Mary in Winchester Cathedral; the magnificent ceremony surpassed any previously witnessed in England. Mary, at thirty-eight, was eleven years the senior of Philip who had also been crowned King of Spain. An heir to the Catholic throne was desperately sought by Mary, but the marriage wasn't popular as people saw the Spanish infiltrating the English throne. Mary had already pointed out that she was in fact part Spanish, as her mother was Catherine of Aragon. Even her most trusted advisor, Bishop Stephen Gardiner of Winchester, advised the queen against the marriage. Gardiner had twice been imprisoned in the Tower for preaching the Catholic faith during the reign of Edward VI.

1555

Richard Chancellor, a merchant from London, managed to become the first Englishman to set foot in Moscow. He set up a trading firm called the Muscovy Company with the approval of both Queen Mary and Czar Ivan VI. He was currently seeking a new route to China, as he also wanted to trade with the Chinese.

In Oxford, on 16 October, Nicholas Ridley and Hugh Latimer were burnt at the stake for heresy, outside Balliol College; both men were staunch Protestants who even fell out with Henry VIII over their views. On the same day, Bishop Stephen Gardiner died.

On 18 July, Queen Mary granted a new charter to the College of Arms to create and register Heraldic Arms. The college still exists today. It operates from its original building in Queen Victoria Street, London.

1556

In March, Sir Henry Dudley was arrested for a planned coup against Mary. He had intended to invade England with mercenaries and banish Catholics, then place Princess Elizabeth on the throne to rule a Protestant England once more. The plan fell apart when Dudley was discovered attempting to defraud the treasury in order to pay for the venture. He was placed in the Tower to await his fate. On 21 March, just three days after Dudley's arrest, Thomas Cranmer was burnt at the stake outside Balliol College in Broad Street, Oxford. Once Henry VIII's most respected chancellor, he went the same way as Ridley and Latimer whose burnings he witnessed from his gaol cell. Although he recanted all his previous statements promoting Protestantism, Queen Mary was said to be glad he was finally gone.

The harvest failed, leaving thousands starving throughout England. Inflation was running high again and new diseases were sweeping the country killing thousands more. The sweating disease (influenza) was the worst. It killed within days. People were running to the countryside to escape the epidemic, thereby exacerbating the food shortage problem.

1557

On 17 November, Queen Mary died. The queen, who became known as Bloody Mary for the 300 martyrs she executed in her desire to enforce the Catholic religion, was never in good health. She suffered many phantom pregnancies and never managed to produce an heir to the throne, which now passed to her sister Elizabeth. Elizabeth was a renowned and passionate Protestant who had secretly vowed to convert England back to the religion that her father, Henry VIII, invented following his disputes with Rome. More reforms were expected along with arrests and executions of devout Catholics, many of whom had risen to power under Mary.

Mary was buried in Westminster Abbey on 14 December in a Catholic ceremony overseen by Bishop John White. Elizabeth inherited a country divided by rich and poor, Catholic and Protestant. Calais had been lost earlier in the year and the finances of the state were in turmoil with inflation high and many forged coins in circulation, which had virtually destroyed the current coinage system. Elizabeth was crowned in Westminster Abbey on 15 January, just five days after turning down Phillip of Spain's offer of marriage. The former husband of her sister Mary was now bankrupt and desperate for a safe haven. Elizabeth wouldn't consider any Catholic for a husband. Archbishop Heath of York refused to modify the coronation ceremony to make it more in line with Protestantism, and so the ceremony was taken by the Bishop of Carlisle.

1559

A churchman from Norwich had come to the attention of Elizabeth at court, who appointed him Archbishop of Canterbury on 17 December; he was only the second Protestant archbishop. Matthew Parker, born in 1504, was well-educated, having studied at Corpus Christi College, Cambridge. He was ordained in 1527 and became vice chancellor of Cambridge in 1544. He also helped to write the new prayer book. He had a rather large nose and was said to be inquisitive of all that went on around him. He was nicknamed Nosy Parker because of it, and the name seemed to have started a new trend at court when referring to a person of an overly inquisitive nature.

1560

The old reforms were to be implemented once again, with the Book of Common Prayer being forced once more on the clergy and the people. Parliament also disassociated the country from Rome and declared that Rome no longer reigned supreme in religious affairs in England. The Act of Uniformity and the Act of Supremacy were both passed in England, and, in effect, Ireland as well. Scotland was also seeing much activity in matters of religious reform and trouble was brewing everywhere. There was much activity at court in September when it was rumoured that Queen Elizabeth had had a hand in the mysterious death of Amy Robsart, the wife of Lord Robert Dudley.

The rumours abounded that Elizabeth killed Amy by pushing her down some stairs in order to free Lord Dudley to openly be her lover; it was well known that they had been secret lovers for some time. Dudley was not liked at court and it was felt the whole affair would end in either their marriage or his execution.

In June the queen visited the Bursary, opened in 1558 by Sir Thomas Gresham. It was renamed the Royal Exchange. The Gresham banking family got their name from the village in Norfolk where they owned an estate. Thomas Gresham lived in Lombard Street while in London, and the family symbol was the grasshopper insect.

There is a legend about how the creature became his trade mark. Apparently when Thomas was about five years old he wandered away on the estate. As darkness beckoned, the servants were sent out to find him. One servant remembered he enjoyed playing with the grasshoppers in a certain field, and listening for the sound they make when they communicate by rubbing their legs. The servant found him in time as darkness fell and the creature was adopted by the family. However, this fanciful story is pure legend; his father had the symbol as the family emblem before Thomas was born.

Thomas's only son died in infancy, and so he left his only daughter his entire fortune. The family name died out with him on 21 November 1579, when he passed away suddenly. Turner's bank later took up the symbol of the grasshopper to remember the man who gave his name to Gresham's Law, a theory that bad money drives out good money. Today in Lombard Street there is still a sign bearing a grasshopper outside Turner's Bank, as well as a grasshopper weathervane on top of the Royal Exchange.

1561

Lady Catherine Grey, sister to Lady Jane Grey, was confined to the Tower. Lady Catherine had a distant claim to the throne and was forbidden to marry without Elizabeth's specific permission. Not only had she secretly married Edward Earl of Hertford, but she had conceived a son.

1562

The long-awaited new coinage finally replaced the old coinage of the realm. Under Henry VIII and Edward VI the coinage had been debased, and therefore contained less silver than the face value. This gave rise to a European devaluation of English coins, and a vote of no confidence in the English economy, causing massive inflation and extortionate rises in food prices, leaving many to starve to death. The new coinage replaced the old which had been called in. All coins now contained an amount of silver equal to their face value. Debasing or forging coins was a capital offence. In September the queen contracted smallpox and nearly died; Lord Dudley was to have been appointed Protectorate of England in the event of Elizabeth's death. However, the queen pulled through.

1563

Parliament passed new laws to cover wages and working hours in most industries. The reforms received mixed comments. Agricultural workers had to work fourteen-hour days, fifteen hours in the summer, with fines for those failing to turn up for work. The reforms allowed the workers two and a half hours for breaks and food. Local magistrates had the power to set wages according to the area and impose fines to prevent idleness.

In September, Captain John Hawkins returned triumphantly to London with hordes of treasure, which he acquired trading with the Spanish in the West Indies. Captain Hawkins had left Plymouth in October the previous year, and while in the Canary Islands discovered that a lucrative trade existed in negro slaves. He purchased a load, and then sailed to the West Indies where he exchanged them for spices, pearls and hides. The Spanish authorities boarded two of his ships when they reached Cadiz, and confiscated the lot.

Hawkins had so much cargo, he had sent two ships to Spain and three ships to England, that he still returned a rich man. Elizabeth was said to be pleased with Hawkins, but furious with the Spanish.

To help the fishing industry, Elizabeth declared that Wednesdays, Fridays, Saturdays and religious holidays were to be meat-less days. It was also now illegal to draw, paint or deal in unauthorised portraits of the queen.

1570

In January, James Stuart, the Scottish Regent was shot and killed by an assassin in a street in Linlithgow. Mary Queen of Scots was confined to Fotheringhay Castle in fear of a coup.

In London, a Catholic merchant named John Felton was tortured and executed for nailing a declaration (a bull) to the door of the Bishop of London's house. The bull declared Elizabeth a bastard and appealed to her subjects to dethrone her as a Protestant fraud. Thomas Howard, the Duke of Norfolk who led a Catholic rebellion in the north, was freed from prison and put under house arrest on the orders of Elizabeth. The northern rebellion was crushed by Lord Hunsdon with the leaders captured, killed or driven over the border into Scotland. Their peasant followers were systematically hanged in their hundreds.

Relations with Spain were very strained; the previous year, Elizabeth had seized Spanish ships forced to seek refuge in Plymouth and Southampton. The ships were carrying treasure and coins to repay a loan to Genoese bankers from King Philip II of Spain. Elizabeth did the deed in revenge for the Spanish confiscating Captain Hawkins' cargo in 1563. She then decided, in order not to entirely fall out with the Habsburgs, that she would take on the loan herself.

1579

The Irish rebels were revolting again. The mostly Catholic rebels were in dispute with English rule and the implementation of Protestant reforms. James Fitzmaurice Fitzgerald, an Irishman, and Nicholas Saunders, an Englishman, had been preaching a crusade against the queen and her reforms; they were drumming up much support. Sir Henry Sydney just managed to hold onto power as the revolt took hold in Leinster, Munster, and Ulster. With Scotland forming alliances with France, and James VI now thirteen years old and ruling in his own right, it was important for England to ally itself as well. A betrothal between Elizabeth and Francis of Anjou, brother of King Henry III of France, was encouraged by parliament with Francis expected to visit England in November.

Robert Dudley, Earl of Leicester angered the queen by marrying in secret. His bride was Lettice Knollys, widow of the Count of Essex, whom he had been associated with for some time. The queen found out when a French courtier came to see her to arrange the visit of Francis of Anjou. He happened to mention that Francis was pleased about the marriage, as it would help to scotch any further rumours about their alleged love tryst. Elizabeth was overheard threatening to send Dudley to the Tower.

Sir Francis Drake, a favourite of the queen, pleased her by capturing the Spanish warship *The Cacafuego* off the coast of Ecuador. Drake had done well against Spain since burning Vera Cruz and returning to England with much treasure in 1573. The campaign had a heavy price though, with Drake's brother, Joseph, dying in the battle.

Drake had been involved in expeditions with Captain Hawkins in 1569 in which they both lost vast fortunes; it seemed Drake was now making up for it.

In November there was much apprehension about the proposed marriage of Elizabeth to the Catholic Francis. A Norfolk gentleman named John Stubbe was arrested for seditious behaviour, when he printed leaflets proclaiming the marriage an offence against God. At his trial the merchant tried to recant his claims, but the justice ruled the deed done and ordered that both Stubbe and the printer have their right hands struck off in public. Stubbe raised his hat with his remaining hand after the axe took off his right hand and shouted 'God save the Queen', before he expired from the shock.

1581

Parliament passed harsh new laws against Catholic transgressors. The Statute of Recusancy raised fines to £20 per year for failing to attend church; in 1559 the fine was just 12 pence. To hold Mass was punishable by a year in gaol, and to convert or be converted to Catholicism was now treason. The queen also outlawed William Allen and Edmund Campion as enemies of the state; if either man set foot in England they would be executed. At Deptford, London, on 4 April, Francis Drake was knighted on the deck of his ship *The Golden Hind* by the queen. Drake had not only trounced the Spanish in South America, but had become the first Englishman and only the second man to circumnavigate the globe. The only person who disapproved was the Spanish ambassador. Elizabeth was presented with much treasure taken from the Spanish by Drake, as part of her investment in the expedition. A study of Elizabethan England by Sir Thomas Smith was published in a book of his findings called *De Republica Anglorum*, in which he set out his theory that the country was now divided into four classes; the gentlemen, who he claimed were the ruling classes, citizens, yeoman and manual workers.

1585

On 6 January the queen knighted another favourite, Walter Raleigh, who described himself as an adventurer and scholar. Sir Walter pleased the queen greatly with his stories of the New World and his many discoveries. The previous year he had returned to England laden with treasure and new discoveries. Among the cargo were two natives of the New World and a strange herb called tobacco. The herb was dried, rolled into a solid stick, and then set alight. The smoke it produced was then inhaled deep into the lungs. Tobacco was said to open the passages of the body and as such was a health aid that would ward off illness. Sir Walter was given land and made Vice Admiral of Devon. In the queen's honour he named land in the new world Virginia.

The Bond of Association statute was passed by parliament in an attempt to further protect the queen from assassination attempts. The statute further declared that all converted Catholics were to leave the country within forty days from 28 February or face a charge of treason and execution. In August, Elizabeth agreed to help the Dutch in their struggle against Spain; the action came about after the assassination of William of Orange in July 1584 by agents of Philip II of Spain.

In 1584 another plot had been discovered that involved the Spanish Ambassador, Bernardino de Mendoza, who was subsequently expelled. Sir Francis Walsingham arrested Sir Francis Throckmorton, and under torture he admitted the plot naming Mendoza and Mary Queen of Scots as fellow conspirators. More trials were expected.

In September, Raleigh sailed with a fleet against the Spanish holdings in the Caribbean. The fleet, which was financed and backed by Elizabeth, attacked Vigo, Havana, Santo Domingo and finally humiliated Philip by sacking Cartagena, the capital of the Spanish Main. War with Spain now seemed likely with Philip threatening to invade and challenge the legitimacy of Elizabeth to rule England. He was said to still be embarrassed at Elizabeth turning down his marriage proposal. In Scotland, James VI was restored to the throne after Elizabeth released his most trusted lords and agreed to support him financially in exchange for peace. His mother, Mary, was still in Fotheringhay Castle awaiting her fate for plotting against the crown. James angered Mary who branded him an ingrate.

1587

On 8 February at 10.00 a.m., Mary Queen of Scots was beheaded at Fotheringhay Castle, her prison for the past nineteen years. The execution, on the orders of Elizabeth, was the final straw after many plots to overthrow Elizabeth and return England and Scotland to Catholicism. Mary, dressed entirely in red, laid her head on the block, as she had practiced many times the night before. The executioner picked up the axe and swung it once for a clean execution. He then held up the head to show the crowd, and it fell from his hand as the wig Mary was wearing came loose. As the head hit the floor, her dress came to life and everyone screamed it was witchcraft. On further examination it was revealed that Mary's pet dog had been secreted under her dress. The dog was then also executed. This ended a long drawn-out conspiracy trial in which seven of her co-defendants were also executed at Holborn the previous September. The seven, including Anthony Babington, a rich Catholic, were hung, drawn and quartered as was the fate of all traitors.

Elizabeth reacted to the end of Mary Queen of Scots in a peculiar manner. On hearing from the Secretary of State, Sir William Davison that Mary was dead, she ordered Sir William confined to the Tower, blaming him for persuading her to sign the death warrant. The queen now claimed that she never intended to sacrifice Mary for the safety of the crown. In Scotland King James VI on hearing of his mother's demise, was said to have been saddened, but pleased that he was now no longer in danger of being impeached, in favour of the abdicated Mary. War with Spain was hotting up with news of a large armada gathering in Spanish ports; Captain Hawkins revealed the invasion plot in October the previous year after returning with Spanish prisoners.

On 29 April, Sir Francis Drake sailed into Cadiz harbour and destroyed much of the armada. The incident, called 'The Singeing of the King of Spain's Beard', angered Elizabeth, who had withdrawn her backing after Drake left England. He had attacked not knowing of her decision. He then attacked and held Cape St Vincent before returning to Plymouth on 7 July. Despite Drake's efforts the Spanish still had a huge navy, and invasion was certain.

1588

In July the Spanish Armada set sail for England. The huge convoy of enormous ships, carrying over 15,000 troops, was engaged in pitched battles with many fine English sailors, Hawkins, Drake and Lord Howard among them. From 21 July for almost nine days, the smaller English warships dodged in and out of the convoy, destroying the ships, and then sailed away to safety. The Spanish were attacked at Eddystone, Portland, the Isle of Wight and Gravelines; they lost eleven ships and some 2,000 men. The English losses were only fifty men and no ships. On 3 August, the Spanish commander, the Duke of Medina Sidonia, gave the order to abandon the attack and retreated back to Spain.

The Armada was further hampered by high winds and storms which drove them as far up the coast as Scotland and the Orkney Islands, where many more were shipwrecked. The English had a secret weapon: ships stacked with timber and pitch and set on fire after being sailed between the Spanish galleons. The fires caused panic and while the Spanish attempted to avoid the flaming ships, the English navy fired cannon and sank them. In Tilbury on 8 August a grateful Queen Elizabeth gave a rousing speech to her Navy and soldiers; the speech is now part of English history.

> Let tyrants fear. I have always so behaved myself that, under God, I have placed my chiefest strength and safeguard in the loyal hearts and goodwill of my subjects, and therefore I am come among you as you see at this time, not for my recreation and disport, but being resolved, in the heat and midst of the battle, to live or die among you all, to lay down for my God and for my kingdom, and for my people, my honour and my blood, even in the dust. I know I have the body of a weak and feeble woman, but I have the heart and stomach of a king, and of a king of England too, and I think foul scorn that Parma or Spain or any Prince of Europe should dare invade the borders of my realm, to which, rather than dishonour shall grow by me, I myself will take up arms, I myself will be your general, judge and rewarder of every one of your virtues. By then valour in the field, we shall shortly have a famous victory over these enemies of my God, of my kingdom and of my people.

The final cost to Spain was sixty-two ships and 11,000 men, who perished either in the ensuing battles or were wrecked off the coast of Scotland and Ireland. Elizabeth held a mass in St Paul's Cathedral in honour of the brave men who fought for England; the Spanish vowed to continue the war.

1593

In January another plot to invade Scotland was discovered. George Ker was arrested and admitted under torture to the plot involving Spain.

The Earl of Essex was admitted to court by Elizabeth and rumours abounded that they were lovers.

In Deptford, London, on 30 May, the playwright Christopher Marlowe was murdered after falling out with his drinking companions. The venue was a known safe house of government spies, set up by the late Sir Francis Walsingham who ran the secret service for Elizabeth. Walsingham had died in 1590. Four men were present at the house of Dame Eleanor Bull. They were: Robert Poley, Nicolas Skeres, Ingram Frizer and Marlowe. Marlowe was out on bail, accused of heresy and was a known spy. A fight broke out between Marlowe and Frizer in which Marlowe tried to kill Frizer with his own dagger. Frizer fought back after being stabbed twice and killed Marlowe. He was fined for the affray after the others gave evidence that Frizer acted in self-defence. All three men were known Conny-Catchers (fraudsters), and were also suspected of spying against Catholics.

1601

Robert, Earl of Essex, was executed by his friend John Derrick at Tower Hill for treason. After failing to quell the Irish and falling out with Elizabeth, he tried to capture London with 200 men at arms. The coup failed when Londoners refused to back him and he was arrested at his house on The Strand. Plans were being secretly prepared to allow King James of Scotland to succeed to the English throne when the sixty-seven-year-old childless Queen Elizabeth died.

1603

The last of the Tudor dynasty died at Richmond Palace on 24 March. The barren Queen Elizabeth, daughter of Anne Boleyn and King Henry VIII, passed away, and with her last breath died the Tudor period of English history. On 26 March King James VI of Scotland was informed by the emissary Sir Robert Carey that he had become King James I of England and now ruled both countries. Elizabeth was buried in Westminster Abbey in the same chamber as Queen Mary on 28 April. The Stuart reign began after James I was crowned on 5 April to the cheers of a tumultuous crowd in London. For his part in the proceedings, Sir Robert Cecil was made a baron. With James now on the throne, Spain hoped that a peace treaty would come about after nearly twenty years of fruitless war.

Ireland was in turmoil again and so James sent Sir Robert Carey to Dublin to find a solution. He persuaded Hugh O'Neill to return to London to make the peace.

To celebrate his crowning, King James ordered a new coinage to be struck.

An outbreak of bubonic plague killed 35,000 Londoners and spread northwards.

The playwright and actor William Shakespeare sought the approval of his work from King James, just as he had sought royal approval under Elizabeth. King James honoured Shakespeare by calling his company The King's Men. Sir Walter Raleigh was arrested with other supposed conspirators over a plot to kill James and put Lady Arabella Stuart on the throne; he was convicted and sentenced to death. In December he was granted a reprieve by James, but stayed in the Tower as a prisoner of the state.

6

GAINING A CROWN, LOSING YOUR HEAD!

The Stuart Period (1603–1714)

1604

King James ordered that England and Scotland converge into the United Kingdom. In an effort to stamp out the loathsome habit of pipe-smoking, which the king had long condemned as harmful and foul, a heavy tax was imposed on all future imports of tobacco. Spain finally settled a peace treaty with England. King James unified a system of collecting the new import taxes from traders. The system, known as a 'farm', was settled on private companies who paid for the privilege of collecting the taxes in their domain; their customers had to pay a custom on certain goods imported and exported.

A plot to blow up the Houses of Parliament and King James was foiled after a Catholic named Guido (Guy) Fawkes was discovered in a cellar under the house on the eve of the opening of parliament. The conspirators were soon rounded up, tortured and sentenced to death. A Jesuit named Garnet and Robert Catesby were the leaders of the coup. The Gunpowder Plot, as it has become known, was discovered when a conspirator named Francis Tresham wrote to his brother-in-law, Lord Monteagle, to warn him not to attend the opening of parliament. Monteagle, who was a Catholic, warned the government and a search of the cellars uncovered Fawkes waiting to light the fuse. After suffering very painful torture under chief executioner John Derrick, Fawkes revealed all those involved. Catesby was shot attempting to escape his arrest.

1611

The new Bible was printed and distributed throughout the realm. It became known as the King James Version as it was authorised and approved by the king himself. Lady Arabella Stuart escaped from custody but was recaptured near Calais. Lady Arabella and her husband William Seymour were put under house arrest, accused of plotting against the crown.

1612

The king was distraught when he heard news that his eldest son and heir had died. Prince Henry contracted typhoid fever and died in his sleep on 6 November. He was succeeded as Prince of Wales and heir, by his brother Prince Charles.

1613

On the evening of 29 June, King James attended a night at the theatre at the behest of William Shakespeare. As the king entered the Globe Theatre to see the latest play called *Henry VIII*, a cannon was fired on the stage to honour the royal party. Apparently, too much gunpowder was loaded into the barrel and a roar of fire flew up to the thatched roof, setting it ablaze. Within an hour the entire thatched roof and wooden building was burnt to the ground. The king vowed to help rebuild it; in the meantime Shakespeare would be allowed to carry on with his plays in the great bear-baiting hall next to the site. The new building was almost complete by December and had a tiled roof to prevent further fires.

1616

Inigo Jones, the designer and royal surveyor, completed the magnificent newly refurbished Queen's House at Greenwich; the property was always a favourite of the Tudors. The house held sad memories for King James, as it was within these very walls that Elizabeth signed the death warrant of his mother, Mary Queen of Scots. The king met with the Indian Princess Pocahontas at a masque held by Ben Johnson. Pocahontas was the wife of Englishman John Rolfe. She had since converted to Christianity and taken the name Rebecca; the couple were the toast of London.

On 23 April, reputed to also be his birthday, William Shakespeare died. He was fifty-two and left a widow Anne née Hathaway. His brother Edmund, an actor, died in 1607 aged twenty-seven and was buried in Southwark Cathedral; William was the third of eight children.

1618

Sir Francis Bacon, the famous parliamentarian, was honoured by James and made Lord Chancellor. He was also endowed with the title Lord Veralum. Bacon was considered one of the most trusted men in the country. He presided over the trial of Lady Frances Howard and her husband, Robert Carr, for the murder of Sir Thomas Overbury in the Tower in 1613. He also tried Sir Walter Raleigh for piracy. Raleigh was executed for his alleged crimes on 29 October in Whitehall. A favourite of Elizabeth, Raleigh had fallen out of favour and lost all his properties after his conviction in 1603 for treason; his sentence was commuted to life imprisonment. He was released in 1617 by King James in order to sail to South America and bring back much-needed revenue for the royal treasury. However, he came back empty-handed and was returned to the Tower. On a complaint from Spain that he had attacked their treasure ships, James ordered his execution and he was beheaded. His wife took to carrying around his head in a bag for all to see while his torso was buried in front of the altar of St Margaret's Church at Westminster. It is said that his headless ghost wanders the church in search of peace and justice. While in the tower, he wrote a book called *The Historie of the Worlde*.

The king angered the clergy and the Puritans by printing his new literary work *The Book of Sports*, in which he advocated certain sports on Sunday, much opposed by the Puritans who considered the Sabbath a non-work and a non-play day. The king requested that the book be read out to the people from the church pulpits to advocate dancing, archery, leaping, and morris dancing, all of which he had licensed. Bowling or animal baiting on a Sunday was forbidden.

1619

On 2 March, Queen Anne, the king's wife, died of dropsy after years of poor health. James had married Anne in 1589, but the couple had been estranged since Anne converted to Catholicism in 1606. They had seven children with only two surviving, Prince Charles and Princess Elizabeth who was married off to Frederick V. The king refused to be with her at the end as he had a morbid fear of being in the company of the dying.

1625

King James I died of a stroke, after suffering from a fever, on 27 March at Theobalds, his favourite house in Hertfordshire. He was succeeded by his son, Charles. For most of his life as the English king, James has argued with parliament. Now his death raised hopes that Charles would have better relations with them.

James was credited with having introduced the game of golf to England. Known as the wisest fool in Christendom, James tried to impose his Scottish morals on the English with little effect. One of his last moves was against the brothels of London. Despite many raids on the notorious brothels of Turnmill Street and Farringdon, resulting in many imprisonments, the trade was alive and prospering in the capital.

On 1 May, Charles married fifteen-year-old Henrietta Maria. On 7 May James was buried in Westminster Abbey. In August, King Charles I moved parliament and his household to Oxford to escape another outbreak of the dreaded plague. The epidemic had taken in excess of 20,000 lives and was spreading like wildfire; the previous outbreak in 1603 had killed over 30,000 and this one looked likely to exceed that total. Orlando Gibbons, the composer, was among those who succumbed.

1629

Trouble between King Charles and parliament festered into revolt. On 2 March the Parliamentarians locked out the king's messenger. They passed new legislation challenging the king's right to absolute rule. The rumpus started after Charles ordered the speaker to dismiss the house on 28 February after the members tried to start the debate. The speaker, John Finch, started to rise from his chair, but Denzil Holles and Benjamin Valentine held him down and Sir John Eliot locked out Black Rod, who Charles had sent to order Finch to dismiss the house. The MPs rose one by one and then the house voted through the statutes. (Author's note: to this day at the state opening of parliament, Black Rod approaches the house and has the doors slammed in his face, he then has to knock three times with his Black Rod, the doors are then opened and he is permitted to enter. Parliament was fed up with Charles imposing taxes to finance his wars with the French, Spanish and Dutch. There was wide consternation in 1626 when some of the royal jewels went missing, believed pawned in Amsterdam to finance this folly. On 10 March, Charles went to the house and closed parliament, saying he would rule the country alone.

1632

King Charles infuriated the members of parliament by ordering them back to their constituencies to attend to their subjects at a local level; this meant the members couldn't meet to discuss issues of state. Charles continued to rule without parliament. On 27 November Sir John Eliot died in the Tower of London. He was arrested three times for arguing against the king's policies, the last time was in 1629 when he locked Black Rod out of the house.

1633

On the night of 11 February a fire broke out in the house of a needle-maker named John Briggs. The fire was later blamed on his maid who had apparently placed some embers under the stairs, in order to keep them warm ready for the morning fire. The house was on the city side of London Bridge near St Magnus the Martyr church. The frozen Thames at low tide prevented the firefighters from getting water from the river, so the conduits were opened and people from both sides of the bridge fought throughout the night, but many houses and businesses near to and on the bridge were destroyed with forty-five merchants losing their homes and businesses in the fire that smouldered for almost a week. The bridge was to be rebuilt and made wider in parts.

1640

The first parliament for eleven years was called to assembly by King Charles, the purpose being to enforce the new election of members. The opposition mounted an attack on the scheming of the king, led by John Pym, the member for Tavistock. Pym had the backing of powerful men from the Providence Company, many of whom were Puritans who the king had annoyed with his promotion of sports on a Sunday, as had his father. The king responded by dissolving parliament.

1642

On 4 January King Charles entered the Houses of Parliament and attempted to arrest five members who had repeatedly disobeyed him: John Pym, Sir Arthur Haslerig, William Strode, Denzil Holles and John Hampden. The five waited until the last minute, then escaped out the back way. The men attempted to have the queen arrested and charged with attempting to sell the royal jewels. The previous year, Queen Henrietta had been stopped from going abroad to avoid her selling the jewels.

On 11 January the royal family fled London as riots took place demanding a democratic parliament. Civil war was again looming in England. Charles sought support in the north as Oliver Cromwell, the member for Ely and a Puritan, gathered support in the south.

Cromwell and his brother-in-law, Valentine Walton, seized silver treasure after taking Cambridge; the treasure was destined for the king to support his army. Cromwell was a big landowner in Cambridge and fervently opposed the king's many taxes. On 23 October at Edgehill in Oxfordshire, the two armies of the Royalists (Cavaliers) and the Parliamentarians (Roundheads) clashed in the first battle of the Civil War. After hours of musket-firing and close clashes with pike and sword, both sides retired to lick their wounds, with no-one actually gaining any significant victory. The war would go on for several years, with both sides getting support from an almost equal number of counties.

In London the people were firmly behind parliament, and the Puritans had complete control. They had enforced their ideals on the populace and pressed some 150,000 folk into military service. John Milton the poet was an ardent supporter of parliament, and even he was digging ditches to defend London against Royalist attack. In May the people embarked on a display of fervour by destroying the royal symbols of the Crosses of Eleanor erected by King Edward I in honour of his wife, Eleanor of Castile. The wooden crosses at Cheapeside and the Whitehall cross, known as the Charing Cross, were the first to be dismantled, the wood being used to build defences. A mounted statue of King Charles in The Strand was ordered to be melted down and turned into musket balls to be fired at the Royalists.

1644

Parliamentary troops moved against the houses of ill repute and the degradation of Southwark. The area across the river had long been outside the jurisdiction of the Puritan governors of the city, under the rule of the Archbishop of Winchester who had raised a fine fortune for decades by licensing the brothels, prostitutes, taverns and theatres. The area was raised to the ground under the guise of the troops seeking out secret Royalists. The Globe, Swan and Hope theatres were among those destroyed by fire, and the criminal elements left the area and retired to the East End of the city.

Many were caught and hanged in the streets for their devilish behaviour. The bishop also fled after his palace was confiscated as quarters for the troops, and his private prison, the Clink, was used to hold prisoners of war. Wealthy Royalist supporters were taken to a prisoner of war gaol set up in Coventry Cathedral. After the war they were released and ostracised by the supporters of parliament. No one would speak to them, and so today in England, anyone who is ostracised is said to have been 'sent to Coventry' as a result.

1647

After five years of fighting, the two sides were still at loggerheads though parliament was winning the war, and both sides started to wind down their armies. Peace talks had failed so far. The Parliamentary army wasn't paid for months and started to mutiny. They formed themselves into a model army in 1646. Parliament was being overseen by mostly Presbyterian members and a clash of ideals had resulted in protests in the house. Negotiations with the king were still secretly going on and so on 6 August Oliver Cromwell and the model army took the Tower and ringed parliament with troops. He demanded that parliament pay the troops and threatened them with arrest if they failed to comply.

The country was in turmoil with law and order being administered locally by corrupt and greedy gentry, and no control coming from central government. The countryside was rife with accusations of witchcraft and neighbours were accusing neighbours of the evil deed to grab land and worldly goods from them. In East Anglia, the fervour was fuelled by a man named Mathew Hopkins, who used torture to extract confessions before hanging or burning the witches and warlocks for a fee. He became known as the Witchfinder General.

The City of London was put under martial law and in December, after escaping from Hampton Court, King Charles signed a treaty with the Scots who vowed to assist him to regain power in England.

1648

After defeating the Scottish troops under the Duke of Hamilton at Preston on 20 August and virtually ensuring an end to King Charles and the civil war, Oliver Cromwell crossed the border to mop up any remnants of troops supporting the crown. The news reached Colchester in Essex where for four months the Royalists under Fairfax, Lucas and Capel had held out against a siege. The starving troops surrendered, having been desponded by the reports. All the officers were executed as were most of the troops. In December the parliament of the Duke of Hamilton, founded out of his engagement treaty with the king the previous year, were all arrested by Colonel Thomas Pride and his band of musketeers as they tried to enter the house. All that now remained of parliament was a Rump Parliament of some sixty members who would be relied upon to enforce legal moves to impeach King Charles, who was arrested on 1 December. The king was now a prisoner of the state and awaited his fate in Hurst Castle.

1649

The trial of Charles I for treason against the people of England, Scotland and Ireland began on 27 January. Sir Thomas Pride summoned 135 members and judges to hear the case, but only sixty-eight turned up. A lawyer named Richard Bradshaw was elected to preside over the trial as Chief Judge. The trial lasted two days and Charles, who refused to recognise the authority of the court; did not defend himself or speak. On the announcement of the guilty verdict, Charles tried to speak and was informed that his chance was gone. The sentence was death by the axe. He was taken to the Palace of St James to be held overnight. At 10.00 a.m. on the morning of 30 January, he was permitted a breakfast of wine and bread, before being allowed a walk in St James Park escorted by dozens of foot soldiers and musketeers.

Just before midday he was marched from St James's Palace up to Hungerford Square (now Trafalgar Square), and into Whitehall. The entourage walked past the main entrance of the Palace of Whitehall and into the Banqueting Room where he was confined. The executioner had not turned up so a guard was sent to find another. The man chosen was an official executioner in the pay of the City of London; he was roused from his bed at Rosemary Lane in Whitechapel along with a neighbour, and escorted to Whitehall. The executioners were allowed to pad themselves out and wear false beards to hide their identity. The main executioner was Richard Brandon, who it was later alleged was the king's illegitimate grandson.

Brandon received a fee of £30 for the dirty deed, a fortune in those days. At 1.45 p.m. the king was taken to the scaffold built over the entrance to the hall, outside the building. He climbed out of a window (now bricked up) onto the scaffold, and proceeded to give a speech. Not a sound was uttered by the crowd, estimated at some 10,000 people in Whitehall alone. After the speech he spoke to Brandon instructing him not to raise the axe till he had signalled him by outstretching his arms. Charles received the last rites and knelt down before stretching himself out flat; the block was a simple log and not the traditional upright block. He outstretched his arms and Brandon struck the fatal blow; another two were needed to completely sever the head. A sound of sadness went up from the crowd, and a fifteen-year-old boy named Samuel Pepys wrote in his diary that, 'The execution was met with such a groan as I have never heard before, and desire I shall ne'er hear again.'

Brandon, still shaking from the experience, nervously lifted the severed head for all to see, and as the blood fell through the scaffold the crowds surged forward to catch droplets onto their handkerchiefs, a seventeenth-century equivalent of an autograph. Of the sixty-eight members who presided over the trial only fifty-five were brave enough to sign the death warrant. They included John Bradshaw and Major General Harrison, both of whom would live to regret it.

Richard Brandon died on 20 June 1649 of gaol fever (TB), which he caught while visiting a 'customer' at Newgate prison in May.

Oliver Cromwell arrived in Ireland to deal with the rebellion in August. His intention was to crush any resistance, banish Catholic priests and rebellious landowners, and impose the Puritan way of life on the country. At Drogheda, near Dublin, in September he crushed the revolt and killed the entire garrison. Civilians and priests were counted in the 2,500 victims of the onslaught. Born in Huntingdon in 1599, Cromwell was now the most powerful man in England and a revered soldier. He returned to London and took over the running of the country.

The Prince of Wales was still free and attempting to muster an army to avenge his father.

1651

On 3 September Prince Charles led his troops against Oliver Cromwell at Worcester and was defeated. The prince then fled the country to become an exile in France. On his way to France, the prince went through the Welsh border area and was nearly caught several times, once hiding in an oak tree (now known as the Boscobel Oak). The oak tree incident is still celebrated every year in England on 29 May and is known as Oak Apple Day. Blasphemy was outlawed in England as was drunkenness, debauchery, immoral behaviour, dancing, singing other than hymns and swearing; all these offences were punishable with fines and public floggings.

1653

In order to bring some organisation, the Rump Parliament was dissolved and replaced with the Bare Bones Parliament consisting of nominated members, with Oliver Cromwell as favourite to lead the new parliament in order to make the necessary reforms law.

In July a book about fishing was published by the writer Izaak Walton called *The Compleat Angler*. It was one of the first books permitted by parliament after the crackdown on pamphlets and books in 1650.

In December, Cromwell was elected by parliament as High Lord Protector of England. The statute passed in 1649 abolished the office of king. England, though technically a republic, preferred to be referred to as a Commonwealth.

1659

All was not well, and on 6 May the Rump Parliament was recalled to deal with disquiet in the army. On 24 May, Richard Cromwell, the son of Oliver, resigned his commission in the army after falling out with General Lambert. The army revolted and nicknamed him Tumble-Down Dick. Speaker Lenthall was re-elected, and kept order in the house during the many meetings of the forty-two members.

The Quaker movement was disturbing parliament with their free thinking ways, although Cromwell gave them a free reign to preach after being impressed with their leader, George Fox. Many were said to be preaching against parliament and the paying of priests. In 1656, a Quaker named James Naylor was flogged, branded and had a hole burnt through his tongue for blasphemy.

On 3 September, Oliver Cromwell died and Richard Cromwell succeeded him as Lord Protector. In October the army threatened to revolt over Cromwell becoming Lord Protector; civil war was once again on the cards.

1660

General George Monck returned to London in February to dissolve the Rump Parliament, an enemy of Lambert and the now out of favour Cromwell. Monck, who was backed up by the larger part of the disillusioned and divided army, called for free elections. He replaced the Rump with the old parliament which was made up mostly of Presbyterians and Loyalists. The country celebrated in the hope of the return of the monarchy. In April, Lambert was imprisoned in the Tower.

On 1 May the declaration of Breda, designed to return the monarchy to England, was read out in parliament to tumultuous cheers and support. On 14 May Prince Charles met with ambassadors to plan his return to the throne. On 29 May Prince Charles was led into London by a great crowd of cheering people. The Lord Mayor met him at Blackheath where his grandfather, King James I, had played the first game of golf in England. The party then proceeded with a great following to Whitehall Palace, where Charles' father had been executed eleven years earlier.

Parliament was keen to bring to justice those accused of the regicide of Charles I. In October, fifty men who had been signatories to the death warrant were themselves condemned. On 13 October, Major General Harrison was taken from the Tower of London and paraded through the streets to Hungerford Square at the top of Whitehall. This part of the city was where common criminals were flogged or put in the stocks. On the spot where the Charing Cross once stood, Harrison was hung, drawn and quartered with another accused of regicide, the Reverend Hugh Peters. Samuel Pepys, now an Admiralty official, wrote in his diary, 'The General was looking as cheerful as any man could in that condition.'

After the execution of Harrison and Peters, the rest of the regicide suspects were executed in the same manner. Oliver Cromwell, Henry Ireton and John Bradshaw, who had all since died, were dug up and their decaying bones were hanged in chains on the Tyburn tree. Afterwards their bodies were thrown into the Thames, except for their skulls which were placed on spikes on London Bridge. Oliver Cromwell's skull was preserved by the family and is still often displayed in Ely, Cambridgeshire.

Coffee houses were becoming popular again and in August, Prince Charles granted a warrant to women giving them the right to perform on the stage.

1661

On St George's Day, 23 April at Westminster, Prince Charles was crowned King Charles II with the consent of the people and parliament. He would no longer rule with absolute power or be able to raise taxes without the consent of parliament, but most of the rights of the crown were given back.

1663

The king granted patents to two theatres in London. The first to open was the Theatre Royal in Brydges Street, Covent Garden. The dramatist Thomas Killigrew would oversee the theatre as manager. The first play performed there was called *The Humorous Lieutenant* by Charles Beaumont and John Fletcher, and was a favourite of the king. The cast was headed by the actors Charles Hart and Michael Mohun. The other theatre was The Duke's House Theatre owned by Sir William D'Avenant, alledgedly the son of William

Shakespeare. The King's Men Company, a title granted to Shakespeare and his company of actors, would be based at Drury Lane. It had been defunct since the Puritan army destroyed Bankside in 1644 banning all forms of theatre.

The king was humiliated by his wife Catherine of Braganza, having spent a small fortune on purchasing the old lepers' graveyard next to St James's Palace, and landscaping it into a royal park in 1662. The king was spotted by the queen picking flowers for his current mistress; enraged at this, Catherine returned to the palace and ordered the gardeners to dig up the entire park to prevent it happening again.

When the Dutch governor of New Amsterdam in the Americas heard the story, he laughed at the king's humiliation and called Catherine the 'Queen of Queens'; in her honour he named a village in Manhattan 'Queens'. The park which ran from St James's Palace between Constitution Hill and Portugal Street (now Piccadilly), was dubbed Green Park because of the lack of flowers.

Colonel Thomas Blood, a Cromwellian soldier in Ireland, failed to capture Dublin Castle and was on the run. It was feared Blood would raise his ugly head again in the near future.

1665

The Black Death once again ravaged London. The royal family and parliament left London to seek refuge away from the worst plague in centuries. The plague started in Southwark in April and quickly spread across the river into the city, some estimates tallied 100,000 or so fatalities. The city was about 25 per cent full and the death toll rose daily. The dead were buried anywhere there was room for a pit, and people were nailed up in their houses to stop the disease spreading. Some 250,000 cats and dogs were killed and burnt.

Doctors were at a loss as to how to cure it or prevent it. The truth was they didn't know how it spread; some family members remained healthy while others died quickly. Doctors and apothecaries took to wearing a mask of leather with two eye holes and a wooden beak to cover the nasal area; they filled the beak with herbs to breathe filtered air. Because they looked like ducks, they were nicknamed 'Quacks'.

1666

The year after the Black Death, a great fire raged through the capital. The summer of 1666 was very hot, and on Saturday 1 September a baker in Pudding Lane retired to his bed at 10.00 p.m. Thomas Farynor was only twenty-one, he left his ten-year-old apprentice to put out the fire in the main baking oven. The boy had stolen some of Farynor's favourite nightcap, as the baker went upstairs to a supper of oysters and brandy. Instead of putting the embers into the wet gutter in the street, the boy drank the brandy then fell asleep. The embers from the oven spilled out and bounced across the room to a pile of wood that the boy had prepared for the lighting of the ovens at 4.00 a.m. the next morning.

Sometime between 11.00 p.m. and 1.00 a.m. the fire took hold and gutted the entire downstairs. A journeyman lodging upstairs raised the alarm then went down to save the boy who had been overcome by the smoke. By 3.00 a.m. the whole street was alight and the wooden buildings, dried out by the long, hot summer, were blazing beyond belief. There was a cool wind blowing from the east and the fire headed up King William Street towards the Mansion House. The Lord Mayor, Sir Thomas Bloodworth, was awakened from his sleep and went to look, remarking, ''Tis nothing a woman couldn't piss out,' before returning to bed. By 6.00 a.m. the whole of Candlewick Parish was gone and the fire was raging west down Poultry and Eastcheape. Leadenhall Market to the east was gutted and the flames were heading towards the Tower as well. By 7.00 a.m. Samuel Pepys was informed that some 300 houses had gone. On 4 September the king returned from Nonsuch Palace where he had been staying, and took control of the situation. He rebuked Bloodworth for not demolishing a group of houses to stop the fire at an early stage; Bloodworth replied it wasn't prudent at the time as the city would have had to pay for them. Now the city was lost.

The king organised crews to stack gunpowder barrels at the end of streets near St Paul's Cathedral, which had fallen foul of the ravishing fire. The blown-up buildings created a fire break and the fire was contained. The total number of buildings destroyed was over 13,000 houses and 109 churches. It took three more weeks to douse the fire entirely, and the city was just a smouldering mess of destruction. Only nine deaths were recorded during the fire, many escaped across London Bridge or by boat to the south side.

The survivors went to anywhere there were green fields. Most went west, to Hyde Park, where they set up shanty towns and huddled together for comfort and safety. The king and queen organised food for them and encouraged them to build whatever shelter they could from the woods around them. Religious zealots were blaming all and sundry; first they pointed out the year 1666 being the mark of the devil, and then they blamed greedy Londoners as the fire started in Pudding Lane and finished at Pye Corner. A Frenchman was arrested on a ship at Greenwich and the halfwit admitted the crime. He was convicted by a jury that included two Farynors and was hanged at Tyburn. After the fire there were no more cases of the plague.

1667

The war with the Dutch was at an end. Devastated by the fire and the plague, England was broke, as were the Dutch, so a new treaty was drawn up at Breda in Holland. England took ownership of New Amsterdam and Holland acquired Surinam in South America. New Amsterdam was attacked by the English in 1664, after which the governor Peter Stuyvesant surrendered the colony. It was renamed New York in honour of the king's brother, the Duke of York.

1671

Captain Thomas Blood the notorious adventurer and mercenary, was caught red-handed attempting to steal the crown jewels. Blood befriended the guardian of the Jewel Tower, Talbot Edwards, after he introduced his supposed nephew to Talbot's daughter. On 9 May, Blood and two accomplices, a vicar and the nephew, went to the Tower and persuaded a slightly drunk Talbot to show the jewels to the two accomplices. When the cupboard was opened they clubbed Talbot then crushed some of the jewels underfoot before they escaped. As they ran down to the quayside, Talbot's son returned unexpectedly and raised the alarm to the Yeoman of the Guard (Beefeaters), who caught all three on the bank of the river.

On 18 July, intrigued by a request from Blood to speak with him, King Charles granted him an audience. The two men spoke for hours in private about Blood's life and crimes, including daring escapes and kidnappings. Promising to be a spy for the king, Blood was released from custody, then had his confiscated lands restored (he was on the run for over ten years as an outlaw), and given a pension of £500 per year. Blood had the run of court and colluded with the Duke of Buckingham in many intriguing plots. The duke had known Blood for years, with Blood carrying out many crimes for him prior to 1671. They eventually fell out but before Buckingham could have him charged with any crimes. Blood died in Bowling Alley, Westminster on 24 August, 1680. After his burial Buckingham had the corpse dug up to confirm it was in fact Blood in the grave as he was a notorious escape artist. The duke himself confirmed the body was indeed that of Blood.

1676

A new London was rising from the ashes of the old. Just ten years on from the catastrophic fire, there were many houses and churches set among the rubble. Sir Christopher Wren, an astronomer and architect, amazed the king and parliament with his designs for piazzas, churches and public buildings. Wren was commissioned to build fifty-two churches including the magnificent St Paul's Cathedral. There was much wrangling over the design and in the end Wren had to amend his original offering to meet with approval. The footings were still being built and it was expected it would be finished in about thirty years' time.

Wren himself laid the foundation stone. He asked a workman to go fetch a stone from the ruins and the man produced an old headstone with the inscription 'Resurgam' which means 'I will rise again', which Wren thought highly appropriate.

1685

On 6 February at noon, the king died of a stroke-related illness; the night before he was given the last rites by the Catholic priest who had saved his life by dressing his wounds after the Battle of Worcester, Father John Hudlestone. The king was succeeded by his brother James, an outright Catholic, and the future of the crown wasn't looking well. During his reign, Charles had to contend with many matters; the fire of London, the plague, the colonies and his own indiscretions with a total of seventeen mistresses who produced many illegitimate children. In 1679 he had to banish his brother James for being Catholic. The king's last request to James was to make him promise to look after Nell Gwynne, his favourite mistress and mother of two of his children. Charles refused to let Nell enter his death chamber.

King James II was crowned in Westminster Abbey on 25 April. The Catholic king was bound to bring fresh upheavals in the kingdom because of his devout beliefs and his insistence on the absolute power of the monarchy, a conflict which had brought his father to the scaffold and England to civil war. In May, two women were tied to stakes on the beach and drowned for refusing to accept the Episcopalian Church of King James II.

In Scotland, James, Duke of Monmouth, the illegitimate son of Charles II, made a claim to the throne as he was a Protestant. Monmouth attempted to amass an army in France and landed with just eighty-two men in Southampton; he was joined by 4,000 anti-Catholics. On 6 July he met with the royal army and attempted a night attack which failed; he fled the scene at Sedgemoor, but was captured on 8 July while hiding in a ditch.

On 15 July at Tower Hill he was publicly beheaded by Jack Ketch. The execution was botched by the drunken Ketch who made six blows to the head before the job was finished by his assistants, using knives. The body was then roped into a chair and the head was stitched back on so an artist could draw a sketch for a painting of the Duke.

Judge Jeffries, the infamous 'Hanging Judge', was busy dealing with the supporters of the rebellion in Taunton, Winchester, Dorchester and Bristol. He had overseen the now infamous Bloody Assizes which had seen hundreds transported to the colonies and sold into bondage, hundreds more hanged and seventy-year-old Lady Alice Lisle burnt at the stake for hiding rebels.

In May, Jeffries sat on the bench in London when the infamous scoundrel, conspirator and liar Titus Oates finally came to trial. Oates had started rumours of a Catholic conspiracy in 1678 with the murder of Sir Edmund Godfrey. The plot was relayed to King Charles by Israel Tonge. Oates, who made up the conspiracy, gave perjured evidence and was found guilty. He was sentenced to life imprisonment after being scourged through the streets of London on his way to Newgate Prison.

1688

The Year of the Glorious Revolution began with King James II's son-in-law, the Dutch King William of Orange, informing Admiral Edward Russell of his plan to invade England and impose Protestant rule after King James had his son baptised in a Catholic ceremony. The church was defying James and the country was in turmoil again with many supporting William.

William landed at Brixham in Devon on 9 November with an army of Dutch mercenaries totalling some 15,000. He rode into Exeter to tumultuous cheers and set his sights on London.

James failed to get the support of the army and navy, so he fled to exile in France in early December.

1689

On 11 April, at Westminster Abbey, William and Mary, the daughter of King James II, were crowned King and Queen of England, Scotland, Ireland and the Colonies. They vowed to rule as William and Mary equally, and to bring the kingdom back to the Protestant faith.

In London a gruesome murder had the East End in fear after a former royal butler, a brothel madame called Sarah Hodges and two of her girls were found dead. The four bodies had been butchered and it was feared a madman was on the loose. Feelings had been running high of late about the depth of the debauchery and venereal disease that was rife in the area of the Hamlets by the Tower (Tower Hamlets).

In December, parliament presented William and Mary with the Bill of Rights which replaced the Divine Right of Kings.

The Jacobite armies in Scotland proved hard to put down after a defeat of William's troops at Killiecrankie, in which 4,000 of his soldiers were killed.

1694

In June the king gave his consent for the setting up of a Bank of England in Lincoln's Inn Field. The bank was basically a group of businessmen who lent the crown £1.2 million to finance his wars. They were granted the right to deal in bullion and bills of exchange. The Act of Tonnage Taxes, a duty on beer, ale and tobacco, was set aside to service the loan. This bank would make London the centre of finance for the whole of Europe.

At 1.00 a.m. on the morning of 28 December, Queen Mary died of smallpox. The king was inconsolable having lost both his parents to the same disease. He would now rule on in his own right as King William III.

1696

The Window Tax replaced the Hearth Tax on houses. The occupier had to pay 2s minimum on any house that had up to ten windows; from ten to twenty windows the tax increased to 4s. Many people with between ten and fifteen windows were bricking some of them up to stay within the lower bracket.

1698

The Palace of Whitehall burnt down. The fire followed a previous conflagration in 1691. This time the damage was greater and the Banqueting House was all that survived. The king ordered the damaged sections to be demolished and the land sold off.

1702

While out riding in Richmond Park on 22 February, King William III sustained a nasty injury and was laid up in bed. On 8 March the king died of complications caused by the fall from his horse. The throne would now go to Princess Anne, his sister-in-law. Anne went to meet with parliament on 11 March, still dressed in mourning clothes for Mary and William. The funeral of William took place on 10 April with Prince George of Denmark, Anne's husband, as chief mourner. Anne announced she was giving one-seventh of her royal income to public services.

On 23 April, Anne was crowned queen in Westminster Abbey. There were no other claimants to the throne as James II had died the previous year in exile in France on 6 September. James did leave an heir, James Stuart, who it was feared might try to claim the throne at a later stage. He had promised his father on his deathbed that he would never give up his religion or his right to the English throne.

Anne made a gift of the mulberry garden to John Sheffield the Duke of Buckingham. The garden was started in 1685 by James II to encourage the silk trade in England. The land was a former leper colony and the Duke promised to build a hunting lodge on it called Buckingham House.

1707

On 1 May, Queen Anne was presented with the Act of Union by the Duke of Queensberry. The act declared that the Scottish and English parliaments were to be joined and seated at Westminster; this act brought into being the United Kingdom of Great Britain. A new flag was designed that incorporated both flags and became known as the Union Flag.

1708

James Stuart made good his promise to his father James II when he attempted to land in Scotland to claim the throne. After catching measles which laid him up at Le Havre in France, he sailed to Scotland where he was followed by Admiral Byng of the British Navy. At the Firth of Forth the supporters on shore failed to signal that all was well, and the French Commander Admiral Forbin refused to land, and then headed back to France. It seemed the expedition was over before it had started and the kingdom was safe. Queen Anne and parliament were most relieved.

Prince George of Denmark died in Anne's arms at 1.30 p.m. on 28 October. Anne was said to be so distraught that she kept hugging and kissing the body. The queen wasn't very well herself and steps were taken to ensure that the crown would not pass to the Catholic James Stuart, the pretender to the throne. Parliament looked to the House of Hanover in Germany to take the crown under the Act of Settlement, passed on 12 June 1701, to ensure the line of Protestant succession.

1710

Queen Anne opened St Paul's Cathedral which had been started thirty-three years earlier in the reign of Charles II. Sir Christopher Wren exceeded the hopes of the people and parliament to produce a cathedral worthy of the capital and country. Outside was a statue of the queen towering over four maidens who represented the four parts of the kingdom, Ireland, Scotland, Wales and the Colonies of America, the latter represented by a native Indian Princess called Pocahontas who had converted to Christianity and married John Rolfe, taking the name Rebecca.

1714

In April, James Stuart was approached by Henry St John Viscount Bolingbroke, who offered him the crown through his agent in London, the spy Abbe Gaultier. It was agreed that if James took the throne, he could pray as a Catholic in private as long as he pretended to be a Protestant in public and not change any laws regarding religion. James downright refused to be part of any deceit so the crown was offered to Germany. Anne died on 1 August at Kensington Palace at 7.30 a.m., having had a life of ill-health brought on by smallpox as a child and perpetual pregnancy. During her marriage she gave birth to six children; one was stillborn, the other five died before reaching eleven. She also suffered twelve miscarriages and she died leaving no heirs. Parliament declared Prince George of Brunswick-Luneberg, second cousin to Queen Anne, to be the rightful successor to the throne of Great Britain.

The Duke of Marlborough returned from exile too late to reconcile himself with Anne, but on 6 August Prince George reinstated Marlborough as Captain General of the forces. On 20 September George made his first official state entrance. With him were his son, George, and his mistress, Madame von der Schulenburg, known in royal circles as The Maypole. George had been with her since he caught his wife Sophia Dorothea of Celle in a compromising position with Count Philip Christopher von Königsmarck. He divorced his wife and kept her imprisoned in Ahlden

Castle. George was crowned on 20 October at the abbey, not speaking a word of English he made a speech through an interpreter, telling the people 'I have come for your good', but the interpreter made a mistake and told the crowd 'I have come for your goods.' The audience burst out laughing as they realised the mistake, to King George's dismay.

The Jacobite army were at it again raising the standard and declaring James Stuart as King James III. The House of Hanover started to reign in Great Britain and just as the Tudors died out when James VI of Scotland took the crown in 1603, so now the House of Stuart also died out. British history was again pushed off at a tangent as regards its royal household, and all due to religious matters rather than matters of state.

7

GOODBYE STUARTS, HELLO HANOVERIANS!

The Georgian Period (1714–1837)

1715

The Pretender to the throne, James Francis Edward Stuart, landed an army at Peterhead in Scotland on 22 December. The Jacobite rebellion (from Jacobus; the Latin for James) was already almost over, but James still intended to claim the throne and stamp out corruption and Protestantism. Earlier, at Sheriffmuir on 13 November the two armies met; Lord Mar led the Jacobites and John Campbell, Duke of Argyll led the outnumbered Hanoverians. The ensuing battle was a draw and Mar made the mistake of retreating instead of regrouping and attacking again. Meanwhile another Jacobite army was attacking Sheriffmuir; although they succeeded in taking the town they were surrounded by the Hanoverians under General Wills, and surrendered. Mar didn't manage to meet up with this group so the rebellion fell apart. James still hoped to rally his supporters and take the crown.

1716

A phenomenon happened in London; a gale hit the capital and caused the River Thames to empty. The gale apparently held back the water and prevented it from going out to sea down the estuary. For the first time in recorded history, Londoners were able to cross the river by walking on the river bed.

1721

The South Sea Company, which was granted a monopoly to trade in South America, went bust and took the wealth of many of the aristocracy in England with it, including the royal family who had not only invested money from the civil list but much of their own personal wealth. The London stock exchange ceased trading shares in the company and the fallback caused shockwaves at the treasury. Sir Robert Walpole was made Chancellor of the Exchequer in an effort to save the day. The company was set up to settle the national debt by exchanging government annuities for company stock. The stock started out at 128 points and within weeks had risen to 1,000 points. Almost everyone with money invested, but the company was granted rights by bribing officials and the whole set-up collapsed. One man who did manage to sell his stock before it collapsed was Thomas Guy. A notorious skinflint, from his profits he set up a fund to finance a hospital to be named after him.

1722

Robert Walpole (later Sir Robert) was made first Lord to the Treasury but called himself Prime Minister, the first time the term was used. Walpole had been an MP for over twenty years and was once locked up in the Tower for suspected fraud. He was forty-six.

In April another Jacobite plot was discovered when the king's mistress, Melusine von der Schulenburg, received an anonymous letter naming the Bishop of Rochester, Francis Atterbury, as the leader. The plot involved capturing the Tower, the Royal Exchange and St James's Palace. The king was to be assassinated before putting James Stuart on the throne. Walpole ordered thousands of troops into London and expelled leading Catholics from the capital. The secret service intercepted mail and kept a watch on known sympathisers. The king postponed his trip to Hanover. In November a barrister named Christopher Layer was arrested for plotting against the crown in the Atterbury Affair. His part was to raise an army and take over strategic buildings in London.

In London, the Lord Mayor, Sir Gerald Conyers passed a new law that affected the traffic in the capital. In future all traffic coming into the city over London Bridge must stay on the west side; those leaving the city must do so by staying on the east side. The decision was reached because as traffic came into the city the sights were better on the west side, therefore giving a better impression of the capital. The west side of the bridge was on the left going in, and the east side on the left going out. The bridge had three marshals to enforce the new law and collect the new tolls. This law became the precedent for all traffic in the UK; it is one of the reasons we still drive on the left.

1727

The king took a keen interest in London architecture and he was partly responsible in 1717 for the setting out of Hanover Square, named after his dynasty. The new church was called St George in his honour as was George Street leading into the square, which boasted many German-style buildings.

The Duke of Westminster, Lord Grosvenor, had nearly finished building mansion houses on his new estate near Grosvenor Square in Mayfair, named after the old horse fair that used to be held on the marshes in April and May. The Duke had so far built on 6 acres and the area would boast the most prestigious properties in the capital. However, no freeholds would be available, only leases. In Hanover on 11 June at 1.30 a.m., King George I died after months of ill health. The Hanoverian king never learned to speak English and spent most of his short reign in Hanover where he was the Elector. His son, George Augustus, succeeded him. Prince George opened Parliament on 27 June. On 11 October George II was crowned in the abbey. France switched allegiance from the House of Stuart to the House of Hanover.

1732

The king granted a gift of properties to the government to be used as an official residence by the Prime Minister and the Chancellor. The group of houses were in a cul-de-sac off Whitehall called Downing Street. The first building on the site was a brewery and tavern called The Axe dating back to the 1300s. In 1680 the MP for Carlyle, Sir George Downing, had bought the small yard and built the houses; the street bears his name. Educated at Harvard he became the second man to graduate from the college and was nephew to John Winthrop, Governor of Massachusetts. He became a chief scout for Oliver Cromwell and teller for the treasury, eventually becoming a politician. He died in July 1684.

No.10 Downing Street has been the residence of the Prime Minister ever since. The king originally offered the house to Walpole as a gift, but Sir Robert turned it down saying he could accept it only as a gift to the government.

In June, Colonel James Oglethorpe announced a new colony in the Americas. It was to be called Georgia after the king who gave £600 towards the setting up of the new territory. Oglethorpe planed to farm the land by giving imprisoned debtors the opportunity to redeem themselves, and start a new life.

1734

Places like London were increasing in population each year, mainly with people from the countryside who were being made redundant by advancing farming technology. Jethro Tull, a Berkshire farmer who invented a soil drilling machine to replace the inefficient scattering method of planting, published a book about farming technology called *The Horse-Hoeing Husbandry*.

Another farmer, Charles Viscount Townsend, devised a four-year system of planting clover, wheat, barley and turnips instead of leaving the field fallow for one year. He apparently used the turnips as winter feed for his cattle instead of slaughtering them as most other farmers did. Between them, Tull and 'Turnip' Townsend, as he was known locally, had shown farmers how to increase productivity.

1736

London had seen many riots since the extortionate duty on gin was raised to £1 a gallon, and liquor retail licences rose to £50. The age of gin began with William of Orange. His wars with France brought an embargo on wine and brandy so he introduced Gineva, a Dutch drink made from the juniper berry (*gineva* is Latin for 'the berry'). London gin houses sprang up in the wake of the lower-taxed liquor and many houses distilled their own, with the saying 'Drunk for a penny, dead drunk for tuppence.' One of the reasons for the increase was to finance the king's civil list. The original concept by William III was to keep the people drunk when they became dismayed at their way of life, and do it cheaply. He once remarked that 'when the people are drunk they are less troublesome to the crown.' In 1735 there were over 8,500 licences issued to gin houses, with many more illegal stills also producing the drink.

1737

The government introduced an act to combat the number of radical plays being shown in London's theatres. The Stage Licensing Act stated no play would be permitted unless it was approved by the Lord Chamberlain, head of the royal household. This came about because of a series of plays lampooning the government and the royal household. However, two theatres were exempt, Drury Lane and Covent Garden as they held royal patents. Henry Fielding, the manager of the Haymarket Theatre, protested strongly though it was mainly his fault for putting on such plays as *The Beggar's Banquet*, which poked fun at Sir Robert Walpole in the guise of the character Peachum; the play was already banned. The Lord Chamberlain's office would hold this position as censor for London plays until 1968 when the act was repealed, and the first nude play was shown in London. It was called *Hair*.

1738

The War of Jenkins' Ear was sparked in parliament on 17 March when Captain Robert Jenkins showed the house his severed ear, allegedly cut off by the Spanish coastguard in 1731. He said he was trading peacefully when his ship was attacked and the crew tortured. War with Spain was looming over the incident as the public applied pressure on parliament

1739

At York on 10 April, the notorious highwayman Dick Turpin was hanged. Turpin, supposedly born either in Finchley, North London, or Hempstead, Essex, earned a reputation as a vicious criminal and had a reward on his head of £100; he escaped from an armed confrontation with a gamekeeper in Essex and headed to York. In York he used the name John Palmer and was a known bully and drunk. He was accused of stealing six chickens by a local farmer and held in York Castle. Investigations revealed that Palmer was often in Lincolnshire; on his return he would have horses and cash with him. Several complaints of sheep- and horse-stealing were rounded on him. As he could not prove an income he was arraigned to the Magistrates Court. He wrote to his brother in London and the letter was placed in the window of the local post office where Turpin's old school master happened by and recognised the handwriting; he reported it to the authorities. For Turpin, the game was up. On the scaffold he gave a speech and, wearing his best clothes, he climbed to the top of the ladder before flinging himself off, breaking his neck and dying instantly.

Captain Thomas Coram started a foundling hospital in London to ease the plight of the abandoned children of the poor.

1747

The Jacobite rebel Lord Lovat met his end at the age of eighty on Tower Hill. Captured after the Battle of Culloden, in which William Duke of Cumberland slaughtered the last of the Jacobite army, Lovat had been held in the Tower. As the execution was about to take place, a platform holding some 200 spectators collapsed and crushed twenty or so to death. Lovat remarked to the axe man that he was most amused to see the ghouls getting their just desserts and entertaining him. He was said to be still laughing as the axe fell; humorists remarked that Lovat literally did laugh his head off. He bears the distinction of being the last man to be publicly beheaded at Tower Hill which lies across the road from the Tower itself.

1750

Henry Fielding, the Bow Street Magistrate, created a force of 'Thief-Takers' to deal with the increasing crime rate on London's streets.

London was hit by two small earthquakes on 8 February and 8 March. Neither caused any great damage. Peter Dolland, an optician, opened a shop making and selling spectacles in The Strand. Samuel Whitbread started a brewery in Chiswell Street; both businesses would survive into the twenty-first century.

In November, Londoners were delighted to see Westminster Bridge opened. Since AD 55 the only bridge over the Thames had been London Bridge. Though only a footbridge, the new bridge was still most welcome. The bridge had some teething problems as it seemed to sink slightly into the river when a lot of people crossed at once, so a guard made sure that only a limited number used it at any one time.

1751

Frederick the Prince of Wales died on 20 March. The cause of death was attributed to an abscess caused by a blow from a cricket ball three years earlier. The Prince's son, George William Frederick, aged just thirteen became heir to the throne of England. After the prince's funeral, a poem circulated about the unpopular Frederick

> Here lies poor Fred, who was alive and is dead
> Had it been his father, I would much rather
> Had it been his sister, no-one would have missed her

Had it been his brother, still better than another
Had been the whole generation, so much better for the nation,
But since it is Fred, who was alive and is dead
There is no more to be said

1752

The Gregorian calendar was adopted by Britain in line with the rest of Europe. The old Julian calendar devised by Julius Caesar had eleven more days in it; now those days would be lost on 3 September when the date would be accelerated to 14 September. Landlords, banks and moneylenders were at a loss as to how they would calculate their month's finances. The most significant change would come with New Year's Day which was being moved from 25 March to 1 January. The difference had come about when in 1582 Pope Gregory XIII added ten days to the calendar.

St George's Hospital and the Seaman's Hospital were founded.

1758

On 4 April, the composer George Frederick Handel died in London. Born in Germany in 1685, he was seventy-four. He came to England in 1710 and had some forty-six operas to his credit as well as thirty-two oratorios. He lived his latter years in Mayfair. In later times another musician, Jimi Hendrix, lived in the house next door.

On 11 May, Richard Vaughan became the first man to be hanged for forging Bank of England notes.

Charles Dingley started a hospital at Magdalen House in an effort to stop prostitution which was blighting London and spreading disease.

The British Museum opened in Great Russell Street at Montagu House. The public could now see the collection of arts and science put together by Sir Hans Sloane and Robert Harley, the Earl of Oxford. Sir Hans Sloane also founded the Chelsea Botanical Gardens.

John Dolland and his son Peter, the Strand-based opticians, invented an achromatic telescope that allowed more light into the viewer and gave a clearer picture of the stars. In December they tried it out on Halley's Comet. It was named after Edmund Halley who in 1705 worked out that the comet had a set pattern; the comet was seen in 1531, 1607 and 1682, appearing every seventy-seven years.

1760

Laurence Shirley, also known as Earl Ferrers, became the first and last aristocrat to be hanged for a capital crime; usually they were entitled to be beheaded. Convicted of the brutal murder of his steward in a drunken state, Ferrers was turned off the ladder at Tyburn on 5 May to a cheering crowd of some 30,000 people.

On 25 October King George II died of a heart attack at 6.00 a.m. while on the toilet and was subsequently buried in Westminster Abbey. George II was the last king to lead his troops into battle, at Dettingen in Germany against the French on 16 June 1743. The king's horse bolted at one point, but he managed to dismount then lead his troops into the affray on foot. He was sixty at the time. His father King George I spoke no English, but George spoke it with a heavy accent and managed to command the respect the crown deserved. He was succeeded by his grandson who would become George III.

1761

On 8 September, Prince George married Charlotte, daughter of the Duke of Mecklenburg-Strelitz. His first choice would have been fifteen-year-old Lady Sarah Lennox, but on Lord Bute's advice he married Charlotte. They were crowned on 22 September. King George purchased Buckingham House from the Duke of Buckingham for the princely sum of £22,000. He didn't intend to live there but just use it to house his collection of books.

While gambling at Whites gentlemen's club in St James'sStreet, the Earl of Sandwich, John Montagu invented a new delicacy. He was on a winning streak and refused to attend the dining room for food, so a tray of meat and bread was brought to the card table. The Earl cut the meat and the bread into equally thinned slices. He then put the meat in between two slices of the bread and ate it. The new meal was dubbed a 'sandwich' after his title. Sandwich in Kent was established in Roman times; the name means a Sandy Place. The title is the only connection to the town; the first Earl was Edward Montagu. In 1660 he was anchored off Sandwich while he awaited orders to bring back Charles II from France. He actually lived in Portsmouth, so the king in appreciation gave him the title of Earl of Portsmouth, but Edward asked the king to change the title because of the connection to Sandwich.

1765

The Stamp Act, inflicted on the colonists in America, was causing great consternation. In London, the voice of the people was aired by Benjamin Franklin who protested strongly to parliament against the tax. It was intended to be a source of revenue to pay for the continuing defence of the realm. The sugar and molasses taxes were collected locally in the New World. The people objected to this tax strongly as it was a direct tax.

In April, King George III was struck down with a strange illness.

The Mozart family of musicians enthralled London with their renditions; the public were most impressed with the young son Wolfgang, a nine-year-old prodigy, and his sister Anna. Queen Charlotte praised the Mozarts for the raising of Wolfgang. The family moved from Ebery Street to Frith Street in Soho.

1766

In March, parliament repealed the dreaded Stamp Act on the colonies after rioting and protests reached crisis point. The colonists were threatening to seek independence from British rule. In Boston the traders imposed a ban on all British goods. In the meantime parliament was looking at other ways to raise the colony's taxes, including a tax on all imported goods. Riots broke out in England after the price of wheat shot up and deprived the poor of bread; farmers were forced to lower the price or face more violence.

The Duke of Westminster closed down the May Fair near Piccadilly. The fair had been a favourite of Londoners for hundreds of years. Recently the horse traders, who were the main stay of the fair, had been arriving earlier and earlier. This year they wanted to start the celebrations in mid-April. The Duke intended to build more housing on the land, which was a wedding gift.

1768

Riots broke out in London in May when John Wilkes, the Member of Parliament for Middlesex, was fined and jailed for libel after printing his newspaper, *North Briton* and the *Essay on Woman*. Wilkes had been a thorn in the side of the government and King George since he first printed the outrageous paper in 1764; he had been imprisoned numerous times, though he had been acquitted recently of the crime of criminal libel. His followers paid the £1,000 fine. They also vowed to provide him with all life's luxuries, wine, women, food and money to ease his twenty-two months in the Tower.

Riots continued in the industrial north over the loss of jobs due to new machines that could do the work of many people. Factories were attacked and set on fire.

In London, King George III founded the Royal Academy which had its headquarters in Somerset House and Pall Mall. Sir Joshua Reynolds was the first president of the society. Another portrait painter, Thomas Gainsborough, was also patron. Gainsborough lived in Pall Mall.

Britain was still dealing in the slave market with Liverpool and Bristol fast becoming the leading ports in the trade. Cotton products left the ports for Africa to trade the goods for negros, who were then taken to the colonies and traded for sugar and tobacco. Some slaves were finding their way to England and it was now becoming common to see negros in service in many households. Newspapers were even carrying adverts for slaves for sale, mostly children.

1770

Captain James Cook, a former haberdasher serving in His Majesty's Navy, discovered a new continent on the other side of the world. After discovering New Zealand he set sail south-west and came across a vast land. He landed at a bay and collected plants to take back. He planted the English flag claiming the land for Britain, and then named it Botany Bay. He had to retire back to the ships after being attacked by natives. The land would later be known as Australia after the legendary tales about the lands in the South Sea, first published in 1700. Joseph Banks the naturalist was also onboard and collected many new species of plants; Banks later established a botanical collection at Kew Gardens to preserve the plants and culture them. Kew Gardens was originally a royal garden founded by George II's wife, Augusta.

1773

A former slave girl had her poems published in England; twenty-year-old Phillis Wheatley had been sold into slavery as a child, she adopted the family name of her master. Later given her freedom, she educated herself and started writing poetry. She had much success with her work which included poems on religion and morals. Her book *Poems on Various Subjects, Religious and Moral* was published in Aldgate, London.

1776

In London, the Quaker John Howard lobbied the government to reform the prison system with his organisation, the Howard League.

At Temple Bar, the entrance into the City of London on The Strand, the severed heads of the Jacobite rebels executed in 1745 were finally removed.

1780

On 2 June in London over 60,000 rioters, inflamed by Lord George Gordon, sacked the city and burned down parts of Newgate Prison; the released prisoners joined in the riot. Gordon was the leader of a Protestant group campaigning against the Roman Catholic Relief Act. The destructive riots lasted for six days before the Lord Mayor reluctantly brought in troops as the rioters started attacking the Bank of England. The Grenadier Guards at the bank melted down the ink pots and used the metal to make musket balls to fire at the rioters; 173 people were killed by the troops with another 139 arrested for treason; Gordon was in the Tower. After a trial lasting weeks, twenty-five of the ringleaders were sentenced to death and hanged in public. One of the men was Edward Dennis who happened to be the official hangman. In order that his own son, who was also a hangman, wouldn't have to execute him, Dennis was pardoned on condition he hanged all the other ringleaders. He obliged and was even paid for the job. Lord Gordon was acquitted as was his movement, The Protestant League, of any wrong doing. He sailed to Holland and became a Jew. On returning to England he retired to Birmingham where he died.

1785

On 24 March parliament passed a law allowing grocers to sell alcoholic liquor for consumption off the premises only; the first off-licence was granted in London. John Adams was received by King George III as the first American Ambassador to Great Britain; he resided at 9 Grosvenor Square, where he established the first American Embassy.

1789

The people of England celebrated the recovery of their much-loved King George III from his bout of insanity. The king suffered years of strange behaviour and outrageous rants. He had been diagnosed insane in 1788 and kept in an asylum. A reverend named Francis Willis visited the king at the request of William Pitt, the Prime Minister. After an examination he diagnosed the king as suffering from a rare disorder called porphyria. The rare disease is caused when the white corpuscles attack the red ones in the bloodstream creating a toxic serum which causes the symptoms. The disease was very prominent in royals due to interbreeding. One of the symptoms is senile dementia which was often mistaken for insanity. The Prince Regent had been ruling in his father's absence; Pitt was eager to restore the king as he was forever arguing with the young prince over money.

On 28 April the crew of *The Bounty* mutinied, and under the command of Fletcher Christian they overpowered Captain Bligh and a few objectors. Bligh was set adrift in an open lifeboat and on 14 June reached Timor. On 14 August the Admiralty sent a ship to bring back the mutineers for trial; Bligh was charged with losing his ship.

1792

Henry Walton Smith opened a shop in Westminster selling newspapers and grocery goods. The business would be taken over and expanded by his son and grandson, also named Henry Walton and made into a formidable chain of shops named W.H. Smith.

1796

The Prince of Wales formally asked the king to agree to a separation from his wife, the German Princess Caroline of Brunswick. The marriage was a farce from the beginning. Prince George only agreed to marry Caroline if the government paid off his debts of £600,000; the government reneged on the deal and so George wanted to separate. When they first met, George was astounded at Caroline's appearance; he remarked to a friend that she was smelly, fat and ugly and he needed a glass of brandy to calm him. The marriage lasted all of thirteen months. Prince George was not very popular with the public, and some of that animosity rubbed off onto the king, who was attacked by an unruly crowd in October the previous year over the prince's increasing debts, and high taxes

1800

On 15 May at the Drury Lane Theatre, a man named James Hadfield fired a shot at King George III. The orchestra struck up 'God save the King' and George simply sat there and kept his stature. The bullet missed by a foot or so and hit a pillar behind the king. This followed an attempt in October 1795 and a stabbing attempt by an angry woman in August 1796.

1805

On 21 October Lord Nelson broke away from the main fleet and chased the French and Spanish fleets, catching them off Cape Trafalgar. The battle raged from morning into the afternoon with heavy losses on both sides. Since General Napoleon Bonaparte had grabbed power in 1799 and declared himself Emperor after returning victorious from Egypt, the British had waged a war on the French and their allies, Spain. The British Navy was victorious in the battle, but at 1.30 p.m. a French sniper shot Nelson. The musket ball entered his body through his left shoulder. It travelled through the body damaging vital organs, exiting on his right side just below the hip. The wound killed him quickly; his body was stripped and preserved in French brandy, confiscated from one of the captured ships.

The damaged HMS *Victory* limped back to England so the greatest of England's heroes could be buried on English soil; the journey took eight weeks. On arrival in England the body was taken to the Painted Hall at the Seaman's Hospital in Greenwich where it lay for three days. The coffin, made from the main mast of the ship *L'Orient*, was put on Nelson's barge, and towed up the Thames to the Admiralty building in Whitehall. Here Nelson lay in state for six weeks. On 9 January 1806 he was finally laid to rest in a tomb in St Paul's Cathedral; the crowd of mourners, from the Admiralty to St Paul's, was estimated at over 100,000 people.

1807

Parliament passed the Abolition Bill on 25 March which effectively outlawed slavery, albeit only in Britain. The bill finally won the support of parliament after the House of Lords had thrown it out, and was the culmination of many years campaigning by men such as William Wilberforce, Lord Shaftesbury and Charles Fox.

Pall Mall became the first London Street to be lit with gas lamps.

1812

On 11 May, the Prime Minister, Spencer Percival was dressing for the day and remarked to his wife that he had a strange dream in which a man wearing a green coat had shot him. Dismissing the dream, Percival went to the Houses of Parliament. After attending to the day's business he was walking through the house towards Westminster Hall. A man in a green coat stepped out from behind a column at about 5.10 p.m. and raising his arm he fired one shot from a pistol into Percival's heart. He fell into the arms of Lord Osborne and was carried to the speaker's room. A man named John Bellingham gave himself up and was arrested. At his trial just four days later, Bellingham pleaded not guilty, but witnesses said they recognised him as the assailant. He was also alleged to have said 'I am the unfortunate man' when the sergeant-at-arms, Mr Watson, shouted out 'who was the rascal who did it?' Bellingham was found guilty of murder. He was hanged in public outside Newgate Prison on 18 May by William Brunskill. Spencer Percival remains the only British Prime Minister to have been assassinated.

John Nash, the designer, outlined a plan to turn the King's Mews and Hungerford Square into a tribute to Lord Nelson. Since the eighth century the area had been used by the royals as a mews, in which they kept their falconry collections. By the early 1800s the area was a huge menagerie where exotic birds were kept in cages and where minor felons were put in the stocks or flogged and branded in public. Nash wanted to set out a granite square in honour of Lord Nelson's last battle at Trafalgar.

1815

In London people rioted against the Corn Laws which controlled the price of corn. The laws banned cheap imports and set out to raise the price to £4 for 2 stones of corn. The rest of the country was also experiencing similar riots. Several rioters were shot in London after smashing the windows of leading MPs who brought in the act.

On 18 June at Waterloo, 8 miles south of Brussels in Belgium, the French forces under Napoleon and the Allied British and Prussian forces under the Duke of Wellington and General Blucher fought a great and decisive battle; one of the last of the Napoleonic Wars. Napoleon had been exiled to Elba, but had returned to power just 100 days earlier. He was again captured, and sent to St Helena where he died in mysterious circumstances in 1821. The battle started at 11.30 a.m. and finished about 9.00 p.m. The allies won the battle and with it the war. Prince George was watching a play at the Theatre Royal Drury Lane when he heard the news, he stopped the play to announce the news and the orchestra played the national anthem, the first time it had been fully played in a theatre. This incident started off the tradition of playing the anthem after performances of plays, and later in cinemas after the last showing of films each day.

King George was very ill again with his debilitating disease taking its toll on him.

The Thames, a steam ship driven by a paddle system, became the first such ship to sail from Dublin to London with passengers and cargo.

1820

The king died of his illness on 29 January at 6.38 a.m. at Windsor Castle. Since 1811 he had been incapacitated with incurring bouts of senile dementia and the Prince Regent George had governed in his place. King George III reigned England for sixty years and was the longest-serving monarch ever. During his reign he had seen many changes. He fathered eight sons and six daughters and was succeeded by his eldest son George, who would be crowned George IV. In February, Prince George started divorce proceedings against Princess Caroline of Brunswick. On 15 February George III was buried but the prince didn't attend due to an attack of pleurisy.

On 23 February the Bow Street Runners, accompanied by soldiers, raided a loft in Cato Street, London. They found fourteen armed men led by Arthur Thistlewood, who were planning to murder the entire cabinet of the government at a dinner in Grosvenor Square. A Runner was stabbed with a cutlass and eleven of the men escaped over the rooftops. Thistlewood was caught and two other conspirators later captured. The three men were executed by decapitation for treason on 1 May.

In November a parliamentarian enquiry into the legality of Prince George's divorce found in favour of Princess Caroline, George had accused her of adultery. The Lords passed a bill to dissolve the marriage and dismiss her claim to be queen. The House of Commons, aware of public opinion, refused to pass the bill.

1821

Princess Caroline accepted a settlement and a house in London.

On 18 January the Theatre Royal opened in Drury Lane.

The Bank of England in Threadneedle Street was completed in March. The massive building had been started in 1791. Designed by Sir John Soane, it was built on the site of the old tailors' guild where many workshops had made clothes for the gentry and the royals. Damaged during the Gordon Riots, the building would be where the country's gold reserves would be kept and guarded by troops.

The Prince Regent was crowned King George IV at Westminster Abbey on 19 July. The proceedings were marred by the arrival of Princess Caroline who insisted she should be crowned queen; the doors of the abbey were slammed in her face on arrival. She threatened to sue George and the government. On 7 August, aged fifty-three, Caroline died of a mysterious illness at her home. She requested in her will that her coffin bear the inscription 'Caroline of Brunswick, the injured Queen of England'.

John Constable from Sudbury in Suffolk displayed his latest work 'The Haywain' at the Royal Academy.

In London, an engineer named Michael Faraday invented an engine that ran on electricity.

London Bridge was in a sorry state and the repairs were becoming too costly, so the bridge wardens asked the government to hold a competition for a new design. The competition was won by engineer and bridge builder John Rennie Snr.

1824

King George put his weight behind the founding of a national art gallery for the country to enjoy. He persuaded the government to purchase part of the Angerstein collection. Consisting of thirty-eight paintings by various artists it was bought for £57,000 and housed at Angerstein House, 100 Pall Mall. John Rennie Snr died and his mantle for the new London Bridge was taken up by his son John Rennie Jnr. The foundation stone was laid in 1825 and the work began beside the old stone bridge, which had stood for over 600 years.

1828

Arthur Wellesley, Duke of Wellington and hero of Waterloo, was appointed Prime Minister on 22 January. Since the death of Prime Minister George Canning on 8 August the previous year, Lord Goderich had presided over the country. Prime Minister Canning caught a severe cold before he took office on 12 April 1827 and never recovered. A district in East London was named after him and a statue of him placed in Parliament Square.

After Wellesley took office, the price of bread rose and the people protested by smashing the windows of the duke's home, Apsley House at Hyde Park Corner, which he had bought from his brother, Richard, in 1823. The duke responded by putting up iron shutters earning him the nickname, The Iron Duke. His address was officially no. 1 London, as the Apsley family built the house after the great fire of 1666 destroyed the city. Workers camping out in Hyde Park's shanty towns had to pay the Apsley family a toll to walk down Piccadilly into the city. They used the tolls to build the house and, as it was the first house they came to in the new city, it was called no.1 London.

The duke presided over a country that was advancing in technology, with the first passenger railway already operating in Darlington, and more being constructed after George Stephenson built the first steam locomotive, named *The Rocket*, in 1825.

The designer John Nash completed a massive refurbishment at Buckingham House for the king, including two new wings faced with Bath Stone, facing The Mall. The new extension dwarfed the original building. Nash also completed a new street that ran from Regent's Park to Carlton House at lower Piccadilly; it was named Regent Street after King George when he was Prince Regent and lived at Carlton House where it finished. John Nash also cleared the area of the Mews and Hungerford Square ready to set out Trafalgar Square, in honour of Lord Nelson's victory.

1830

The king died at 1.45 a.m. on 26 June at Windsor Castle. William, Duke of Clarence succeeded his brother as King William IV. Neither of the brothers had any legitimate heirs and as William was sixty-four years old it seemed the dynasty may die out with him. However, to deal with the issue George III had married off his cousin Edward, Duke of Kent to Victoria of Leningen in 1818. They produced an heir to the throne in 1819, named Alexandrina Victoria who was next in line after William if he failed to produce an heir. King George IV was buried at Windsor on 15 July. The Duchess of Kent was estranged from her husband and took Alexandrina Victoria under her wing, banning her from royal functions.

1831

King William IV was crowned at Westminster Abbey on 8 September at the age of sixty-five. The affair was very low-key and wasn't popular with the aristocracy. In August, to celebrate his birthday, he opened Windsor Castle to some 3,000 local people and had a party for them in the gardens.

William was in trouble over the Reform Bill which would in effect make voting in members of parliament fairer. The system at the time allowed much corruption. MPs were returned from areas with little or no population, while areas of huge population got no representation. The system was based on the old Feudal System. The new reforms would double the amount of people allowed to vote. However, the bill failed and William closed parliament to save it. Riots broke out all over the realm with many rioters being shot dead by troops sent to quell them.

In London Walter Hancock launched his steam omnibus service running from the city to Stratford in the East End.

Cholera outbreaks were rife in London and spreading across the country fast, killing hundreds.

A proposal was submitted to parliament that a building be constructed at the King's Mews to house the National Gallery. John Rennie, son of the designer of the London Docks, John Rennie Snr, completed the new London Bridge. It was officially opened by King William IV and Queen Adelaide on 1 August. John Rennie Snr also designed and built Waterloo Bridge which was completed in 1817, alongside Southwark Bridge which opened in 1819. This new London Bridge was taken apart between 1969 and 1971 and now stands on Lake Havasu, Arizona, where it was rebuilt as a tourist attraction with its original Victorian format; complete with gas lamps. John Rennie Jnr was knighted for his work.

1833

Slavery was finally abolished throughout the empire. It had been banned in England for some time, but was still legal outside the country to appease the colonists. Another act, the Factory Act, limited the hours children could work in factories, putting an age limit on workers of nine years old.

The country was enjoying a boom in public houses, licensed to brew and sell beer since the Beer Act of 1830, which was brought in to counter the watering-down of brewery-produced beer by unscrupulous landlords. Gin palaces were also on the increase. Any homeowner could obtain a licence for £2 to make and sell gin and beer.

Work began on the National Gallery at Trafalgar Square; the King's Mews were being converted on a design by William Wilkins incorporating the layout of the huge stable blocks. The King's Mews were made redundant by George III in 1763, when he moved the coaches and horses to Buckingham House after he bought it and added the indoor riding school.

1834

The Houses of Parliament in Westminster Palace burnt down after two workmen left a fire unattended on 16 October. The fire was made up in an incinerator after they were ordered to burn all the Tally Stick. These dated back to the twelfth century when the treasury borrowed money from the lords and barons. The chancellor would take a tally which was a two-inch thick stick and make markings on it in code to show the loan and the conditions, the stick was then spliced down the middle and each party would get half. When the loan was due to be repaid the sticks would be put together to see if they 'tallied'. The practice generally ceased in 1783, though it was still in use until 1836. Crowds cheered as the roof collapsed and although the building was completely destroyed. Westminster Hall was saved by four teams of private fire companies; they soaked the beams in Thames water using fire engines equipped with hand pumps and hoses. The king offered the government Buckingham House which was virtually a palace now, as an alternative place for parliament. He hated the extravagant building which his brother George had commissioned. The government declined the offer and William was stuck with it.

An architect named Joseph Hansom patented a design for a new carriage, called the Hansom Cab.

In July, Earl Grey, who had a type of tea named after him, stepped down as Prime Minister and William Lamb took over. Lamb was the second Viscount Melbourne and Home Secretary. Earlier in the year he had presided over the case of the Tolpuddle Martyrs. The martyrs were members of an agricultural union formed in 1833. They swore an oath and were prosecuted under an act dating back to 1798, which was implemented to stop mutinies in the navy. The six farm labourers were sentenced to seven years' penal servitude and transported to Australia.

Trade unionism was growing in Britain after Robert Owen formed the Grand National Consolidated Trades Union.

Columns from the demolished Carlton House were used in the construction of the National Gallery; the gallery would house the country's art collection and would be open to all, rich and poor. It was virtually in the centre of the capital, so was an equal distance from the affluent west and the poorer east. The statue of Charles I that stands on the site of the old Charing Cross is the point where all distances to and from London are taken; it used to be the Lode Stone in Cannon Street.

A competition was launched to find a design for the new building of parliament. The general public were asked to enter, but instead of using their names they had to put a symbol on the top of their design, and then register the symbol with a registrar. Charles Barry won the competition and his symbol was a portcullis with a crown above it; the symbol was adopted by the government and used on all parliamentary papers and official government documents.

1837

On 24 May, Alexandrina Victoria, daughter of the Duke and Duchess of Kent was eighteen years old. She would finally be able to become queen and rule in her own right. Just four days earlier, the king had offered her a private income of £10,000 a year to enable her to cut the apron strings from her mother. However, the duchess forced Alexandrina to sign a letter refusing the offer. Alexandrina hadn't long to wait however, as at 2.12 a.m. on 20 July, William breathed his last and died at Windsor. William had been ill since his only daughter, Sophia, died in childbirth in April. He was seventy-one and succeeded by his heir, Princess Alexandrina Victoria of the House of Saxe-Coburg-Gotha ending the dynasty of the Hanovers. The Princess was awoken at 5.00 a.m. by Lord Conyngham, the Lord Chamberlain, and told she was now the Queen of England. Alexandrina moved out of Kensington Palace and decided to reside at Buckingham House, which she renamed Buckingham Palace. She also ordered the removal of all references to Alexandrina from official papers, she would be known as Queen Victoria as she felt the name Alexandrina sounded too foreign and the people would find it unacceptable.

The Duke of Cumberland inherited the crown of Hanover, as a woman was barred from ruling the German state.

Thomas Crapper, the engineer, was commissioned to install drainage and bathrooms, including his patented water closet, the W.C., at Buckingham Palace. Sir Benjamin Hall was commissioned as the chief clerk of works to rebuild the Palace of Westminster. Charles Barry and Auguste Pugin would be the architects, with Pugin designing the Victoria Tower where the sovereign's entrance would be.

King William was buried on 8 July.

Four plinths were erected in Trafalgar Square as part of the layout and one was being reserved for a statue of King William, but his will didn't contain any provision for paying for it, so the plinth would remain empty.

Charles Dickens, a published author, became a parliamentary correspondent.

On 4 July Euston station opened as London's first mainline train station which would provide services to Birmingham and the north-west. The first train arrived in Birmingham on 17 September after a journey of 112 miles. With the completion of the link to the Liverpool and Manchester railway system, it was now possible to travel from London to Liverpool by train, though a change of trains was necessary. This would open the capital to many people in the industrial north.

8

WE WEREN'T AMUSED ... FOR A LONG TIME!

The Victorian Period (1837–1901)

1840

Queen Victoria was married to her beloved cousin Prince Albert Augustus Charles Emmanuel of Saxe-Coburg-Gotha in the chapel of St James's Palace on 10 February. The queen, who was crowned on 28 June 1838, insisted on a short honeymoon and the royal couple spent just two days at Windsor as Victoria insisted that matters of state took priority. Albert wouldn't be crowned king; instead he was to become the Queen Consort. On 10 June, Edward Oxford, described as an eighteen-year-old simpleton, fired a pistol at the royal couple as they drove up Constitution Hill in an open carriage. The first shot missed and as Oxford aimed again with a second pistol, Albert flung himself at Victoria to protect her. A father and son named Maillais tackled the assailant and a group out riding surrounded the carriage to protect it as it made its way back down the hill to Buckingham Palace. The pregnant queen was said to be shaken, not so much by the attempted assassination, but by the thought of one her subjects disliking her so much.

William Fothergill Cooke and Professor Wheatstone unveiled an electric telegraph machine at King's College, London. The electric telegraph consisted of five needles which printed out the letters of the words into plain text.

The Queen and Prince Albert were taking a keen interest in the art of photography after the success of William Talbert, who managed to reproduce an image on paper using silver nitrate.

The Penny Black stamp was issued on 6 May and launched the first pre-paid postal system in Britain; up until now the receiver of the mail had to pay the postage.

Elizabeth Fry, the prison reformer, set up a teaching home for nurses in London. The trainees would live in the home and train in London hospitals.

1841

Trafalgar Square opened to the public. Having started the work in 1828, John Nash died in 1835 and the project was taken over by Charles Barry. The Pillar, designed by William Railton, is 185ft tall, the height of the middle mast of Nelson's ship, HMS *Victory*, under which he was standing when the fatal musket ball hit him. On the top is a statue of Lord Nelson. He is facing down Whitehall where he laid in state. Before the statue was erected, the workmen had tea on top of the pillar to the delight of city workers who had been watching the progress on a daily basis. The statue, made by E.H. Bailey, is 17ft tall, three times the actual height of Nelson.

Barry was worried about the amount of people who might gather in the square, so he designed and installed large fountains to break up the crowds; later Edwin Lutyens improved on the fountains.

Londoners were starting to use a new expression from America, said to emanate from the bad spelling of politician Martin van Buren. The word is OK or Okay and comes from Ol Korrect which van Buren misspelled on a document; it means everything is fine.

1845

The Irish Potato Famine caused millions to perish as the crops failed and the tenants were evicted and forced to roam the countryside. Thousands managed to escape and sought passage to America and England. London was seeing a vast influx of Irish refugees, forced to leave owing to the famine, settling in the already overcrowded East End. The mainly Jewish population, themselves refugees from European pogroms, were complaining to the authorities that the Irish immigrants were undercutting them as they tried to carve out a living.

The debtors prison, the Fleet, was demolished in the light of the repeal of the Act for the Imprisonment of Debtors.

In London's East End, because of overcrowding, landlords were setting up rooms with ropes strung across them. For one penny a person could drape their arms over the rope and hang there as they slept, which was easily done when drunk on cheap gin. The system was dubbed 'The Penny Hang'.

Thomas Smith, a London sweet maker, invented a new Christmas novelty: the Christmas Cracker. He started off wrapping up sweets for his children in elaborate wrappings. Then he added mottos, small toys and paper hats before finishing it off with a strip of thick paper that went 'bang' when pulled.

The Texas Embassy closed in London; it had been there since 1842 as an official embassy to the Court of St James. The office was above the wine merchants Berry Bros & Rudd in St James's Street, near the Palace of St James. The actual address was 3 Pickering Place, where the entrance to the main office was accessed via an alley. The Ambassador placed a brass plaque on the wall inside the alley entrance next to the building to commemorate it. The Republic of Texas became part of the Union of the United States of America on 29 December after the tenth US President, John Tyler, signed the legislation to annex it to the Union on 1 March.

1851

The Great Exhibition was opened in Hyde Park by Victoria and Albert. It was the result of many years' planning by Albert. The main entrance was the Marble Arch, designed by John Nash for George IV. The arch was first established at Buckingham Palace. The queen, however, hated the arch, seeing it as a symbol of unnecessary extravagance. She persuaded the government to move it to the site of the old Tyburn Tree, complaining that her coach couldn't get through it. The statue of George IV that adorned the arch was moved to Trafalgar Square and placed on a plinth looking towards the National Gallery which King George helped to establish. Albert was making his mark with the people after introducing the fir tree to Britain as a symbol of Christmas; in future, people would erect one in their house and decorate it with baubles and candles. He also started the tradition of sending a card celebrating Christmas to friends and family.

The queen was not so popular, with four attempts on her life so far. The second and third attempts happened on 29 and 30 May 1842 when John Francis fired on the couple in The Mall. The first attempt failed when the gun jammed and he escaped. Francis returned the next day with an empty gun and pointed it at the royal coach, this time he was captured and sentenced to death, but later reprieved. On 3 July the same year, a deformed midget named John William Bean fired a gun loaded with gunpowder, tobacco and paper at the royal couple, again missing them.

On 27 July 1850, while riding with her family in Piccadilly, a man stepped out of a crowd and attacked the queen with a walking stick giving her a black eye. The man, Robert Pate of Cambridge, offered no explanation and was arrested by the crowd and sent to an asylum for treatment, the third such man to do so since Victoria became Queen. In Hyde Park the biggest exhibit was the Crystal Palace, a huge building taking up the area of two football pitches and made of glass. In order that the government and the crown could escape the window tax introduced in 1696, the government, earlier that year, had repealed the tax and replaced it with the House Tax. While discussing the tax in parliament one MP said that:

> This tax is disgraceful and unfair, it is causing people to brick up their windows and thereby the government is depriving them of their right to light; it is tantamount to daylight robbery.

From then on the expression 'daylight robbery' came into the language meaning an outrageous price or invoice not worthy of the goods or service.

Thomas Cook, a Leicester man who started the country's first holiday company, reported that business was booming. He organised trips to the Great Exhibition from far and wide for over 150,000 people, and was looking to start package tour holidays abroad.

1854

In May the London authorities closed the oldest medieval fair in Britain, the Bartholomew Fair. With drunkenness and crime rife in the capital, a stand was being made and this followed on the heels of the recent restrictions imposed on public houses. The new Liquor Act restricted the opening times from 12.30 p.m. to 2.30 p.m. and from 6.00 p.m. to 10.00 p.m. To serve alcohol outside these hours was punishable by a fine or loss of licence.

Florence Nightingale, an accounts clerk, arrived in the Crimea with a group of fifty nurses to tend the wounded. At Scutari, Florence moved 300 wounded soldiers from the field hospital to an empty building in the town and 203 died within a few days. The building was over a sewer and the contamination infected their wounds or gave them cholera, dysentery or typhus.

At Balaclava in the Crimea on 26 October, Lord Cardigan was mistakenly ordered by Lord Lucan to attack the Russian guns with the Light Brigade. Of the 673 men that went into the affray only 426 returned, it was a great disaster for the Allies.

Queen Victoria started a group of knitters at Windsor Castle who were making socks for the troops. The queen also ordered a new campaign medal to be struck.

In London the British Medical Association was founded.

1859

On 31 May the new bell at Westminster Palace, the Houses of Parliament, rang out. The Palace was rebuilt after a massive fire. The bell was made at the Whitechapel Foundry in the East End by George Mears, master founder and owner, and cast on Saturday 17 April 1858. It weighed 13 tons, 10¾cwt, 15lb. It cost £2,401, but Mears allowed a discount for the material reclaimed from the old cracked bell of £1,829; so the final invoice submitted on 28 May 1858 was for £572. The foundry is the oldest in the world and famous for making the original Liberty Bell. In 1975 the foundry also made the Liberty Bell II, which was presented to the USA from the people of Britain to commemorate the Bicentenary of the Declaration of Independence in 1976. The foundry still does tours of the works and now only uses recycled bells to make new ones. On its arrival at Westminster, pulled on a giant custom-built wagon by sixteen Suffolk Punch horses, the crowds and members of parliament cheered and gasped at the sheer size of the bell. Sir Benjamin Hall, the chief clerk of works, was also present. Legend has it that a newspaper reporter overheard an MP saying to Sir Benjamin 'My God, isn't it Big Ben,' the paper printed the story and that is supposedly how the bell got its name.

1860

London was well on its way to getting an enclosed sewer system. After the problems accumulated in 1858 with the year of The Great Stink, engineer Joseph Bazalgette was commissioned to build an underground sewer system from London to the coast, to take all the waste straight out to the North Sea. For centuries Londoners had been throwing their waste into open sewers in the streets; when it rained it was washed down to the Thames and carried to the sea by the changing tide. With the population at peak numbers this system was no longer viable. Private privies in houses were not being emptied quickly enough and overflowed into the basements, eventually getting into the water system. With cholera cases high, the health boards were convinced that contaminated water was to blame. While building the sewer, Bazalgette assisted the companies constructing the world's first underground railway system using new tunnelling methods. A 4-mile run of the Metropolitan railway linked King's Cross, Euston and Paddington.

Having returned from the Crimea with much praise, Florence Nightingale founded a teaching college for nursing at St Thomas's Hospital.

Jeremiah Smith, a publisher, invented the self-adhesive envelope.

1861

After revelations about his private life, Albert Prince of Wales was sent to Dublin to get some military training at The Curragh Camp in August. In November he was caught in bed with an Irish actress named Nellie Clifden and his father was sent by the queen to bring him home. On the long journey back they stopped at many coaching inns and it is suspected that Prince Albert took some contaminated water at one of them, and caught typhoid. The illness worsened and at 10.50 p.m. on 14 December he died with his family around him. The queen was distraught and inconsolable. Victoria blamed the Prince of Wales for his death, and vowed to carry on with matters of state alone. Albert was buried at Windsor on 23 December.

Having now patented his new flushing water closet system, Thomas Crapper set up in business; he now manufactured and sold toilets, sinks and baths to the rich of London. It was becoming popular to use the word 'crap' to mean ablutions; however, the origins of the word didn't come from Mr Crapper's name. It was in fact an old medieval French word 'crappe', meaning the grain in a storage barn which was trodden underfoot, thereby becoming useless.

1870

An orphanage was opened at the Stepney Causeway in East London by the Irish physician Dr Thomas Barnardo. His deep religious beliefs influenced him to help the orphans and abandoned children of the East End.

Parliament passed the Tramway Act which allowed municipal authorities to build, operate or license tramways.

Queen Victoria was furious at Prince Edward, whom she now called Bertie. The Prince was accused by Sir Charles Mordaunt of an illicit affair with his wife, the twenty-one-year-old Lady Mordaunt, and had to appear in court to affirm that the allegation was not true. The divorce petition brought by Sir Charles failed due to his wife's continuing mental state.

Charles Dickens, the author of many great stories about life in the capital, died on 9 June aged fifty-eight.

The MP William Forster was successful in getting his Education Bill through parliament; the act ensured that all children would be guaranteed a state education. The bill facilitated for local authorities to raise money through rates on houses to pay for, and maintain the scheme.

The Thames Embankment was widened to facilitate the pipe work for the new sewage system; Chief Engineer Joseph Bazalgette ingeniously reclaimed part of the Thames to enable him to bury the pipes. The reclaimed land ran from Westminster Bridge along the Thames to Blackfriars and then up to London Bridge. Somerset House no longer had a waterfront; for the first time you could walk into the building from The Embankment.

1874

On 20 February, Benjamin Disraeli, the seventy-year-old parliamentarian, became Prime Minister. Queen Victoria was delighted that Disraeli would be a frequent visitor to the Palace.

The Criterion Theatre opened in Piccadilly.

The Christmas period was being updated with many new trends being introduced. The giving of gifts was also popular, brought about by the wonderful stories of such people like Charles Dickens. Parents began telling their children about Santa Claus. The tradition came from America where it was introduced by the Dutch settlers who called him Sinter Klass, which derives from St Nicholas. Children had to put a Christmas stocking on the fireplace and Santa Claus came on Christmas Eve to leave gifts of nuts, an apple and an orange if they had been good. The origin of a character who brought gifts to good children on the birth of a god comes from Africa where tribal history is steeped in the tradition. Europeans adopted it sometime in the late seventeenth century.

1880

The London Telephone company, which opened its first exchange in 1879, published the first telephone directory with the names, addresses and phone numbers of its 225 customers. The telephone was invented in America by Elisha Gray, but on 10 March 1876 after successfully making his first call, Scots-born Alexander Graham Bell beat Gray by two hours when he managed to take out a patent on the design of the invention.

Londoners were able to buy cheaper imported meat from Australia. The long journey had made it impossible for the colony to trade in meat with Britain until the invention of large refrigerated units, which enabled ships to transport the goods and keep them fresh. The first consignment arrived in London on 2 February aboard the SS *Strathleven*.

1885

In January the Irish Fenians planted bombs which damaged the Houses of Parliament and the Tower of London.

On 26 January General Charles Gordon, born in Woolwich, London, was killed in the Battle of Khartoum by rebel followers of the Mahdi.

A new bicycle went on sale in the capital; unlike the Penny Farthing bicycle this one was much safer and driven by a chain attached to the back wheel which was the same size as the front wheel.

The Earl of Shaftesbury died. Aged 84, he was one of London's best-known philanthropists and helped many of the capital's poor to lead better lives. A group of appreciative people raised money for a memorial to the great man who was also involved in getting better conditions for women and child workers.

1888

A series of horrific murders caused concern in the East End of London. Between August and September five prostitutes were killed and mutilated by an unknown perpetrator. The last murder was a young woman named Mary Jane Kelly who was found in gruesome circumstances on the day of the Lord Mayor's Parade. The murders suddenly stopped and although the police had several suspects, no one was ever charged. The murders became world famous and a whole industry of books and paraphernalia sprung up that lasted for many decades. The murderer was dubbed 'Jack the Ripper' by newspapers.

1890

London was thriving and so too were the people who lived many miles from the capital. The success of the railway system enabled people from far and wide to commute into London on cheap day tickets, with an estimated 10,000 arriving at Fenchurch Street before 9.00 a.m. alone. The residents of the poorer areas of London were fairing much worse, with some 5.5 million people huddled into the capital. Housing became overcrowded which only bred more disease and despair. Parliament passed new legislation to enable local authorities to build houses and rent them for reasonable rates. These households would then also pay housing tax as did the more affluent households. William Booth, the founder of the Salvation Army, was campaigning hard for the poor of London.

The *Daily Graphic* became the first newspaper to carry half tone photographs; up until then papers only had sketches or facsimiles to illustrate stories.

On 11 April, Joseph 'John' Carey Merrick, better known as 'The Elephant Man', died in the London Hospital where he had lived under the protection of his benefactor, Sir Frederick Treves. Treves took Merrick into the hospital after the wretched man came to his attention over reports of ill treatment by a freak show owner. Born in Lee Street, Leicester, in 1862, he suffered from a rare illness which left him badly disfigured and covered in tumours; the illness eventually suffocated him at the age of twenty-seven. During his time at the hospital, Merrick became the toast of London society with many famous and rich friends and benefactors. Joseph Merrick was a self-educated man who was well-read and knowledgeable. He attended the theatre and social events and even visited Queen Victoria for tea.

The future of the underground railway system looked good after the first electric-powered trains started operating between Monument and Stockwell. It outdated the steam-driven trains of the Metropolitan railway company which began in 1863.

Deptford, South London, saw the opening of the country's first electric power station. The station used steam to drive huge generators, designed by Thomas Edison.

On the London Theatre circuit, Oscar Wilde, the Irish playwright, was enjoying great reviews of his work.

1893

The sculptor Alfred Gilbert finally unveiled the statue of The Angel of Christian Charity in Piccadilly Circus. The statue was paid for by the poor of the district who owed so much to Lord Shaftesbury, who it was in honour of. The people of London nicknamed it Eros as Gilbert used the God of Romance as the basis for his aluminium statue; it was mounted on an elaborate fountain with drinking cups for the public and troughs for horses.

Lady Margaret Scott became the first woman golfer to win an open championship for ladies at Surrey.

Oscar Wilde, whose plays were doing well at the Haymarket Theatre, upset the ruling classes by calling fox-hunting, 'The unspeakable in full pursuit of the uneatable.' Wilde liked to bring attention to himself with his witty banter and described the game of golf as 'a good walk wasted.' Another Irishman, William Butler Yeats, was wooing London society with his recent publication *The Celtic Twilight*, a collection of wonderful legends and fairy stories of old Ireland.

1894

Tower Bridge was another of the monumental achievements of Victorian designers, engineers and builders. It was opened by Prince Albert on 30 June. In the first year of opening the bridge raised its middle up 6,023 times to allow tall ships into the Pool of London; there were, at one time, up to 2,000 ships on the Thames.

In parliament on 16 April, Sir William Harcourt, the Chancellor of the Exchequer, introduced death duties on inherited wealth.

William Ramsey, a chemist at University College London, discovered a new gas in the atmosphere called Argon; he had discovered Helium in earlier experiments.

1897

Irishman Bram Stoker was fascinating Londoners with his novel *Dracula*, about vampires who come back to life as the undead; they in turn fed off the blood of the living thus making them vampires. Stoker was once the manager of the Lyceum Theatre in Covent Garden.

On 1 July, Sir Henry Tate, the sugar Baron, opened his new art gallery, The Tate. It was built on the site of the old Millbank Gaol.

In June, Oscar Wilde, the disgraced playwright, was released from Reading Gaol. Wilde was sentenced to two years' hard labour in June 1895 for unnatural homosexual practices. The offences came to the public notice when he sued the Marquis of Queensbury for libel after he called Wilde, 'a ponce and a sodomite' in a restaurant. At the libel trial the Marquess produced witnesses who swore that Wilde had committed homosexual acts with them. The case collapsed and Wilde was later arrested and charged. A broken man, and banned by his wife from seeing their children, Wilde moved to Paris.

On 10 August the Automobile Association was founded. The AA was formed to assist motorists who had broken down. The previous year saw the speed limit for mechanical vehicles raised from 4mph to 20mph.

On 10 September a London taxi driver was convicted of being the first drink-driver, after the first taximeter cabs were launched on 19 August. On 23 September a nine-year-old boy was killed by a taxicab in Hackney, London; he became the first recorded fatality on the road caused by a motor vehicle.

1901

While at Osborne House on the Isle of Wight, Queen Victoria died surrounded by all her family. Her death saw the last of the Hanoverians; a new house was about to take over the British throne. Her death at 6.30 p.m. on 22 January saw the end of a great reign in British history. At eighty-one, Victoria became the longest-serving monarch beating the previous reign of sixty years by George III. The era of the Victorian Age saw many changes for Britain and the British Empire, which expanded throughout the world. Victoria was succeeded by Edward, Prince of Wales. Queen Victoria was buried next to Albert at Windsor on 4 February. Owing to illness, Edward was not crowned until 9 August 1902.

Londoners were amazed at the first table tennis championships; the new craze was called Ping-Pong.

9

SHORT BUT SWEET, 'TWAS BERTIE'S TREAT!

The Edwardian Period (1901–10)

1902

The new king, King Edward of the house of Saxe-Coburg-Gotha, was crowned on 9 August at the abbey with his wife Queen Alexandra. The delay in the coronation was due to the king developing appendicitis on 24 June 1901, just two days before the original coronation date. He was operated on by Sir Frederick Treves. In gratitude to the nation for all their messages of goodwill, he donated Osborne House on the Isle of Wight, his mother's favourite house, to the state. Edward was the second oldest monarch to ascend to the British throne at fifty-nine; his ancestor William IV ascended at the age of sixty-four.

1903

King Edward became the most popular man in England with the landed gentry; it was deemed an honour to be invited to his estates for shooting and banquets.

1904

King Edward paved the way for an agreement with France whereby the two countries would become allies. On a visit to Paris his speech was well received and the agreement was thrashed out with his help.

Edward also had an interest in military matters and wanted to see the army and navy given more funding; he feared that a war in Europe was imminent.

Jigsaw puzzles were becoming very popular in England. Designed to teach children about geography, they were now being used as a pastime. One of the most popular designs was a picture of the royal family.

1905

Southwark Minster was declared a cathedral at last; the decision was taken when the Church of England Diocese of Southwark was created.

1906

The Thames caught fire when an oil spill ignited in January.

In March a new tube line opened between Waterloo and Baker Street.

Parliament approved the principle of old age pensions.

The Suffragettes were very active in their campaign for votes for women, with some being arrested at Westminster for chaining themselves to the railings. They were sent to Holloway Prison for refusing to recognise the court and pay their fines; they went on hunger strike.

César Ritz opened his new plush hotel and tea rooms in Piccadilly. Born in Switzerland, Ritz ran a hotel in Paris where he met Arthur Gilbert, and with his chef, Auguste Escoffier, he came to London and taught the capital's rich how to enjoy themselves. Gilbert bought the Savoy Palace from the family and transformed it into the Savoy Hotel. Alex Marnier, the inventor of Grand Marnier, persuaded him to open his own hotel and financed the whole operation, the Ritz being the result. It was the first steel-framed building in Britain.

Harrods, which opened the previous year, announced good figures for the fiscal year.

1908

The Old Age Pensions Act became law.

The king was not well and the nation feared it would soon have a new monarch, but Edward was soon back to his public duties, which he took seriously. His preference was for the Conservatives which put him constantly at loggerheads with the Liberals.

1910

Londoners became concerned that the German military machine was building up and war looked imminent.

In January the Suffragettes besieged the Prime Minister and he had to be rescued by police.

On 1 February the first labour exchange opened in London and it was swamped.

Captain Robert Scott set off from London on his attempt to reach the South Pole on 1 June.

Dr Hawley Crippen, who was wanted for the murder of his wife Belle in London, was captured in Canada in a remarkable series of events that saw the first use of the telegraph in criminal matters. A message was sent from the ship SS *Montrose* to Scotland Yard to say that Crippen and a boy had been spotted on board. Police raced to Quebec aboard a quicker ship and arrested them both when the ship docked. The boy in question turned out to be his mistress and accomplice, Ethel le Neve. Both were returned to London. Crippen was found guilty of murder and hanged on 23 November; Le Neve was acquitted.

The king was taken ill with suspected bronchitis while on a trip to Biarritz. He returned home on 27 April but never fully recovered. On 5 May he was confined to his bed. The Prince of Wales visited his father the next day and told him of his victory at the races. His horse, Witch of the Air, had won the 4.15 race at Kempton Park. Edward listened intently to the details; then replied 'Yes, I have heard of it and I am very glad.' He then drew his last breath at 11.45 p.m. and passed away. The Prince of Wales was now king and would rule as George V.

1911

On 22 June Prince George became King George V of the house of Saxe-Coburg-Gotha. He was crowned in the abbey with his consort Mary of Teck who would be known as Queen Mary.

10

A SCANDAL OR TWO, TOO MANY!

The House of Windsor (1910–present)

1914

At London's Middlesex Hospital, doctors were claiming a victory after successfully treating a man for cancer with Radium.

On 4 August the government declared war on Germany; on 17 August the first forces landed in France. Londoners were eagerly joining up to fight 'the Boche' and Olympia became a detention centre for German detainees. Stories from the front shocked the City seeing shares plunging. On Christmas Day the troops called a truce to exchange food and drink; they then played a game of football. The next day they slaughtered each other.

1916

Women were leading the home front with over 2.5 million working in war-related occupations.

London museums closed for the duration of the war.

In March, Zeppelins flew over southern England bombing cities and towns. London was hit and, on the Embankment, Cleopatra's Needle was damaged when a bomb fell close by. The damage was never repaired and can still be seen today.

The king relinquished all titles with the house of Saxe-Coburg-Gotha owing to the German connotations; in future the records would show that the British monarchy would be known as the House of Windsor.

1918

London restaurants were ordered to have two meatless days a week to help with the food shortages.

On 6 February the Suffragettes finally got their way when women over the age of thirty gained the right to vote, the age for men was lowered to twenty-one and at the same time the school leaving age was raised to fourteen.

In April the Penny Post was abolished.

In November thousands of Londoners perished as Spanish 'flu hit the country.

At 11.00 a.m. on the eleventh day of the eleventh month, the war was finally declared over; Germany lost and had to pay reparations to the Allies. President Wilson visited King George V in London to receive thanks from England for America's help in winning the European war. Over 10 million were dead in what was described as the 'War to end all Wars'.

1919

On 1 December Lady Nancy Witcher Astor, an American-born woman, was elected to the House of Commons and took her seat as the first woman MP to sit there. Married to the wealthy Lord Waldorf Astor, Annie represented the Sutton division of Plymouth for the Conservative party.

1920

The Bowes-Lyon family, headed by the Earl of Strathmore, moved into 17 Bruton Street off Piccadilly. It was rumoured that Lady Elizabeth Bowes-Lyon was seeing a lot of Albert, Duke of York

On 11 November an unknown soldier, whose body was taken from a Flanders field, was interred at Westminster Abbey in a special tomb near the entrance into the Western Towers. The tomb would commemorate the lives lost in the First World War; many countries around the world were doing the same. It became known as 'The tomb of the unknown warrior'.

1925

The government approved the permanent implementation of the Summer Time Act, originally brought in during the First World War. The act declared that in the winter clocks be put back an hour to allow the farmers more daylight. Now it would happen every year, with clocks going forward again in March.

Wireless transmissions of entertaining programs as well as news bulletins became a regular thing with the BBC and reached over 40 million people worldwide from their London headquarters.

The Charleston dance craze hit London as many hotels held dances.

White lines were painted on London's roads to keep traffic in regular lanes.

In July, Patricia Cheeseman became the first person to be treated for diabetes with insulin injections at Guy's Hospital.

1926

At 17 Bruton Street at 2.40 a.m. on the morning of 21 April, the Duchess of York gave birth to a baby girl named Elizabeth. The house was the family home of the Bowes-Lyons. Elizabeth would later become the first sovereign to be born in a numbered house.

1931

Third party insurance became compulsory for motor vehicles, and trolley buses started operating in the capital for the first time. The economic situation was worsening with unemployment figures increasing as firms shut down. London was thrown a lifeline when Henry Ford opened a car production factory in Dagenham, Essex, just a few miles from the East End.

In September there was a run on the pound and it devalued to US$3.40.

Edward, the Prince of Wales, met an American couple, Mr and Mrs Ernest Simpson, at a party given by Lady Furness.

King Alfonso XIII of Spain abdicated and arrived in London.

1936

The king died of heart failure on 20 January at 11.55 p.m. aged seventy. During his twenty-six years on the throne, King George V saw many changes. He also made history with his regular radio broadcasts. He was succeeded by Prince Edward who became Edward VIII.

In June Haile Selassie was exiled to London after a defeat by the Italians.

Adolf Hitler was now considered a great risk to peace in Europe by the City of London.

Fred Perry won his third successive singles title at Wimbledon.

On 21 August, the BBC broadcasted for the first time from Alexander Palace.

On 30 November Crystal Palace burnt down.

After much thought and many meetings with the government, King Edward VIII decided to give up the throne for his love of Mrs Simpson. On 10 December he signed the Instrument of Abdication and effectively handed his brother Albert the throne of England. Edward would henceforth be known as the Duke of Windsor. Prince Albert said he would rule under the name George VI in honour of his father. He would rule with his wife Elizabeth (later the Queen Mother).

Pinewood film studios opened at Shepperton.

1939

The IRA bombed London in a bid to oust Britain from the six counties of Northern Ireland which were still under parliament's rule.

In February the government recognised General Franco as the supreme head of Spain; it was hoped this would keep Spain neutral in the impending war to come with Germany.

In August the country prepared for war as talks with Germany broke down. Britain reassured Poland that it would stand by its agreement to defend the country against aggression. At 4.45 a.m. on 1 September, Germany invaded Poland and on 3 September at 11.15 a.m. Britain declared war on Germany over the incident. British forces landed in France to bolster the French forces against an invasion by Germany. In December rationing came into force.

1940

The war wasn't going well and Nazi Germany was pushing its way across Europe. The Germans launched a blitzkrieg on France to drive the British and French troops towards the coast after taking Paris. At Dunkirk in May and June the troops fought with what little supplies they had, trapped between the English Channel and the Germans. A flotilla of ships headed by the navy steamed to the beaches to rescue them. The flotilla was joined by an armada of small private boats manned by civilians who between them saved over 330,000 men by bringing them back to England. On 20 August Winston Churchill made a moving speech to the nation in which he praised the RAF for their tenacity and bravery in the Battle of Britain. He said, 'Never in the field of human conflict has so much been owed, to so many, by so few.'

A German pilot accidentally dropped bombs on the City of London which were meant for factories further up the coast. On the night of 7 September the Luftwaffe deliberately bombed London. The destruction was devastating and the loss of life enormous. This raid caused 1,000 fires, killed 430, injured 1,600, damaged 200 houses, 2 power stations, and the Wellington Barracks chapel where it killed 119 people. In June and July the British Library and Highbury Corner were hit killing 24 people and damaging 5 houses as well as the Dogs' Home at Battersea. By early July, 200,000 houses in London needed repairs or were damage beyond repair. Londoners started to use the underground stations as air-raid shelters and the area around St Paul's Cathedral was patrolled by volunteers. After 12 November the German planes started to bomb other cities and London went for days when the bombs didn't fall at all. In the air, the RAF was still busy fighting the Battle of Britain. The daily dog-fights were for the supremacy of the skies; if the RAF had lost the fight, Britain would have become a sitting duck.

1941

By May the German air raids were starting to get less and less as the Luftwaffe prepared to invade Russia. The total number of civilians killed across the country exceeded 41,000 with 1.4 million people made homeless. Rationing was taking its toll on morale and children were sent to the country for safety. America was reluctant to get involved in the war, though they were supplying the British with war materials and food. On 7 December Japan launched an unprovoked attack without warning on Pearl Harbor and America declared war on Japan. Admiral Yamamoto of the Japanese navy feared that the raid would awaken a sleeping giant. It did, and America was now in the war, allied with Britain against the Japanese who had already attacked British forces in Asia. This in turn brought America into the European war against Germany. Within months American forces were stationed in Britain for the duration.

Britain had stood alone until now and was at the mercy of the German forces that had already invaded and occupied the Channel Islands; Hitler had put off his invasion plans for Britain to concentrate on Russia. This turned out to be his biggest mistake, as he could have walked into Britain with little or no resistance. Had he done that the Americans would never have been able to get a foothold in Europe to station their troops and air force. Britain was saved by that simple bad decision.

1944

In May MI5 officers were alarmed to read the *Daily Telegraph* crossword puzzle, for it contained words that were being used as codewords in documents relating to the proposed invasion of Europe in June. They went to see the compiler, a teacher named Leonard Dawe in Surrey, and asked him to explain why he has used words like Overlord, Omaha, Neptune, Big-Wig and Mulberry as the answers to clues. After extensive questioning they came to the conclusion that he wasn't a spy and that the coincidence was just that, a coincident. On 6 June the HMS *Belfast* fired a volley of shells at the beach head off the French coast; the Allied invasion of Europe had begun. The ship was later saved from the scrap yard and is now anchored as a tourist attraction on the Thames, between Tower Bridge and London Bridge.

The war in the east wasn't faring well, but the German war was moving towards an end. Londoners had seen their city devastated by the Luftwaffe bombs with Parliament, the docks and even Buckingham Palace damaged. The queen remarked that because of the damage at the palace, she could now look out of her bedroom window and see the East End. Morale was high until the German V1 and V2 rockets started falling on London. These pilot-less flying bombs were more destructive than the other bombs, falling at random, killing thousands. In July Sloane Court was hit, killing 26 people. The rockets travelled over 200 miles at a speed of 3,500mph. Many were shot down by coastal and anti-aircraft guns as well as the RAF but over half reached their destination. Londoners nicknamed them Doodlebugs; an Americanism.

1945

In March a V2 hit Stepney in the East End killing 134; by the end of hostilities the V1 and V2 rockets killed more than 2,500 and injured 6,000.

On 8 May Londoners crowded the rubble-strewn streets to celebrate Victory in Europe Day. Winston Churchill declared it a national holiday as the war was now over and the country could start to recover. Rationing would still be in force for years to come, but at least the destruction had stopped.

The Asian war effectively ended when Japan surrendered in August/September.

1950

London was getting back to work after the war years which created vast wastelands of demolished houses and factories. The industrial waste being pumped into the atmosphere caused concern to scientists fearing the return of the old Victorian smog that made London's air so dense; it often became impossible to see further than one foot in front of you.

1951

The Sherlock Holmes Society celebrated the fiftieth year of Abbey House, Baker Street, London, where the public could see memorabilia of the great detective.

On the South Bank, Londoners celebrated the Festival of Britain where the public could see exhibitions of great British inventions and feats of engineering.

1952

King George VI died after a long illness on 6 February. His personal butler tried to wake him at 7.30 a.m. and called a doctor who pronounced the king dead from heart failure. His daughter Elizabeth succeeded him as queen. The princess, on a tour of Africa, was in Kenya when she was told the news. Philip, the Duke of Edinburgh and Princess Elizabeth returned to comfort her mother. Little did anyone know that the princess born in a house in Bruton Street on 21 April 1926 would one day become queen. The king was buried at Windsor on 16 February. In May, Elizabeth and Philip moved into Buckingham Palace to allow renovations to Clarence House where the Queen Mother and Princess Margaret would live. In November Elizabeth opened her first of many parliaments and in December agreed to have her coronation televised on 2 June the following year.

In June, London got flashing orange beacons at zebra crossings. Also, parliament was told that Britain now had the nuclear bomb while in July Londoners saw the last tram taken out of service.

Derek Bentley, convicted of the murder of policeman Sidney Miles while in the committal of a crime, was sentenced to death. His accomplice, Christopher Craig, who actually shot the officer while Bentley was in police custody was also convicted, but couldn't hang because of his age. Bentley allegedly shouted to Craig, 'Let him have it Chris', which the jury construed to mean shoot the officer. Bentley insisted that he meant for Craig to give the officer the gun; the controversy was set to drag on for many decades.

1953

On 28 January Derek Bentley was hanged at Wandsworth Prison.

On 24 March Queen Mary, the widow of George V, died.

The police issued an alert for John Halliday Christie, a former tenant of 10 Rillington Place in Notting Hill, London, after the bodies of three women were discovered hidden behind false panelling in the kitchen. Christie was a witness at the trial of another former tenant and neighbour, Timothy Evans, who had been convicted of murdering his wife and child. After being arrested Evans, who was a simpleton, admitted to police that he committed the murder. Then at his trial he changed his story and blamed Christie; the jury convicted Evans, who was hanged.

John Christie was convicted of the murder of four women, including his own wife, and was sentenced to hang on 15 July. The Evans family asked the Home Office to reinvestigate Timothy Evans' claims, but were refused as parliament reaffirmed the conviction.

1955

In February, parliament announced it had developed a Hydrogen bomb.

On 13 July Ruth Ellis, a model, was convicted of the murder of racing driver David Blakely outside a London night club. Despite reassurances that an appeal of the death sentence would succeed, Ellis made history by being the last female to hang in a British gaol.

Designer Mary Quant opened her first London shop in trendy Chelsea.

1958

Parking tickets were issued for the first time in London, yellow 'no parking' lines were painted on the roads and meters were put in streets for motorists to pay for parking their cars.

The CND (Campaign for Nuclear Disarmament) was formed in London against nuclear weapons development.

In Notting Hill Gate in September, white and black youths attacked each other with weapons and petrol bombs in racial riots.

In October the first women Peers took their seats in the House of Lords.

The popularity of Elvis Presley inspired English rock and roll singers. A young man from South London was making himself a name on the music circuit. His name was Harry Webb. Harry sang under the stage-name of Cliff Richard; MPs commented in the House that the trend would not last, neither would Cliff.

1963

Londoners were going crazy with Beatlemania. The four Liverpudlians, John Lennon, Paul McCartney, George Harrison and Ringo Starr who made up the Beatles were top of the pop charts.

Cinema-going Londoners were being entertained by a new film based on books by Ian Fleming. Actor Sean Connery was wooing the ladies with his sexy performance of the British secret agent James Bond in *Dr. No*.

In June the Minister John Profumo, Secretary of State for War, was forced to resign amid a scandal involving the call-girls Christine Keeler and Mandy Rice-Davies, who it was alleged he shared with a senior Russian diplomat and suspected spy.

On 8 August a gang of robbers got away with £2.6 million in used and untraceable notes after holding up the London – Glasgow mail train; the money was made up of old notes that were due to be incinerated and renewed. Within months the gang were rounded up and convicted. They included Buster Edwards and Ronnie Biggs, well known petty thieves from London's East End.

On 22 November London was left shocked at the news of the assassination of US President John Fitzgerald Kennedy in Dallas; it was a day that would stay in people's minds forever. Almost everyone in the world remembered where they were when they heard the news about this popular president and family man. John Kennedy attended the London School of Economics in 1938 when his father Joe Kennedy was working at the embassy in Grosvenor Square.

1964

On 10 March the queen gave birth to her fourth child; Edward Antony Richard Louis. Her majesty, who was now thirty-eight, was very tired during the pregnancy and had to cancel many engagements. On 1 May the queen's sister, Margaret, and husband Lord Snowdon announced the birth of their second child, Lady Sarah Armstrong-Jones. These royal births made it a great year for the royal family; the Duke and Duchess of Kent had also had a baby girl, Lady Helen Windsor.

In a free vote in parliament on 21 December, it was passed that there would be a suspension of capital punishment; the act would be reviewed in five years' time.

1965

On 24 January Sir Winston Churchill died; he lay in state before being buried in the village churchyard near Blenheim Palace.

In February smoking adverts were banned from television.

The Beatles were awarded MBEs for services to the music industry; it was alleged in a national newspaper that they smoked cannabis in the palace toilets before the ceremony.

1966

In Dublin on 8 March, the IRA blew up Nelson's Column in O'Connell Street, Dublin. It was feared that they might strike in London next.

In London, a state of emergency was declared when the dock workers went on strike.

On 30 July the England football squad won the World Cup at Wembley Stadium after extra time. Shortly before the games started the trophy was stolen, but later found by a dog named Pickles, hidden in a hedge.

In October, Timothy Evans, who was convicted and hanged for murder on the evidence of mass murderer John Christie, was finally proved innocent of all charges. Christie killed Mrs Evans and her baby, then coaxed the simpleton Evans into believing he had killed them.

1969

In London the leaders of a notorious criminal gang were sentenced to life for murder. The brothers were known as the Kray Twins and were convicted of the murders of George Cornell, and another notorious petty thief named Jack 'The Hat' McVitie. They were to serve a minimum of thirty years each.

1972

Britain signed to join the European Economic Community. The entry was the work of the Prime Minister, Edward Heath, whose Conservative party won the general election in 1970.

Electricity blackouts were prevalent in England when the miners' strike caused coal shortages. Some places were without electricity for up to twelve hours and the economy was badly hit with factories on short time.

In Uganda in August, dictator Idi Amin expelled 50,000 Asians. The expulsions meant many came to Britain, many to London, with only £50 in their pockets, this being the amount that Amin declared they could take with them. Britain condemned the expulsions, but Amin insisted it was for the good of Uganda.

1973

The government imposed a three-day working week, 50mph speed limits and credit restrictions as the country was held to ransom by the power workers; the winter of discontent had set in.

The queen opened the new London Bridge; the old one had been sold in an auction to an American named Robert Paxton McCulloch. He paid $2.46m for the bridge then had it taken down block by block, and reassembled in the Mojave Desert at Lake Havasu in Arizona. It was declared the 'world's biggest antique' for tax purposes.

1975

Margaret Thatcher was elected leader of the Conservative party. As leader she was given the privilege of becoming an honoray member of the Conservative party gentleman's club, The Carlton Club in St James's. This was the first time a woman had ever been allowed to become a member of such a club.

Lord Lucan was believed to be on the run after his nanny was found beaten to death at the family home in Westminster in November 1974.

The IRA was keeping up its campaign of terror on the streets of London. In December four IRA men surrendered to police after a six-day siege in Balcombe Street.

1976

The London Dungeons opened in Tooley Street in Southwark, based under the arches of London Bridge station. The new attraction was an exhibition of 'The Horrible History' of England. It was an instant hit with tourists and it was hoped that Southwark might now be developed into a tourist area. The closure of the docks had brought a great deal of unemployment to the area.

1979

The country was in turmoil again with rubbish piling up on London streets due to strikes by the bin men. A delivery driver strike caused shortages in shops and the capital tightened its belt.

A general election was called early, and Downing Street got its first female Prime Minister when Margaret Thatcher was elected. Airey Neave, Secretary of State for Northern Ireland, was killed by the IRA at Westminster.

1982

On 7 July the queen was disturbed by a male visitor to her bedroom in the middle of the night. He drew the curtains in the room and that woke her majesty, who kept her cool and chatted to him as he sat on the bed. After about 10 minutes her majesty was allowed to call down for a light for her cigarette, this alerted the guards who took the man away. He was identified as an unemployed Irishman named Michael Fagan.

Prince William Arthur Philip Louis was born to Charles and Diana, Prince and Princess of Wales, at St Mary's Hospital, London, on 21 June.

1984

Londoners were relieved to hear the Thames Barrier was now operational. The huge moveable barrier would prevent any future flooding to the capital. Since Roman times the Thames had flooded London and the south-east coast many times. The last major flooding, in 1953, caused untold damage to houses and businesses in the capital.

The miners' strike was affecting the daily routine of the capital with constant protests.

On 22 April, Yvonne Fletcher, a young police constable, was murdered outside the Libyan Embassy in London by someone inside the building. The ensuing siege ended with thirty diplomats being deported. No one was charged as diplomatic immunity was claimed. The incident happened as a demonstration took place outside; Yvonne was doing her duty controlling the crowds when someone from inside the embassy fired a wild shot into the street; it hit the WPC killing her.

On 15 September Princess Diana gave birth to Prince Henry Charles Albert David better known as Prince Harry. It was traditional in England for royal Henrys to be known as Harry.

1988

The old Liquor Licensing Act was finally repealed; it was brought in during the First World War to stop people taking days off work from the munitions factories. The hours of business for a pub changed to allow them to stay open from 11.00 a.m. to 11.00 p.m. Monday to Friday, and 12.00 p.m. to 10.30 p.m. on Sunday. The statutory closure of pubs from 2.30 p.m. to 6.00 p.m. was abolished.

Prince Charles was nearly killed while skiing in Switzerland with friends; they escaped an avalanche by just a few minutes.

1990

The city erupted in violence as mass protests turned into riots with millions protesting against the Poll Tax. Not since 1381, when Wat Tyler came to London to protest against Poll Taxes, had the capital seen such civil unrest. Prime Minister Thatcher who instigated the tax was forced to resign as hundreds were jailed for refusing to pay it.

On 26 June the IRA bombed the Carlton Club. As it was the official club of the Conservatives, it was suspected the bombing was to bring publicity to the Irish cause.

London reservists were called up as Saddam Hussein invaded Kuwait. John Major was elected by the party to take over the reins in Downing Street from Mrs Thatcher.

1993

In London, GMTV launched their new breakfast channel on New Year's Day.

In February the World Trade Center was bombed in New York. As a result, millions were wiped off stocks in the London Exchange.

In April a London student was stabbed to death in the street. The murder of Stephen Lawrence was suspected as being racially motivated.

1995

Barings Bank, one of the oldest in the City, was declared bankrupt after a rogue trader named Nick Leeson unlawfully gambled away a fortune.

The sixty-one-year-old Ronnie Kray, who was twenty-seven years into his life sentence for murder, died in Broadmoor. His brother Reggie attended the funeral in London where the streets were lined with thousands of mourners. Notorious South London gangster Dave Courtney organised the security for the event, which was also attended by many old faces from London's crime syndicates.

There were riots in Brixton after racial tension in December.

1997

Londoners woke up on 31 August to hear the devastating news that at 4.00 a.m. that morning, their beloved Princess Diana had been killed in a tragic road traffic accident in Paris. With her was Dodi Al-Fayed who was also killed along with the chauffeur. Dodi's father was Mohammad Al-Fayed, the Egyptian-born owner of one of London's most prestigious stores – Harrods. The world was in mourning and conspiracy theories abounded regarding the incident.

On 6 September, London and the world came to a standstill as the royal family publicly buried Diana, with a ceremony in Westminster Abbey. Elton John the songwriter/musician adapted his hit 'Candle in the Wind' to refer to the princess who was a close friend; he had originally written it about Marilyn Monroe. Elton sang the new song in the abbey to a hushed and tearful world. A whole new industry sprung up as the world remembered the 'People's Princess'.

In London, the Home Secretary Michael Howard announced to Myra Hindley, the notorious Moors murderess, that she would never be released from prison. Her co-conspirator Ian Brady had long been diagnosed as criminally insane; he would serve out the rest of his life in Broadmoor.

1998

General Pinochet, the former dictator of Chile, was put under house arrest in London. It was at the request of a Spanish court who were considering charges against him for Human Rights violations.

In parliament the European Human Rights bill of 1998 received royal assent.

2000

London welcomed the new millennium with millions on the streets of the capital to celebrate. British Airways sponsored a giant Millennium Wheel on the waterfront called the 'London Eye'. The ferris wheel turns so slowly that passengers are loaded and unloaded while it is still turning; it has 32 pods holding 25 people in each and takes about 27 minutes to do a complete turn. The 32 pods represent the 32 boroughs that now make up the capital; it stands at about 443ft tall.

2002

On 9 February Princess Margaret died; the queen's sister was buried on 15 February at Windsor.

On 30 March the nation was again in mourning when the Queen Mother died at Windsor. The much-loved 'Queen Mum' lay in state and was then buried at Windsor after a funeral at Westminster Abbey. It was the Queen's Golden Jubilee year and much celebrating took place, with many parties in the grounds of Buckingham Palace.

In London, Paul Burrell the former butler to Princess Diana was cleared of theft from Kensington Palace of the princess's property. Burrell insisted all along that the property was given to him by Diana over the years. A letter from the queen to the court was considered by the jury to verify the claim.

Ian Huntley, a caretaker from Soham in Cambridgeshire, was charged with the murder of two ten-year-old girls. Jessica Chapman and her friend Holly Wells went missing in the village; their bodies were found a week later. Huntley was declared by a judge at the Old Bailey in London to be fit to stand trial.

2003

The London-based soap opera *Eastenders* had a new storyline where 'Dirty' Den Watts came back from the dead after fourteen years.

US President George W. Bush visited London; he was welcomed by huge protests against the invasion of Iraq.

On 17 December at the Old Bailey in London, Ian Huntley was convicted of the Soham murders. His girlfriend Maxine Carr was found guilty of perverting the course of justice and given a three-and-a-half-year gaol term; she had made a false statement to police giving him an alibi. Huntley may never be released.

2004

On 6 January the Diana and Dodi inquest was opened to rumours that they were murdered by the state; the *Daily Mirror* published a letter written by Diana, in which she claimed someone was trying kill her.

Ken Livingston won the London mayoral elections again; he would serve for another four years.

2005

Prince Charles married Camilla Parker-Bowles, his long-time mistress, at a registry office in Windsor on 9 April.

In July, on the 7th and the 21st, Islamic terrorists carried out suicide bombings on the London Underground and buses. The 7 July bombs went off killing fifty-two people and the bombers. On the 21st all the bombs failed to detonate and the perpetrators were arrested; they all claimed that it was a hoax to scare people. The Al Qaeda cell consisted of Mukta Ibrahim, Yassin Omar, Ramzi Mohammed and Hussain Osman. They will all serve a minimum sentence of forty years after being found guilty; they appealed and lost the case.

A Brazilian man, Jean Charles de Menezes, was mistaken for one of the hunted terrorists and shot dead on a tube train in front of passengers. It happened a week after the attempted bombings. It later emerged that he was innocent.

In May the general election was won by Labour; returning Tony Blair to Downing Street.

On 6 July Londoners went wild with delight when the Olympic committee announced from Singapore that London would host the 2012 Olympics. Politicians from all sides joined in the celebrations with the stars of stage, screen and sports, along with millions of Londoners.

2006

On 20 January Londoners rallied to help a stranded whale, trapped in the Thames near London Bridge. All efforts failed and the whale died of shock.

Actress Helen Mirren won a series of awards for her portrayal of the queen in a biopic of the royal family called *The Queen*.

In London, a former KGB double agent, Alexander Litvinenko, died after being poisoned with radiation. The suspected killer escaped back to Russia where it was alleged the plot was hatched by the Russian government. The investigation had all the hallmarks of a good James Bond film; a trail of radiation was followed by the police all over London.

On the morning of 7 December Britain came under attack from a strong Atlantic low-pressure system. It brought unstable weather conditions to most of the country, and the south in particular. At about 7.30 a.m. a small group of thunderstorms gathered in Cornwall, then moved east-north-east across the country. By 10.00 a.m. the squall line had reached Salisbury where a major drop in humidity was recorded, this resulted in an increase of atmospheric pressure behind the squall, causing it to accelerate forward. The increased intensity combined with a change of wind direction ahead of the storm, initialised the rotation of the mesocyclone in one of the stronger storm cells. The end result was the touchdown of the tornado in Kensal Rise, London, at 11.00 a.m. The London Fire Brigade and structural surveyors assessed the damage, and structural safety of the affected properties. Several hundred people were evacuated from their homes until they had been declared safe. Brent Council held a press conference to quell the panic; they confirmed that none of the affected properties were likely to be demolished. However, twenty-nine homes had been declared unfit for habitation due to the damage caused by the tornado. Brent Council was in the process of re-housing fifteen of the people affected; sixty-five people remained officially homeless with some injured, including a fifty-year-old man who suffered a serious head injury. It was also reported that eight people were treated at the scene, by the ambulance brigade for trauma.

2007

January saw a fair few disasters to celebrate the New Year; first seventeen people were killed across the country when Hurricane Kyrill struck. London and India then became the focus of riots and protests over the reality show *Big Brother*. Jade Goody, a former *Big Brother* contestant and celebrity, who, along with Danielle Lloyd, a model, and S-Club 7 singer Jo O'Meara, was accused of making racially abusive remarks towards another contestant. The contestant was Indian actress Shilpa Shetty, and the switchboard of Channel 4 was swamped with complaints from viewers. The police were even called in to investigate. Shilpa got the public behind her and eventually won the show with a 63 per cent vote. Jade, Jo and Danielle were slated by the press and Jade Goody's perfume was removed from shops.

On 18 January Londoners were delighted to be able to see Comet McNaught which was the brightest comet seen in the capital for over forty years.

Prime Minister Tony Blair was caught up in another political scandal: the 'Cash for Honours' investigations. It was alleged that certain peerages were 'sold' to businessmen for cash contributions to the Labour Party.

On 24 June Tony Blair moved aside as Premier and let Chancellor Gordon Brown take over as the British Prime Minister. Also in the news was the opening of the O2 arena on the site of the former Millennium Dome.

On 29 June, Londoners were again subjected to a terror attempt. A car full of petrol, gas cylinders and nails was discovered suspiciously parked outside the Tiger-Tiger night club, an ambulance crew attending an incident there reported smoke and fumes coming from the Mercedes saloon. The Haymarket venue was evacuated and the bomb squad sent in to disarm the lethal car bomb. Another Mercedes 300E car was ticketed and removed by traffic control from nearby Cockspur Street. Leaking petrol and fumes caused the bomb squad to attend and they discovered a similar bomb, which was disarmed. Both devices were set to be triggered by a crude detonator made with a mobile phone; the device failed. On 30 June a Jeep was driven into Glasgow airport's main entrance by two extremists. Bilal Abdulla, an Iraqi doctor working in the UK, was arrested after the vehicle caught fire, in the attempt to blow up the building. His accomplice, Kafeel Ahmed was severely burnt and died later of his injuries. On 2 August. Bilal Abdulla was sentenced to thirty-two years in gaol.

2008

On 5 February the US stock market plunged 3 per cent and threw shockwaves through the London Stock Exchange; major companies were in danger of being wiped off the FTSE 100. The Banking Crisis struck the City of London hard; on 18 February the government passed emergency legislation to bail out the Northern Rock bank. Four days later the bank was nationalised to save the investors and the bank from going under.

In April the famous London eye hospital Moorfields made history; they successfully carried out operations to implant 'Bionic Eyes' into two blind patients. Both patients were able to see for the first time in their lives.

On 1 May, Conservative party candidate Boris Johnson became the second Mayor of London, and had to resign his parliamentary seat. This office is totally separate to the long-standing office of The Mayor of the City of London, which goes back to King Richard in 1189. The Mayor of London is a political office. Londoners aired their grievances with former Mayor Ken Livingstone who, among other thing, brought in the dreaded and hated Congestion Charge. This was a tax on all vehicles entering an area of London from dawn to dusk, Monday to Friday. Even residents and the emergency services were subject to the charge.

In November Barack Obama was elected as the forty-fourth President of the USA and he promised to help the UK and the world out of the present economic situation. Gordon Brown was under constant attack from his political opponents, over the increasing problems in the banking system. The government were also under attack from promises made to the President elect about taking in more terror suspects from Camp X-Ray. *Celebrity Big Brother* star Jade Goody was diagnosed with terminal Cervical Cancer. She died on 22 March (mother's day) 2009.

2009

Londoners were tightening their belts to weather the storm of economic strife that faced them all. Companies such as Woolworths had already gone to the wall, and many people faced losing their jobs and homes. However, Londoners have always been a resilient lot. Through the fires, invasions, sieges, political and civil wars, peasants' revolts, bombardments from the air and economic strife, they have always come back from the brink. The old John Bull spirit and the Winston Churchill 'We'll fight them on the beaches' stance will always be a part of London and Londoners. 2009 and beyond will be no different.

YOU'RE NICKED, MY SON!

The London Thief-Takers

The authorities in London have had many organisations throughout history that have been responsible for law and order. The most recent is of course New Scotland Yard. This agency of the law has evolved from many private, and government, financed agencies and continues to improve life for the law abiding citizens of the capital.

The eighteenth century 'Thief-Takers' were generally well to do citizens who set themselves up as a sort of local private security company. The most famous of these people was Jonathan Wild who, through his connections with the underworld and criminals in London, set up a lucrative business whereby he retrieved stolen property for a fee. Wild was eventually hanged for the offence of handling stolen goods, which was a capital offence brought in by the authorities to combat the rising crime rate of the time.

After the 'Thief-Takers', came the Bow Street Runners. In 1748 Henry Fielding, the famous novelist, was commissioned as a magistrate in Bow Street. Fielding was fairly wealthy; as a successful writer he wrote the classic tale *Tom Jones*. His half-blind brother, John, was already a magistrate who also sat at the assizes in Bow Street, next door to their house. In 1749, fed up with so many felons failing to attend court and the increasing crime rate, the brothers recruited a group of ex-naval men with exemplary records and formed the first paid metropolitan police force. There were eight uniformed constables who operated from Fielding's house at 4 Bow Street. Henry was the chief officer and his brother John his assistant. At first the runners didn't patrol the streets; their main job was to serve writs issued by magistrates and to arrest felons who failed to attend court. Part of the uniform was a very bright scarlet waistcoat and they got the nickname 'Robin Redbreasts'. Henry Fielding retired from public life in 1754 and John succeeded him as chief of police and chief magistrate. Because of his disability, John Fielding was known as the 'Blind beak of Bow Street'. The runners were legendary in their pursuit of felons and travelled the length of the country to apprehend them; like the later Mounties of Canada, they always got their man – or woman.

In 1757 the government funded the organisation and they started the first criminal records office. They also trained their constables in surveillance techniques to form the first detective unit. In 1829 Sir Robert Peel started the Metropolitan Police Force, and the Runners, who by then consisted of eight constables, two sergeants and two commissioners, were integrated into the new force to form the first Criminal Investigation Department (CID). The new police force had sweeping powers and were numbered in their thousands. They also got nicknames of Peelers or Bobbies, after their founder. Bobbies is still used today, as is the expression the Old Bill. This name is the oldest of the lot and goes back hundreds of years to when the beadle or constable of a parish walked the streets in a red uniform with a long stick on top of which he had his badge or 'Bill of Office'. As he came upon a corner at night, he would put the stick with the bill of office on it round the corner to warn any waiting muggers that he was coming. Attacks on the police were common at that time.

The headquarters of the new force was a large building on the embankment near Westminster in the district of Whitehall. It was called Scotland Yard after the building, and the telephone number became famous when it was used many times in films and TV shows all over the world; it was Whitehall 1212. Many police forces in the UK still have numbers ending in 1212.

The reason it is called Scotland Yard is a fascinating story in itself and one that must be told. It all started around 1232 when Hubert De Burgh was sacked from his job as the Chief Judiciar of Justice in England, which was an office created by the Magna Carta and King John in 1215. Hubert bought some land in 1231 which was near the Westminster; he gave the land to some monks in 1240 and they sold it immediately to the Archbishop of York who added it to his estate called York House. It measured 14 perches by 6 perches and was rumoured to have once been owned by the Scottish royal family. In 1413 it was recorded that the land had been put out to a tenant as a smallholding. In 1519 the land was seized by Henry VIII and given to Cardinal Wolsey as a gift. He elaborated on the building and turned it into a palace with a large white hall. It became known thereafter as Whitehall Palace and the area as Whitehall. In 1529 Wolsey fell out with Henry VIII and he used it occasionally to stay in.

The Palace of Westminster had burnt down in 1512 and work was still being carried out there, so when Henry was in London he stayed at the Tower or Whitehall. The building fell into disrepair and the land was again tenanted to a family named Scott and became known as Scotelande. A canal was built across it in the late 1500s that went down towards the Charing Cross and into the Thames. A map dated 1593 clearly shows the canal which is referred to as being on the land called Scotelande. Houses were built on the site over the next hundred years and, in 1660, Charles II was restored to the throne and inherited the building which had been previously used by his father, Charles I, as a royal palace, and was where he was executed in public in 1649.

In 1662, in an effort to curb the rising crime rate in the city, a group of wealthy men took over the building and set themselves up as constables of the parish. They called themselves the Commissioners of Scotland Yard. Maps dating from about the 1670s show the entrances marked as Scotland Yard and Whitehall Palace. The main part of Whitehall Palace was destroyed in a massive fire in 1698 and was never rebuilt; all that remains is the Banqueting Rooms, which still stand today opposite Horse Guards Parade in Whitehall.

In 1729 some of the refurbished buildings were let out to a semi-retired naval officer named Thomas de Veil who took the buildings as offices where he served as a magistrate and commissioner of peace in Westminster. The building was called Great Scotland Yard by this time. De Veil was also a serving magistrate at Bow Street courts and was later knighted for his services to policing. In 1812 a building called the Clock House stood in the area of Scotland Yard and it was converted into a civil court named the Marshallsea Court House.

In 1829 Sir Robert Peel, the then Home Secretary, introduced his Metropolitan Policing bill in parliament and the force was commissioned. Their headquarters were at 4 Whitehall Place and it was rented for £560 6s 0d per annum. The rear part of the building, overlooking the Great Scotland Yard, was converted into the station house, and the other buildings were known as the Metropolitan Police Office which opened for business on 29 September 1829. The first two commissioners were Charles Rowen and a lawyer named Richard Mayne. Over the next fifty years or so they took over other buildings within the grounds, including the old clock tower. Later, in 1874, an inspector Neame started a Museum of Crime at 1 Great Scotland Yard, and this is now known as The Black Museum. The building is exclusively for the use of Scotland Yard and you will need special permission to get in there. It contains tools and murder weapons used by infamous criminals over the years and some rather ominous looking ropes used to hang most of them. The museum is unique in that it is not open to the public and most of the invited guests who visit from time to time are crime writers or researchers.

12

POO...WHAT A PEN AND INK!

The Sewage System and disease in London

'A right ol' pen and ink' was what the cockneys called a stink, and London was a very smelly place. Health has always been a problem where large amounts of people live and work in the same environment and London has been no different. The city has expanded over the centuries so quickly that, at times, the disposal of waste and the reckless lack of personal hygiene among the populace have often made them their own worst enemy. Since probably about the thirteenth century, the streets of London were laid with open gutters, firstly to dispose of rain and secondly to wash away the filth and human waste that was thrown into the streets, often from windows above. The people who lived in cramped conditions in the multi-storeyed wooden buildings simply did their ablutions in a potty; it was called a 'Gazunder' because it 'goes under the bed'. The potty was then emptied by opening the window and shouting a warning to people below. 'Gardy Loo' was the shout and, if you heard it, you needed to take heed lest you got a head full of someone's ablutions. The expression has evolved to 'going to the loo'.

The waste would lie in the gutter until a heavy downpour washed it into the Thames, which was used as a giant sewer. The tide turned twice a day and carried the waste of London out to the estuary at Shoeburyness in Essex. Once in the open sea, the plankton would break it down. There were two problems here. Firstly, as the population increased the tide was often overburdened with waste, and it often brought some of it back up the river. When it reached London Bridge, the twenty arches slowed down the flow and so the waste built up and often blocked the river; the smell was horrendous. The second problem was that the plankton was eaten by the fish, and the fish eaten by the people, so they were in fact eating their own untreated sewage. Is it any wonder that as the staple diet of most poor Londoners was fish, that up until the late 1800s the life expectancy was about forty? The problem extended further, because the many cesspits that existed in the affluent areas were not emptied very often, and invariably they overflowed into rivers and streams, contaminating the drinking water. This led to widespread disease such as dysentery and cholera. Most people got their water from city wells or through standpipes, often put up by well-meaning benefactors in an effort to keep disease down; but invariably the opposite happened.

When James VI of Scotland became the English King James I in 1603, he took up his seat in London and was astounded at the filth and lack of hygiene. He ordered that the boroughs must keep the streets clean by hiring people to sweep all the refuse, dumped each day, into the Thames. He was very concerned about the lack of fresh water and commissioned the first water board to the city. The New River Head at Finsbury was completed and opened in 1613. Clean water was collected from as far as 50 miles away, put into giant tanks at Finsbury; and from there it was piped into the city through hollowed-out tree trunks.

The Bubonic Plague was another health hazard that kept the population down. There have been some recorded outbreaks, and many not recorded. The ones we tend to hear about are the 1348 and the 1665 outbreaks; these brought about the deaths of tens of thousands of Londoners. In the summer of 1665 they stopped counting the dead when the total weekly count surpassed 10,000. One of the main problems was the lack of medical knowledge and the acceptance of the periodic outbreaks. No one seemed to want to take the matter in hand and actually try to find a logical reason for the disease, or indeed a preventative procedure or cure. In reality of course, most people who were influential simply left the city and returned when it was all over; life went on. The other main problem throughout history is that the influence of the church and its leaders seems to have made the situation even worse when the plague was prevalent.

Since the time of Augustine's arrival in England as an emissary of the Pope in the seventh century, it was normal for the church to claim miracles for medical cures though most of these were fake claims. They also claimed that when the plague and other disasters came our way, it was a punishment from God for our wicked ways. With this in mind no one would dare to come up with a cure, lest they be accused of challenging the will of God. There were no medical boards in medieval Europe, so anyone who could read and write a little, could claim to be a medical practitioner, and many did just that in the outbreak of 1665. If the patient died then it was the will of God, or it was blamed on the fact that the doctor was called in too late. These so called Physicians got the nickname of 'Quacks' because they wore a leather, herb-filled mask to protect themselves; it looked like a duck's bill, hence the expression. Today, a quack is a fake, struck-off or wannabe doctor who doesn't have a licence to practice, but in times past these dangerous idiots were all the uneducated and poor had.

The plague gets its name from the buboes which are one of the main tell-tale signs. These are swellings of the lymph glands which are part of the lymph system which protects us from major diseases. Black spots also appeared all over the body, giving rise to the name 'Black Death'. The victim would become feverish and unable to hold down any food or water. The disease was very contagious and anyone within a household would also get it very quickly; houses were nailed shut by the local authorities to prevent victims leaving their homes. This practice didn't stop the spread; it just enhanced your chance of dying.

The disease is thought to have come from China in the twelfth century; by the late 1300s Europe was trading within the area of the Black Sea, where Asian and European merchants met and traded, it seems not only goods, but also diseases. By 1347 Italy was in turmoil with the quarantining of Genoa, the main port. Some ships managed to slip the net and sailed to England, docking on the south side of the Thames. It was here in Southwark that the rats came off the ships, carrying the fleas that were host to the plague. At first the outbreak was fairly well contained, but the practice of city dwellers going over the bridge to seek their entertainment meant that the disease was carried into the city, probably in the clothing where fleas liked to hide.

The population of the city at that time was around 300,000 and that figure fell dramatically within months; many left for the country taking along the fleas and spreading it further afield. Before long the whole country was infected; some 50 million people worldwide died of the disease in this outbreak alone. By the onset of winter the number of victims always seemed to deplete, yet no one ever seemed to associate that with the fact that fleas were dormant in cold spells. In the 1348 outbreak in London it was feared cats and dogs were to blame, so they were hunted down in the streets and killed; the rats must have been laughing all the way to the larder. The 1665 plague was blamed on the wrath of God, and ironically another wrath of God saved the city from many more deaths. The last Great Fire of London was in 1666 and this devastating disaster probably killed off the last of the host-carrying rats and with it the disease disappeared. There were small outbreaks in the following centuries, but the plague never devastated London again like it had done in the fourteenth and seventeenth centuries.

General Boards of Public Health were set up in the late 1700s and improved upon in the early 1800s, but the commissioners were often corrupt or incompetent and the problem prevailed. The first water-flushing toilet to be built in England was in 1598; it was the idea of Sir John Harrington who was godfather to Elizabeth I. It consisted of a simple valve that released water down a pipe to flush the area around the toilet, which was usually a plank of wood with a hole cut in it. The water then merely moved it on to a cesspit or, in the case of most palaces and castles, the moat. Before this you simply poured a bucket of water down the hole and it did the same thing. The idea didn't catch on as the system leaked sewage smells back into the room and made it impossible to use at times. Sitting on her throne was how the queen often explained her ablutions, and today that is still an expression meaning you are on the toilet.

In 1832, a royal commission was set up to re-evaluate the poor laws passed in the 1600s to deal with relief and hygiene for the less well off. The assistant commissioner was a lawyer and sanitary campaigner named Edwin Chadwick. Chadwick was well aware of the problem and wrote the report that would change London's sewer and water system for the better. For years Chadwick wandered round the capital witnessing the filth and appalling conditions of the poor. His report, *Survey into the Sanitary Conditions of the Labouring Classes of Great Britain*, was finally published in 1842 and was so damning it forced the government to make drastic changes.

In 1848 the Public Health Act was passed. In order to be able to take control away from central government, the City of London commissioners formed their own public bodies and appointed a Medical Officer of Health (MOH), when later that year they managed to get passed the City Sewers Act. The first MOH was a doctor from St Thomas's named John Simon who was later knighted for his work. Simon was so fastidious in his work that he became a national figure and was the chief medical advisor to the government from 1851 until 1870.

During the 1840s and early 1850s London was hit with many cholera epidemics. The theory that the disease was airborne prevailed and exasperated the problem until 1854 when another epidemic killed thousands in weeks. John Snow was a doctor in the Soho area who was treating patients during an outbreak in 1854. He started a chart plotting the addresses of over 500 victims in the area, and came to the conclusion that they'd all used a particular water pump in Broad Street (now Broadwick Street), at the junction with Poland Street. He managed to persuade the city officials to take off the handle and within days the epidemic was over. He had proved that, contrary to popular belief, the disease was in fact waterborne, probably created by raw sewage leaking into the water system. John Simon was not so easily swayed by Snow's theory, and it wasn't until Louis Pasteur published his theories on germs in the 1860s, that John Snow finally got his recognition. In Soho today, near the spot of the old pump, is a pub named after the Soho doctor, The John Snow. In the summer of 1849 there was another outbreak of cholera; by October nearly 900 people had died from the disease which had become waterborne. John Simon wrote a report condemning the authorities for their corruption and lack of care. By November 1849, 6,500 victims in the Metropolitan area had succumbed to the diesease.

The problem of getting rid of the waste of nearly 2 million people on a daily basis is a vast task and up until the 1850s no one had taken the problem seriously enough. The city was exploding with poor immigrants, Jews from the east, Irish from the west and most were poorly-educated in hygiene. As one can imagine, the problem escalated out of control. There were new communities of poor people squeezing themselves into ever-shrinking properties, and this, with the hot summers, escalated the health problem. People were dropping like flies; something needed to done – and quick. The 2 million people who lived in London in the 1850s were served by over 200,000 cesspits. Mix this with coal fires, the industrial revolution with its chemicals and sulphur pollution, the lack of washing facilities making people smell and you start to get an idea of what Victorian London was really like. Literally everything was thrown in the river, whether it was legal or not.

By 1858 the river was so polluted with raw sewage, industrial waste and dead bodies, that parliament moved to Oxford as the stench was unbearable.

The lack of hygiene in food preparation didn't help either, and only increased early human death along with the rat population. Parliament passed an act to rid London of the problem and awarded £ 3 million to the district health board to build a safe, enclosed sewage system. The new railway system was also bringing in more people to work in the city and this further increased the waste problem during the week.

Joseph Bazalgette was chief engineer to the board of the metropolitan commission for sewers and they put him in charge of the proposed closed system. The problems were all too familiar to Bazalgette; he was working full time to clear the Kings Mill Sewer near Rotherhithe which had years of sewage back-up in the system. Bazalgette's solution was simple: he was to build a series of connecting pipes from every area of the city and take them down to a mains system which would run alongside the Thames and not directly into it. Street drains to collect rainwater would also form part of the framework and would be used to keep the system flowing. The statistics are phenomenal. When you think that in an age when everything was virtually done by hand, Bazalgette achieved a miracle in his task. Eighty-three miles of brick-lined sewers were built below ground. These flowed eastwards using a combination of gravity and rainwater. They were connected to over 450 miles of main sewers that were themselves connected to over 13,000 local smaller sewers. Over half a million gallons of waste flowed through the pipes every day.

The entire system took years to build, using mostly labourers to hand dig most of the channels; digging machinery was not available at the time. They used 320 million bricks, 860,000 cubic yards of cement and dug out over 3.5 million cubic yards of earth. The river flowed, at that time, right up to where the Temple Gardens are now fenced on The Embankment. The area of land which now goes down to the river was all reclaimed by Bazalgette. It allowed the sewage mainframe to be easily constructed without digging tunnels. What he did was quite ingenious; he simply waited for the tide to go out and piled along the river to form a void. Then he placed the pipes along the dry void and backfilled it, creating an area of land as well as an extension to the new underground railway system on the District Line. Part of the money that the system cost was recovered by the sale of prime riverside land on which today many buildings stand.

For many years afterwards though, the problem of raw sewage floating in the Thames was still often prevalent. The dumping of sewage had been solved, but factories along the river were still dumping their filth and waste in to the waters. Toxic waste killed off the fish and the river's natural wildlife suffered as a consequence. The factories and the railways brought many people into the city during the daytime to work; their waste increased and overloaded the system. It wasn't long before the estuary started to find it difficult to get rid of the daily waste, so what it couldn't pass into the currents of the North Sea, got sent back up river. No one seemed to notice this, probably because the London smog had now engulfed the capital and made it almost impossible to see anything for most of the time. The smog was a problem for many decades and wasn't really tackled until the 1950s; since then there has been a slow progression towards cleaning up the river and the air. Today we have the problem of carbon emissions which are choking the capital, the congestion charge on vehicles going through London Monday to Friday seemed to be helping, but how much will not be known for years to come.

Thomas Crapper set up a factory making bathroom furniture and opened some new public toilets in the city. The toilets were all connected to the main system and it was a wonderful new concept for Londoners. At first Crapper charged two pennies to use the toilets. This was to keep out the riff-raff, but the poor complained and he was forced to reduce the sum to one penny, hence the expression 'to spend a penny'. The history of the flushing toilet and that Crapper did not invent it, but merely redesigned it, is well known. The oldest flushing toilet system was discovered in China and is over 3,000 years old. Crapper had an admirer in Queen Victoria, and when she moved the official royal palace from St James's Palace to Buckingham House in 1837, it was Thomas Crapper who installed all the bathrooms and toilets, most of which still exist today; now that is value for money!

There is an official Thomas Crapper day each year on 17 January which is actually the wrong day. It is thought to be held on the day he died in 1910 but he actually died on 27 January. He held nine patents for improvements to the drainage and sewage systems, including a design for manhole covers. He didn't actually get to patent the invention of the siphon system either, this was granted to an ex-employee of his named Albert Giblin in 1898. Crapper later bought the patent and marketed the product under his brand name. Crapper furniture is now considered antique and very collectable. The Thomas Crapper Company went out of business in 1966. However, an apprentice of his started his own plumbing business, and his descendants still operate the business today from their premises in Richmond, Surrey; they call themselves Original Bathrooms.

13

SHE'S IN A RIGHT OL' TWO AN' EIGHT!

Rhyming Slang

This fascinating subject is actually all about communication and intrigue. It is believed to be unique to the East End of London, but in fact originates from South London and the borough of Southwark in the sixteenth and seventeenth centuries. The borough was awash with constant entertainment and debauchery, with taverns, wine bars, theatres, animal-baiting and brothels. With these came the dominant 5 per cent of the population who lived off the weaknesses of others, the criminals. In Southwark in those dark days, you could get anything you wanted – for a price. The criminals prospered and the customers went home satisfied … well most of the time they did. However, when you get organised crime you get competition and jealousy, and that is how rhyming slang started. It was out of necessity (which is the mother of invention) that the criminals needed to develop their own unique language to keep themselves safe from informants and their rivals. The many gangs that operated in the area used code words that only they were familiar with, and that kept them safe from outsiders.

Today the language of cockney rhyming slang is still spoken by proud Londoners, no matter what part of the city they come from. From City gents to costermongers, all use words that will sound unfamiliar to foreign visitors. However, with a little bit of background knowledge you will soon be interpreting what is being spoken, often by Londoners trying to impress you with their banter and impart a feeling of friendship. The words are, quite simply, rhyming words that mean something else, i.e. 'a whistle and flute' is a suit of clothes and this is often shortened to 'a whistle'. Sometimes an expression is used in conjunction with a slang word. For example, 'there I was, all dressed up to the nines in me whistle wiv me sky full of wedge.' This quite simply means, there I was dressed up smartly (it used to take nine yards of material to make a suit of clothes) in my suit (whistle) with my pocket (sky rocket) full of money (so much money you could use it to make a wedge for a door). Now you get the general idea. The main object was to be able to speak to your fellow criminals without being informed on.

Over the centuries we have developed many words that mean the same thing, such as a bird which comes from the birds and the bees and means a woman; this has developed into a tart which would normally be an insult, but to a Londoner is an affectionate term although it is sometimes used to mean a man who is being stupid. Then we get more complicated with similar words that need a bit of working out to get to the meaning. For instance, a Richard; this comes from the expression Richard the Third, a reference to the old king. It rhymes with bird so therefore means the same, a woman. Now that you have grasped the basics, here is a short list of familiar cockney rhyming slang for you to digest and, at the same time, I wish you luck in speaking the lingo to the natives. Remember that it doesn't sound the same with a New Jersey or Sydney accent, so try to get the accent right as well. See Dick van Dyke's attempt in *Mary Poppins* to see what I mean.

Cockney Rhyming Slang

A Syrup (of Figs), An Irish (jig), A rug	A wig or toupée
A Pigs Ear, Britney Spear	A beer
Rub-a Dub	The pub
Ol' Joanna	A piano
Titfer (tit for tat)	A hat
Centre Half	A scarf
North and South	Mouth
Tom and Dick	Sick (not feeling well)
Right as nine pence	Feeling much better
A Right ol' two an' eight	To be in state of panic or depression

Shell-like	Ears
Trouble and Strife	Wife
Old Man	Husband/father
Mince Pies	Eyes
Porky Pies	Lies/Deceit
Pegs	Legs
Plates (of meat)	Feet
Barnet (fair)	Hair
Drum (drummer's hat)	A flat/apartment
Moggy	A cat
Mutt	A dog
Dustbin lids, Sproggs	Kids/children
Butchers (hook)	A look/to watch something
Jam Jar	A car
Frog and Toad	The road
Apples and Pears	The stairs
Cup o' Char, Rosie Lee	A cup of tea
Gold Watch	A measure of whisky as in Scotch
The Outlaws	Anyone associated with the family of your spouse, as in 'in-laws'
Merry-go-round	A ginger ale, as in American Dry Ginger Ale
Old Bill, Rozzers, Bobbies, Peelers	The police
Black Maria	A police vehicle for taking away numerous prisoners, usually arrested at a raid or illegal drinking/gambling houses
Spiel	An illegal gambling club, from *spielen*, the German for 'to play'
Dicky Dirt	A shirt
Knackered	Tired/worn out, as in the knacker's yard where old horses were sold when they couldn't work anymore
Lemon Tart	Smart/clever, 'Don't get smart with me' or 'Don't get lemon wiv me'
Tatters (pronounced Tay-ters)	Cold, as in potatoes in the mould.
Paraffin Lamp	A tramp

Just to summarise on Cockney Slang, a lot of the new expressions are associated with the names of famous people, and to Londoners the expressions are usually easy to fathom out. Here are a few examples:

Gregory Peck	Neck
Julian Ray	Gay
Omar Riza	Pizza
Frankie Vaughan	Porn
Judy Dench	Stench
Thomas Edison	Medicine
Euan Blair	Leicester Square

The last one, Euan Blair, is a reference to an incident in 2003 when former Prime Minister Tony Blair's son, Euan, was arrested for being drunk and disorderly in Leicester Square, London. The Cockneys of London have a unique sense of humour as the Euan Blair expression shows.

14

PLACE NAMES, STREET NAMES AND PUB SIGNS

There are thirty-two boroughs in London and Greater London; all are commemorated by a pod on the London Eye. The names of the boroughs are mostly Saxon names, and the simplicity of them all is what makes them so fascinating.

Barking   The place of the people of Berica's tribe.
Barnet   The place where the land was cleared by burning it.
Bexley   The place of the box wood.
Brent   Celtic word for a river.
Bromley   A field where the Broom plant grows in abundance.
Camden   After an eighteenth-century MP, Charles Pratt-Camden.
Chelsea   A place where chalk is unloaded.
Croydon   A place where wild Saffron grows in abundance.
Dagenham   The smallholding of a Saxon named Daecca
Ealing   The place of the tribe of Gilla.
Enfield   The fields of a Norman named Eana.
Fulham   The place of a house owned by a Saxon named Fulla.
Greenwich   The settlement of the green fields and hills.
Hackney   An island in a river belonging to a Norman named Haca.
Hammersmith   Where the smithy has his forge and anvil.
Haringey   An enclosed settlement in the wood of a man named Grey.
Harrow   A place where there was a temple for heathens.
Havering   Where the tribe of Haefer live.
Hillingdon   The hill home of Hilda.

Hounslow	Where a mound shaped like a dog once stood.
Islington	A Saxon named Gisla owned this place.
Kensington	The hunting estate of a Norman named Cynesige.
Kingston-upon-Thames	The king's estate.
Lambeth	Where lambs were unloaded.
Lewisham	The place of the house of Leofsa.
Merton	Settlement by a natural pool.
Newham	A new town built in the 1960s, means new house.
Redbridge	A place where there was a red bridge in the 1700s.
Richmond	Named after the Richmond estate in Yorkshire.
Southwark	The south works; a Roman gravel pit work place.
Sutton	A Norman farm to the south of the county.
Tower Hamlets	A hamlet of houses near the Tower of London.
Waltham Forest	The forest of friendly people.
Wandsworth	A settlement of the tribe of Waendel.
Westminster	The minster that lies to the west of the city.

That in total makes thity-five, but there are six boroughs that have amalgamated into three, making the number of true London Boroughs thirty-two. They are Barking & Dagenham, Hammersmith & Fulham and Kensington & Chelsea.

Street names within the capital are usually commemorative of the history that is associated with those places. Looking around the city you will see such names as Cheapside. Cheap is the Anglo-Saxon word for a farmers market; it comes from the term 'cheape' meaning to barter. Cheapside is therefore the farmer's market place. Traders within the City boundaries usually sold their goods and wares in the same street; unlike today where you are likely to find a grocer shop, a tailors and a newsagents in the same row of shops. The only other trades that frequented the streets in days of old were coffee/tea houses and taverns. To get an idea of what this was like, a good place to start is the area around the Bank of England in Threadneedle Street.

Threadneedle Street was originally where the tailors to the aristocracy and the royal family had their workshops; the area was demolished in the 1770s to make room for the new Bank of England. The tailors moved to Savile Row, which is now renowned for bespoke tailoring.

Nearby is Lombard Street which runs from right to left across King William Street. In the fourteenth century, London was a thriving city and with the traders came the commerce, administration and the bankers. The biggest group of bankers who came to London were the Italian bankers, from the Lombardy. These bankers brought with them a reputation for honesty and integrity; this was the basis on which they issued the first bank notes, which were promissory notes promising to pay the bearer on a certain date the sum mentioned in gold. To this day the British notes still contain the sentence, 'I promise to pay the bearer on demand'.

Lombard Street was established as the banking area. Close by were the money changers in Exchange Alley, money retailers who exchanged gold and silver bullion for coins. These money changers would borrow from the banks by issuing their own promissory notes. They had to settle their accounts on the first of the month. If you couldn't settle your account then your creditor would send his men to break up your trading bench and expel you from the alley. The Italian words for broken bench altered over the years to the word 'bankrupt'. Today in Lombard Street you can still find some of the oldest banks in the world. Behind the Mansion House (formally the first stock exchange) which is the official residence of the Lord Mayor of the City of London, there used to be a coffee house run by the Lloyd brothers who started Lloyds of London. After discussing the insurance requirements, a scribe would write the policy ready for Lloyds and the customer to sign. The policy was written on a board under the table so no-one else would know your business. From this we get the expression 'underwritten'.

At the end of King William Street, we find Cannon Street. If you look just above the first-floor window, you will see a concrete frieze of lighted candles running around a building on the corner, called Candlewick House. The area is within the Parish of Candlewick and the street was originally where the wax chandlers lived, worked and sold their wares. By the end of the 1700s most of these people had moved out and workshops making wicks for cannons were set up in the street, which is when it changed its name to Cannon Street.

Halfway up Cannon Street on the right is a former Chinese bank; set into the building is a large stone behind a grill. This old millstone is the London Lode Stone and was once the centre of London, from where all distances to and from London were measured. Today that point of measuring is taken from the statue of Charles I which stands in Trafalgar Square. This spot itself was known as the 'Charing Cross' from 1190. On this spot in 1190, King Edward I erected the twelfth Cross of Eleanor, marking the spot where his wife Eleanor of Castile laid in state, before being buried at Westminster Abbey. The cross, along with eight others, which marked the route of her funeral cortège from Nottingham to London, was destroyed by Parliamentary troops during the English Civil War. Another part of London, the Elephant and Castle on the south side of the river, is a derivation of Eleanor of Castile.

By the Bank of England are a lot of streets which can trace their history back to the old market of Cheapside. Poultry is one such street; a proclamation in 1345 laid down that only Freemen of the City of London were allowed to trade poultry in this street. That was due to an outbreak of salmonella which the Freemen blamed on the outside farmers trading in the street. The outsiders were forced to start trading at Leadenhall Market about a mile away. In 1598 the street had changed with many taverns, haberdashery, upholstery and grocer shops being established. The street was destroyed in the Great Fire of 1666, and Sir Christopher Wren rebuilt St Mildred Poultry church which survived until 1832. Going off this thoroughfare is Wood Lane, Honey Lane, Milk Lane, Grocers Hall and Old Jewry where the Jewish money lenders traded. All these streets were frequented by the traders whom they were named after. London was thriving by the fourteenth century, but it was still illegal for certain members of society to learn how to read and write.

This area was also very near to the docks and the Pool of London where many ships, as many as 2,000, would come to the city to trade. Many of the people in this area were therefore foreigners and also unable to read and write English. So the traders established a simple way that people could see, at a glance, the name of the street and therefore what was sold in it. This method was so simple and clever, we still use it today. The system was a sign or statue depicting the trade. For example, at the end of Poultry today there is a replica of an old street sign, a statue of a young boy strangling a goose. It is halfway up a building on the corner near the entrance to Bank tube station.

Most of the other streets had painted signs: a milkmaid for Milk Lane, a pile of wood for Wood Lane, a honey pot for Honey Lane and so on. This was a very simple and effective idea. It came from the tradition of pub and tavern signs which, again, evolved from the lack of the ability to read and write. So, today we still have the tradition of seeing a red lion, a white hart, the king's head and many other pictures on pub signs outside these premises. The tradition has evolved into trade marks. A recent survey came to the conclusion that the big yellow M of Mcdonalds is the world's most recognisable symbol and widely used trade mark; all this from a system which evolved from the necessity of giving information to people who were illiterate. In our modern world, you can visit most places on the globe and, without knowing anything of the local language, you can easily get around and find places, by using the now widely used method of sign language. Go into any public building, and you will see a picture of a man running towards a door over all the exits, you know immediately this is the emergency exit. Simple, isn't it?

There are no roads in the City of London, only streets, lanes, exchanges, thoroughfares, passages, ways, alleys and squares. A lot of the streets are also named after famous people or incidents. By the London hospital is Mount Street. This is where they piled up the bodies from the outbreak of the plague in 1665; they simply ran out of space and then piled the bodies high and covered them with lime and earth, leaving a mound. It became known as Mound Street and then Mount Street. Near Bread Street and Milk Lane is a road called Friday Street, this is where the Catholics had a fish market, but it only took place on the one day of the week that they had to eat fish – Friday. The area of Soho is named after a mediaeval French hunting call. Soho was the equivalent of today's shout of 'tally-ho'; the area was a hunting estate and became known as Soho because of it. It was bordered by blue posts to mark the boundaries of the estate which is why there are many pubs in the area called The Blue Post, one such example being in Rupert Street.

London is now, in retrospect, two cities in one. First we have the original City, which is literally a square mile in size, and referred to as such. Then we have the area around the City which is Westminster, Southwark, Chelsea, Kensington and the many other boroughs that make up the Greater London area. Coming in from the west, you would pass Hyde Park and come down a road called Piccadilly, just that, no road, street or lane. One story about how the name came about involves a lepers' graveyard. In the thirteenth century the Knights Templar started a leper hospital on the site of the present St James's Palace in Pall Mall, a street named after a game similar to croquet and golf called Pallamaglio. The hospital was closed down after the Templars were arrested and burned at the stake as heretics under Henry III. The remaining lepers moved to what is now Buckingham Palace, which was then a swampy marsh. Here they set up a leper colony, one of many in London. When the hospital was open, the area now covered by Green Park in Piccadilly was used as a graveyard for the dead lepers. The bones, I believe, are still there. In 1666 the Great Fire of London destroyed 97 per cent of the City and people moved east, west, north and south of the City to set up temporary shanty towns.

Many people went west to the area which now covers Hyde Park. When they started to rebuild the City, the west Londoners would walk into the City down Portugal Street, named after the Portuguese Princess Catherine of Braganza, wife of Charles II (1660–85). They remembered that the graves of the lepers were still there, although Catherine had bought the grounds and turned it into a royal park. To protect themselves from the disease, they planted lavender all around the park. On their way home they often picked the lavender to make pot-pouri. The old English name for lavender was dilly-dilly as in the children's nursery rhyme 'Lavender blue dilly-dilly', so they were said to stop and 'Picc-a-dilly'.

Another story is that the street got its name from a house called 'Piccadill Corner' from where a Robert Hall traded in Piccadills. These were a fashionable ruffled collar. However, Piccadill Corner, which stood roughly where Glasshouse Street is today just off Piccadilly Circus, wasn't built until the 1730s and Piccadilly got its name before that time. There is a lot of evidence to back up the leper's graveyard story. In 1675 a London newspaper described the house of Sir Thomas Clarges as being near Burlington House, above Piccadilly. That is over fifty years before Piccadill Corner existed and probably before Robert Hall, the proprietor, was even born.

Coming down Piccadilly into central London we come across a place called The Haymarket; no prizes for guessing where this name comes from. From Elizabethan times this wide road had been a market, not only for hay and straw, but also cattle, pigs and oxen, right up, on and off, to the 1800s. Wagons full of straw and hay would frequent the street twenty-four hours a day, and the products were used for many purposes; stuffing mattresses, giving to horses, street cleaning and more. The smell from the animal manure was at times unbearable and spurred some monarchs who lived in St James's Palace to complain about it, the palace being a mere few hundred yards away.

The Haymarket today has two theatres, one of which is the second oldest in London, the Theatre Royal Haymarket. The whole street in the 1700s and into the late 1800s was a street, not for straw and hay, but for entertainment, with many buildings showing exhibitions of wonderment. Bisset once had a great show there called the *Cat Opera*, where trained cats did acrobatics and danced with dogs. He later added more amazing acts which included a hare that could walk on its hind legs and play a drum, canaries and linnets that picked up letters and spelt words on command. He even trained a tortoise to write people's names with its blackened feet.

At 61 Haymarket was a house where a giant was exhibited in 1804. His name was O'Brien, and he was said to have been a direct descendant of the eleventh-century Irish King, Brian Boru. He measured 8ft 9in, and had such long legs that he needed to rest on the shoulders of two gents when walking up the Haymarket. When he needed to light his pipe he simply took the top off a street lamp and lit it. He died in 1806 and his skeleton was exhibited in the museum of the College of Surgeons for many decades.

Week's Museum in the Haymarket was a gaming house with a massive room upstairs that was over 100ft long. It was nicknamed Shavers Hall having been built by the barber, from his own money, to Lord Pembroke.

The widow of Colonel Thomas Panton lived her latter years in the Haymarket. Panton was the keeper of a gaming house in Piccadilly and in 1720 he bought land and a house in the area; Panton Street is named after him. His daughter took his fortune into the already wealthy family of Lord Arundell of Wardour, when she married. Both Arundell and Wardour Streets are named after the Lord. Nearby is Warwick Street, named after Sir Philip Warwick, a friend of Charles II.

The Aldwych is a famous street near Covent Garden, known for its theatres. The first theatre, built after the English Civil War of 1642–51, was commissioned by Charles II near Drury Lane, just off Aldwych, which is Anglo-Saxon and means 'old village'. The name comes from a street that was demolished in 1902 to make way for a new development of the area. The street was called Wych Street and so Aldwych is therefore named after the Old Wych Street, and not as many believe an old Roman village abandoned in 410 and re-occupied by the Anglo-Saxons in 510. Many streets and alleyways dating back to the late 1600s were also demolished. The area had become something of an embarrassment to the local parish council with many seedy shops selling pornography, and sleazy taverns hidden away from the main street. There was a lot of great history lost when the area was demolished. An old tavern in which the highwayman Jack Sheppard met with his criminal friends was destroyed; it was the White Lion in White Lion passage. Sheppard also served his apprenticeship to a carpenter in a narrow courtyard, just of the old Clare market place; all of this is now integrated into Theatre Land.

In nearby Covent Garden you will find wonderful street entertainers, cafés, bars and clubs, but there are now two Covent Gardens. The other one is the new fruit and vegetable market which moved from its original home just behind the Aldwych. The gardens go back to the twelfth century when a convent was built for the Franciscan Nuns. The nuns grew fruit and vegetables for themselves and the monks at Westminster. In 1534 Henry VIII confiscated the land under his act of the Dissolution of the Monasteries; it became a series of small holdings and a fruit and vegetable market. It evolved into a wholesale market in the 1800s selling products from all over the world. In the early 1970s it was closed when the new market opened at Nine Elms to the west, just by Vauxhall Bridge. The old market was re-developed into a wonderful area of piazzas for the tourist trade. Nine Elms is so named because in the area there used to be a group of elm trees, nine in total.

To the north of London you will find the Seven Sisters Road. This is named after a tavern called the Seven Sisters in front of which was a group of seven elm trees, with a walnut tree in the middle. They were about 500 years old and are said to have sprouted up on the spot where a Catholic martyr was burned to death. The trees died of Dutch Elm Disease and the locals have planted another seven elm trees in their place. The tavern is long gone, and the trees now stand at the entrance to the village green.

15

THEY CAME, THEY SAW, THEY LIVED HERE!

Famous London Residents

John Smith, Governor of Virginia (1580–1631)

Smith was born in the great Elizabethan age when the British Empire was being extended by the adventurers of the period. We often hear of people like Drake, Raleigh and Devereaux, but it was people like John Smith who were building empires on land in Europe and in the New World of the Americas. John was apprenticed as a cordwainer, a goat-leather worker. He was as good at this trade as he was later on as a soldier. John Smith was a man of enormous self-pride. Maybe it was the era he lived in, an era where the country was ruled by a woman with the heart of a king as Queen Elizabeth I once described herself. We know Smith was very colourful, brave, respected and to a degree an honest and fair man of average religious beliefs. Tiring of his mundane lifestyle and listening to stories of adventure and riches in far off lands in the taverns of London, Smith decided to have a try himself and joined the Army. He fought in many European wars as far away as Hungary, where the Empire was allied to the enemies of the Turks. It is reported that during one battle he took on three Turkish warriors at once and having slain them all, cut off their heads as souvenirs for the Grand Duke of Transylvania who led the battle. The duke gave him a gift of a special shield with a coat of arms featuring the three heads in gratitude. He returned to London in 1604, after hearing of the death of his beloved Queen Elizabeth and the coronation of the first Stuart King, James VI of Scotland, who became James I of England.

Granted an audience with the new king, John swore the same undying allegiance to James as he had done for the old queen. Two years passed before King James agreed to finance another expedition to the New World. John Smith was asked to accompany the expedition as an experienced soldier. The expedition left Blackwall Docks in London in 1606, led by Captain Christopher Newport with some 150 men under his command. When they landed in the Americas, Newport founded a colony and named it Jamestown in honour of their benefactor the king. Smith proved himself a self-sufficient man, and so Newport left him in charge of security at the new colony, when he returned to England to report to the king. Smith was ambitious and wanted to go down in history like his heroes Drake and Raleigh.

After building a fort at Jamestown he started to venture further afield, and explore the surrounding countryside to collect any new species of plants or animals. On one of these trips in 1607 his party was ambushed by a tribe of Algonquin Indians and taken to their leader, Chief Powhatan. While Powhatan was deciding what to do with his captives, the Chief's daughter Matoaco, better known by her tribal nickname of Pocahontas (wanton-one), took a shine to the handsome Smith and helped him to escape. Whether this is true or not has been a matter of conjecture to historians ever since. The story emanates from a journal Smith wrote in 1624, *The Generall Historie of Virginia*. There may be some truth to the story; some historians advocate that Powhatan was only performing an initiation ceremony and not preparing to execute Smith. Whatever the truth, Smith did form an alliance with the then twelve-year-old Pocahontas. The young girl visited the colony many times and saved Smith a second time in 1608, when her father had sent warriors to kill Smith. Pocahontas is also accredited with saving the colonists from starvation during a particularly bad time for them when their crops failed.

Thackeray later wrote of this adventurer in his book *Virginians* and Smith returned to England to retire in 1609, after an accident with a powder horn that nearly blew his leg off. During his time in America he became a Governor of Virginia and also held the title Admiral of New England. He died in 1631 and is buried in the church of St Sepulchre's – entombed on the right side of the choir stand. His gravestone was damaged during the Great Fire in 1666, when the church was used as a hospital, and is now under the new floor. His epitaph was copied onto a brass plate for visitors to see. Part of it reads, 'Here lies one conquer'd that hath conquer'd Kings'.

The church of St Mary-le-Bow, where he prayed many times, has a statue of him outside.

John Rolfe and Pocahontas
(1585–1622 & 1595–1617)

John Rolfe was born in Norfolk to John and Dorothea (Dorothy) Rolfe, in May 1585. Little is known of his younger life or indeed of his first wife. It is possible he wasn't even married to the pregnant and unknown woman, whom he sailed to the New World with in 1609. The convoy that Rolfe sailed on was led by the navigator George Summers. The expedition had been commissioned by the Virginia Company to set up a profitable business in the newly established colony of Jamestown. John Rolfe was at this time a trained farmer, and his part in all this was to grow tobacco for the company. His ship *The Adventurer* was shipwrecked in a hurricane in November 1609. Hundreds of the crew and settlers managed to row ashore to safety on the island of Bermuda, where they were stranded for many months. His wife gave birth to a girl in February 1610, who they named Bermuda. Sadly the baby died shortly afterwards. The settlers built two new smaller ships using new wood and salvaged some of the salvaged hulk of *The Adventurer* and her sails. They named the new boats *Patience* and *Deliverance* for obvious reasons. The two ships got the settlers to Chesapeake Bay in just ten days in May 1610. John had more bad luck when his wife died three weeks later, it had all been too much for her. Probably the saddest part of it all is that there seems to be no record of who she was.

John was soon farming and his main crop was tobacco. The indigenous tobacco plant was far too rough and strong in taste to be traded in Europe, so John was actually experimenting with seeds from the West Indies, where the Spanish grew their successful, sweet tobacco. John Rolfe was banking on successfully growing a hybrid species of tobacco that would compete in Europe with the Spanish in this new industry. By 1612 John had managed to come up with a species, which he had grown by splicing the local harsh tobacco plant with the softer West Indies seeds.

The plant he produced was easy to grow in the unusual soil of Virginia. By 1617 most of the tobacco farmers of the colony were growing John's new strain, and that year they exported their first major commercial tobacco crop to England. It was received with a fairly good response, but the far superior and sweeter Spanish crop was still the top dog. During the 1620s, tobacco was used in Europe as a medicine and recreational drug. Snuff was made from ground-down tobacco. It was literally snuffed up into the nasal system as a powder and the nicotine had an instant effect; it was very popular and fashionable later on.

In 1613, while John Rolfe was busy experimenting with his tobacco plants, the colony of Jamestown was expanding and one of the other commodities it dealt in were furs. This trade brought the colony in constant conflict with the local Algonquin Indians, who considered trapping more animals than you could eat or need to make your clothes was not good environmentally. The colonists were also accused of stealing animals from the traps of the Indians. When they caught them, the Indians took the colonists prisoner, in a vain attempt to stop the practice. In revenge a group of colonists kidnapped the Princess Pocahontas in an effort to trade her for the prisoners. Chief Powhatan wouldn't give in, so a stand-off occurred for many months. During this time Pocahontas learned English and even took to Christianity. The colonists baptised her in the name Rebecca and she continued to use the name with the settlers from then onwards.

In early 1614, while still a captive, the now nineteen-year-old Pocahontas met John Rolfe and the pair soon fell in love. John had very mixed emotions as he was a pious man. He still considered Pocahontas a heathen, and wrote a letter to Sir Thomas Dale the Governor of Virginia who held John in great esteem. He told the governor of his great love for Pocahontas and of his mixed feelings; Dale decided to use the situation as a means to an end. The end in this case was a peace pact with Powhatan. Dale advised John to follow his heart and not his conscience. After all, the royalty of Europe had practiced marriages of convenience for centuries, so why shouldn't the colonists? To make it all official John also sent a message to Powhatan and sought his permission to marry the princess. Powhatan was as shrewd as Dale and probably also saw the pay-off in such a union, so he agreed to the marriage.

John Rolfe and Rebeccca married in the parish church in Jamestown on 5 April 1614. In accordance with English custom the father usually gives the bride away. However, Powhatan didn't quite trust the colonists, so his brother Opachisco took his place. The union led to many years of peace and harmony between the colonists and the Indians. The colony expanded and received many more immigrants from England. It wasn't long before they had such a hold on the area that the Indians were starting to lose their way of life. The couple had a son, Thomas, who was born on 30 January 1615 and the couple seemed happy and very well respected. John was asked by the Virginia Company if he would go to England and speak on their behalf about the success of the colony to encourage investment and royal approval. The couple set sail for England in 1616, with Sir Thomas Dale and many other dignitaries of the colony.

After arriving in England, John wrote to the king about the colony and in response, King James I invited him along to the Palace of Whitehall for an audience with the royal couple. John introduced Pocahontas as Rebecca, Princess of the Powhatan. The king was intrigued, as was the royal court, of the story of the colony and the union of John to Pocahontas. But the main attraction seemed to have been Tomocome. Tomocome was Chief Councillor to Powhatan and went everywhere with John and Rebecca Rolfe in his native dress. The king however, wasn't very amused when he realised that for all intents, John Rolfe had married a princess, and was advised by his councillors that sometime in the future Rolfe may realise this and make claim as a royal to the colony. They even considered at one time if that by marrying Pocahontas, Rolfe had in fact committed treason. The matter blew over but John forbade his wife to see the king again.

The couple and their son, along with Tomocome, were the talk of all London and the Bishop of London laid on a grand ball in their honour. A statue of Pocahontas in her native dress was later added to the bottom of the statue of Queen Anne in 1710 when it was unveiled outside St Paul's Cathedral, on its reopening after Great Fire. The original statue was later destroyed, but the replacement still shows the princess representing the colonies, in the reign of Queen Anne.

After a year in London, it was time to depart for home. Virginia was still their home so they prepared to return to Jamestown. The day before their departure Pocahontas fell very ill with pneumonia and died within days. John was heartbroken and she was buried in Gravesend, Kent. Thomas, their son, was left behind with relatives to get an English education.

On his return, John was hailed a hero for his efforts in getting investment for the colony, and within four years of his return the colonies, the tobacco trade was enormous. John served on the council of Jamestown from 1614 to 1619 as secretary and recorder. He married again, to Jane Pierce, daughter of a fellow colonist and they had a daughter, Elizabeth, born in 1618. After the death of Powhatan in 1620, relations with the Indians went sour and the old wounds opened up, with each constantly attacking the other. In 1622 during an Indian attack on his plantation, Bermuda Hundred (it was one hundred acres in size), John was killed. He is buried in Jamestown. Jane and daughter Elizabeth survived the attack. His son Thomas eventually returned to Virginia and married there. Thomas Rolfe became a very distinguished gentleman and the State of Virginia still has many citizens related to one of their greatest founders.

John Harvard, School Founder (1607–38)

John Harvard was born in Southwark, London, in August 1607, and baptised in September at St Saviour's church to Robert and Katherine Harvard, Robert's second wife. John was very well-educated in the classics, grammar, writing, arithmetic and the Bible. He is reported to have been a studious boy and excelled in all these subjects. The Harvards were very rich and influential; Robert owned a butcher's shop and the Queen's Head coaching inn in Borough High Street. Katherine came from Stratford-upon-Avon and was a friend of Anne Hathaway and her husband William Shakespeare; young William and his brother Edmund (buried in Southwark Cathedral) were accomplished actors in their early days in Southwark, and the Harvards often supported them. They attended their plays, and spoke highly of them, no doubt helping the Shakespeares out with a sausage or two when times were hard.

Southwark wasn't a rich area, or indeed an influential area. It was busy because of the theatres, taverns and brothels that swamped the area. These were not permitted in the City of London, just across London Bridge. It was also part of the Pool of London where ships came from all over the world to trade. Southwark had many warehouses including the Hays Wharf, where they stored fruits and vegetables from every corner of the known globe. Hays Wharf warehouse was the biggest in England; it was known as the London Larder. Since a fire closed it in 1850, that title now belongs to the Borough Market. With the food stocks came the rats and they carried the plague all over the world. In 1625, there was an outbreak of the black death, (the bubonic plague) in Southwark. It never reached the City, but hit Southwark hard and especially the Harvard family. At just eighteen years old, John Harvard watched his father, Robert, and three brothers and a sister die from the plague. All that remained of the family was John, younger brother Thomas and mother Katherine. Apart from the businesses, which were still flourishing, Robert left some houses and £550 in gold coins. The survivors were devastated, but well provided for. Katherine remarried within the year to another wealthy man John Elletson, but was tragically widowed again six months later when he died. John Elletson left Katherine most of his estate as well.

John Harvard was now wealthy enough to do anything he pleased. He was drawn to the Ministry and decided to enrol at Emmanuel College, Cambridge, to study theology. John was attracted to Puritan ideas, probably having seen all the iniquitous and sinful happenings in Southwark. A lot of people from this particular college were to later make their mark in politics, especially during the Civil War (1642–51). John studied hard and in 1631 graduated with a B.A. He continued to study there and in 1636 he got his M.A. While at college John became friends with John Sadler, son of the vicar of Ringmer, Sussex. John often visited the Sadlers during holiday periods from the college, not so much to see his friend John, but his pretty sister Ann.

The year John Harvard graduated with his M.A., 1636, his mother died. John and his surviving brother, Thomas, inherited even more riches. He got £250 and a half-share in some houses in Barking, property that Katherine had inherited from her second husband John Elletson. It was time to take a wife and leave the politically troubled England. King Charles I was in constant turmoil with the Puritans, who were a powerful force in England, but at times persecuted for their beliefs. Many Puritans were looking to America, where freedom of religion was easier in certain colonies. On 19 April 1636 John Harvard married his friend John Sadler's sister Ann, at the church of South Malling, Sussex. John decided to go to America and establish himself. He chose a place named Charlestown, Massachusetts, where he knew a lot of the townspeople from his time at Cambridge University.

In March 1637, he sold four houses that his father had left him to a retiring sea captain. He kept the Queen's Head and leased off the business to get a regular income, as it was too valuable an asset to sell quickly. He also kept the half-share in the four houses with his brother Thomas, again to provide a regular income. He went round London and bought 350 books to take with him to the New World, as he planned a career as a teacher. He set sail with the books and his wife Ann and finally arrived in his new home, Charlestown, on 6 August 1637. He soon settled in and bought a large house. His influence and kinship had preceded him for on 2 November that year he was appointed to the post of teacher to the church school, and made a freeman of the colony. He received news that his brother Thomas had died during his sea voyage to the colony; John now owned even more property.

John became so respected and sought out as an advisor on all matters, probably because of his vast library, that he was soon asked to become a senior member of the town committee, and advised on legal matters among his other duties. It was all to be short-lived however, for John caught a chill in the autumn of 1638 which developed into pneumonia, and he died aged only thirty-one on 14 September. He left no will, but made a dying deposition that half his estate and the entire library be left to the college that was being proposed at that time. The town of Newtown, the site of the proposed college, was renamed Cambridge, for many of the townsfolk had been educated there. Although he never even saw the plans of the college, which developed into what we know today as Harvard University, it is almost certain that his bequest of money and the vast library made it all possible. In 1639 the town council at Cambridge recorded in the minutes of a meeting, 'That the college, agreed upon formally to be built in Cambridge, shall be called Harvard College.'

Benjamin Franklin, Statesman (1706–90)

Benjamin Franklin is remembered mostly as an American statesman and inventor. However, Benjamin spent a lot of time in London in his eighty-four years on earth. A very charismatic character and inquisitive man was how many described him during his lifetime. He was born the tenth son of Josiah and Abiah Franklin (née Folger) in New England. Young Benjamin Franklin was to have sixteen brothers and sisters to compete with; Josiah could only afford to send him to school for three terms. However, Benjamin was an eager student and could already read by the age of five. His first ambition was to enter the clergy, but his lack of schooling made this impossible, so he was apprenticed to his brother James, a printer. Benjamin was a self-taught man, he read every book he could get his hands on and was prolific in his trade of printer. He would later in life be involved in the print trade in London in the famous 'Street of Ink', Fleet Street, where William Caxton had set up a print shop in England in the fifteenth century.

He was such a hard worker that after a day printing off papers, he would then go onto the streets and sell them. He believed that success was measured in hard work and he wanted to be accomplished.

James started *The New England Courant* in 1721 which many consider to be Boston's first real newspaper. There were already two papers in circulation in Boston at the time, but they are not considered to be true papers, as they just recycled old news from England. The *Courant* was a pioneer in respect of the fact it had articles about current English and Boston affairs, articles written by James's friends. As well as adverts, it also carried news of ships arriving and leaving the busy port.

Being a journalist was an early dream of Benjamin. His brother James had considered him a bit of a buffoon and would laugh when Benjamin talked about his ambitions and considered his brother under-educated. Benjamin would not be beaten and knew it was useless to try to persuade James to let him write for the paper. So, he hatched a plan to get round the problem.

He wrote articles on local Bostonian affairs in the name of a widow named Silence Dogood, whom he made up. He then pushed the letters under the door at night. When James found the first one he was intrigued, so much so that he actually printed the letters as articles. The widow remained anonymous and as she asked for no payment, James continued to print them. Silence was an almost instant hit with the readership of the *Courant*. Everyone wanted to know who she really was and after fifteen letters were published, Benjamin confessed to the hoax. The regular journalists thought this whole affair was hilarious, and congratulated the now twenty-two-year-old Benjamin on his pieces. James, however, was furious and gave Benjamin a dressing-down for his trouble.

Boston was a Puritan town and the powerful family of preachers, the Mathers, were constantly trying to run things their way, to which James objected. He constantly fell out with them on many affairs. This animosity came to a head over the Smallpox Affair. The Mathers were believers in the idea that inoculation was a preventative form of medicine which needed promoting; this particular disease was wiping out small communities in the New World every week. James believed inoculation simply festered the disease and wrote in his paper against it, heavily criticising the Mathers. Most readers were in agreement with James, but objected to the way James made his point and at the same time, belittled the Mathers.

The affair ended with James being arrested for blasphemy and libel and thrown in the local lock-up. Benjamin couldn't believe his luck, this gave him the opportunity to prove himself and he ran the paper while James lingered in gaol. On his release, James beat Benjamin up and the feud caused Benjamin to run away from home in 1723. At the time, running away from home, no matter what your age, was illegal. The Puritans believed that everyone in the community had a purpose and a runaway was considered to be disrespectful of that society, so they made it illegal.

Benjamin managed to make his way to New York. After failing to find work he literally walked across New Jersey and then took a boat to Philadelphia. His money all but spent, he arrived in Philadelphia on 6 October 1723. A pretty young woman spotted him and later wrote in her diary that he 'looked odd'; her name was Deborah Read. After finding a job as a printer's assistant, he made friends with the Governor of Pennsylvania who promised to set him up in business. However, in order to do this he had to go to London to buy the equipment. At the time Benjamin was staying with the family of Deborah Read. Deborah was desperate to marry while

Benjamin was not. He wanted to concentrate on the opportunity afforded him by the governor, so he waylaid Deborah, and set off to London to get what he needed to start his new venture. The governor later reneged on the promise and Benjamin found himself stuck in London with little money. While he was away, Deborah got fed up of waiting and married another man.

His first home in London was near St Paul's Cathedral, which had been finished by Sir Christopher Wren in 1710, when Benjamin was a mere four years old. He lived in an area known as Little Britain. He supported himself working for various printers in London, mainly in Fleet Street at a print works in the grounds of the church of St Dunstan-in-the-West, where Dr Johnson later printed his English dictionary in 1755.

He returned to Philadelphia in 1726 and got a job running a shop. He soon tired of this menial work and, longing for the print trade, he got a job as a printer again. By this time he knew a lot about the print business and had some good ideas, which his employer didn't share, so the frustrated Benjamin borrowed some money and bought out another business. At last he had his own equipment and the means to indulge his ambitions. He worked hard and soon became the talk of the town. The state governor was impressed enough to recommend him to be appointed the state's printer and he thrived with his new government contracts. He is reputed to have fathered a child named William in about 1728 although nothing is known of the child or mother. Presumably they weren't married, for in 1730 he finally married Deborah Read. Deborah's husband had abandoned her and under the law she was therefore entitled to marry again.

In 1729 Benjamin bought a newspaper, *The Pennsylvania Gazette*. Deborah Franklin was a very astute and well-educated woman; she helped Benjamin in the print shop and also ran a book shop they set up. In 1732 Deborah also set up a store that sold everything from household goods to dressmaking fabrics. While Deborah concentrated on the shops, Benjamin worked hard in the print business. *The Pennsylvania Gazette* became the most important paper in the state, and eventually became the most popular in the colonies. It is accredited with carrying the first political cartoon which Benjamin drew himself. It consisted of a snake cut into eight pieces; each piece represented the existing colonies, the words underneath simply said 'Join or Die'. It made such a point that he became the talk of the colonies and was consulted by many politicians.

During the late 1720s and throughout the 1730s, Benjamin joined the Freemasons and started a self-help group to work on civic matters, called the Junto. In 1733 he had an idea to print an almanac, as a sales ploy he called it *Poor Richard's Almanac* and sold it under the guise of the pseudonym, Richard Saunders. Richard, according to the almanac was in need of money to support his ever-complaining wife. The book was distinguished from other almanacs because it was full of witty stories and anecdotes, as well as the usual information about the weather, recipes and general information. Benjamin Franklin is also accredited with many sayings, which he spread through the almanac such as, 'a penny saved is a penny earned.'

Benjamin was full of ideas and was usually doing something to put them to the test or get them going. In 1731 he started the Library Company. Members pooled their resources and added to the stock by clubbing together and buying books from England. This was the nation's first subscription library. In 1736 he started the first Fire Department in Philadelphia; the company was actually a sort of insurance company and he used the saying 'An ounce of prevention is worth a pound of cure' to sell the idea. He got the idea from Fleet Street in London during his first visit to the capital. He saw the famous fire plaques, some of which existed up until the early 1900s. After the Great Fire in 1666, private Fire Departments started in London. They put a plaque on your house and if it caught fire would rush to put it out. Woe betide you if the wrong company was called, for if their plaque wasn't on your house, they would simply carry on running down the street and let your house burn. Franklin's Fire Insurance Loss Company, which he started in 1752, also compensated you for loss due to damage, another first. The company he formed is still in existence today. He retired from business in 1749 and franchised out his printing business to other colonies. In 1751 he founded the Philadelphia Hospital.

After retiring he concentrated on his science and inventions. He was now rich enough to do what he wanted and although he had initially had a very frugal education, he had some brilliant ideas; he was the Thomas Edison of his day. He had by this time already invented many practical things such as the Franklin Stove, an efficient stove for heating houses. He also invented Swim Fins, which later evolved into Swimming Flippers and a musical instrument called the Glass Armonica as well as one of his best-known inventions, the bifocal spectacles. His greatest achievement was his studies into the power of electricity; his experiments with lightning conductors attached to kites brought him international recognition.

In 1757 he was asked to go to England and represent the State of Philadelphia in a case against the surviving members of the Penn family, who for all intents and purposes, owned the state. The Penn family had always insisted that they were the power in the state, and only they had the power to elect the governor. Benjamin stayed for eighteen years in England and eventually represented not only Philadelphia, but Georgia, New Jersey and Massachusetts at the court of St James.

While in London he lived at 36 Craven Street (off The Strand). He did return to America for a visit in 1762 to try to persuade Deborah to move with him to London; she was terrified of ships and refused to make the journey. Benjamin was very disappointed. He loved London as it had all the nice things the colonies lacked: free thinkers, theatres and shops with an abundance of everything. He returned to London in 1764 and lived at 7 Craven Street. Craven Street still exists today and although no. 7 was demolished in the 1900s, no. 36 still stands as a memorial to the great man, with a plaque outside to commemorate him. In 1765 he was called before parliament to explain the colonies objection to The Stamp Act. His rousing speech eventually persuaded parliament to repeal the taxing act.

During this term of office in London, Benjamin started to see the cracks in the establishment. He constantly witnessed corruption on a grand scale and started to see the sycophancy of the Royal Court of St James. Up until this point he had considered himself a loyal Englishman, but as early as 1754 he had the idea to unite the colonies and seek independence. His first two visits to England had clouded his judgement, and although he had many allies and friends in England, he was starting to think about home again.

He fell out with a lot of influential people and the court during the Hutchinson Affair. Thomas Hutchinson was the English appointed Governor of Massachusetts. He was a two-faced bigot who courted the favours of the crown and parliament, while pretending to represent the people of the state. Benjamin came into possession of some letters addressed to the king, in which Hutchinson called for 'an abridgement of what are called English Liberties.' Outraged at this hypocrisy, he sent the letters to a friend in America and they caused a huge rift between the colonists and Hutchinson. Benjamin was summoned to the English Foreign Ministry in Whitehall and admonished for what he had done. Fed up with England and fearing a war was looming, he left England in 1775 and returned to the colonies to prepare for independence. Twelve months later he would not only help to draft, but add his signature to the now famous Declaration of Independence at Liberty Hall, Philadelphia. Ironically, his son William became the Royal Governor of New Jersey and Benjamin tried to use his influence, but William was a loyal Englishman and they fell out, never to speak to each other again.

After the declaration was made, Benjamin sailed to France and became an ambassador to the Court of Louis XVI. He dressed down while in France and the exuberant French liked him for his wit and independence. Now a widower of many years, he flirted with all the women, and this being a French trait, it delighted the king and the court. In 1778 the King of France signed a Treaty of Alliance with America, to the anger of both George III and parliament. George III had befriended Benjamin over their joint interest in science, the king even consulted him on the design of lightning conductors; they disagreed over which was the best, pointed tops or blunt tops, and this was the topic of much jesting at court. Benjamin was responsible for negotiating peace after the War of Independence ended and signed on behalf of the New America, the Treaty of Paris in 1783. He was succeeded in his Paris position by Thomas Jefferson in 1785 and returned to America.

In his last five years on earth, Benjamin became President of the Executive Council of Philadelphia. He also served as a delegate to the Constitutional Convention and was a signatory on the American Constitution Document. Ironically enough, one of his last acts was to later split America and cause another war, which is still accredited today, for being the war that killed more American soldiers than any other since. He wrote a treatise on anti-slavery in 1789, which started an argument in political circles that lasted until the Civil War started. Benjamin Franklin died on 17 April 1790 at the grand old age of eighty-four; some 20,000 people attended his funeral, a fitting end to a man who helped carve out a constitution and a democracy of people in a land where it is still possible to be as great as he was, and achieve the dream.

Charles Dickens, Author (1812–70)

Charles John Huffam Dickens was born the second child of John and Elizabeth Dickens in a small terrace house in Landport, Portsmouth. His sister, Fanny, was delighted to welcome her new brother on 7 February 1812; there would be another six children to follow. In his early life, Charles was to be influenced by his paternal grandmother, who was a prolific story-teller. At the age of three, Charles got his first sight of the London he would come to love and hate, and later write so passionately about. John Dickens was a clerk in the Admiralty of the Royal Navy. He was transferred to the London headquarters at Somerset House in The Strand. Charles was a sickly child, not unusual in those bleak, cold times on the coast. After a short time in London, John was again transferred to another posting in Chatham, Kent. Charles would pass away the time in his sick bed by reading; his mother

Elizabeth taught him to read at an early age. John Dickens was a prolific reader and had a small library of most of the classic books of the day and Charles read every one, some over and over again. Among his favourite books were *Tom Jones*, *Don Quixote*, *Gil Blas* and *The Vicar of Wakefield* as well as *Robinson Crusoe* and *The Arabian Nights*. Among his most favoured books were the Smoletts Novels; Charles wrote his first short story called *Misnar*, which he partly based on *The Tales of the Genii*.

When he was about six years of age, a friend of John Dickens took young Charles to the theatre, and he was fascinated with the stage actors and the appraisal of the audience, maybe he even thought about writing plays. That night Charles returned home completely exuberated by his experience, and his health started to improve greatly. However, his father's troubles were just beginning. Although he had had a pay rise, John Dickens couldn't make the household accounts stand up. There was always a deficit at the end of the month; the only solution was to move to a less desirable and cheaper rented property in Chatham. The house was next door to a Baptist school and so Charles continued his education. He started to improve greatly in his health and learning.

In 1823, John was again transferred back to London, where he was stationed at Somerset House in The Strand. The family moved to live in Bayham Street, Camden Town. The family's debts followed them and John was forced to face up to his creditors. John sent daughter Fanny to be educated at the Royal Academy of Music, Charles was slightly jealous and bewildered at this decision. His own education came to an end, and he was forced to stay at home and help his mother around the house. Charles continued his education by reading all the books he could borrow from his Uncle Barrow, who lived above a book shop. His love of writing was revived and he wrote a short story about his Uncle Barrow's barber.

Things weren't going well at home, with the debts mounting, so Elizabeth Dickens started a school in a vain attempt to bring in some extra money. The school didn't get one single pupil and was doomed before it even opened. John was arrested on a warrant for debt and taken to the Marshalsea Prison in Southwark. The family furniture was sold and they moved to a boarding house, still within Camden. The house was owned by a Mrs Roylance, on whom Charles later based the character Mrs Pitchin in *Dombey and Son*. Charles took a job in a factory, which made shoe blacking.

Charles had a drab job of tying blue ribbon around the jars for 6s a week. After a while, Charles could afford his own accommodation, and moved to a room near the Marshalsea and his father. He visited him most days, bringing him little luxuries to ease his life. During these visits, the now twelve-year-old Charles, got to know some of the other debtor families. The Garlands, who featured in *The Old Curiosity Shop*, were based on a family he met at the prison.

John Dickens wasn't in prison very long, just six months, after which he was freed under the Insolvent Debtors Act. On his release he returned to the family at Mrs Roylance's boarding house. Charles was to later use all these experiences to write *Little Dorrit*, set in the Marshalsea prison. He was said to have based the great Mr MiCawber (*David Copperfield*) on his father.

John got a job as a reporter for the *Morning Chronicle* and a legacy from a dead relative paid off all the remaining debts in full, and allowed Charles to attend school again. His life in the blacking factory and having to give up his education had made Charles a bitter young man. Charles left the factory at aged thirteen and attended the Hampstead School. His attitude changed dramatically and he took an interest in drama. He also started pulling off practical jokes on the teachers and other pupils.

In 1826, at fifteen years old, Charles was ready to take a trade. He started in the office of a lawyer named Molloy, at the Lincolns Inn. He renewed his hunger to write again and learnt short hand, which enabled him to write quicker. Charles then became a reporter for the *True Sun* newspaper, and attended parliament on a regular basis to report on the House of Commons.

He became very popular with the other reporters and when a strike by them broke out, he represented them all and won their case. This led to his securing positions as reporter on the *Morning Chronicle* and the *Mirror* at parliament.

In 1834, John Black, the editor of the *Morning Star*, was so impressed with him that he got his first published works commissioned by the *Old Monthly Magazine*; it was called 'A Dinner at Popular Walk', and was the first of nine articles. Later on he used the pseudonym Boz, which was a nickname for one of his brothers.

Charles thrived both in health and career. He did try his hand at acting, but this career never surfaced; it is rumoured that the manager at Covent Garden, having seen his acting, conveniently lost his application form. In 1836 he wrote *Sketches by Boz*. These were published in two volumes and were so popular they had to reprint the series. The series was all based on humorous characters, and the situations they found themselves in. Maybe in the drab and hard life of the period, people found a little happiness in the comical outrages of the characters Charles invented. The stories included 'The Parish', 'The Boarding House', and 'Mrs Minns and her Cousin'. They showed Charles at his wittiest.

In 1836 he also wrote *The Pickwick Papers*. He was approached by a publishing firm called Messrs Chapman and Hall who, with the artist and cartoonist Seymour, were planning a series of monthly articles about a group of gentlemen who caused chaos and mayhem in their pursuit of hunting, shooting and the life of the country gent. The original article was called 'The Nimrod Club', but Charles renamed it the 'Pickwick Club'. The illustrated articles took a little time to gain popularity, and it wasn't until he introduced Sam Weller into the articles that it took off, selling in excess of 40,000 copies a month. In 1837 while still writing *The Pickwick Papers*, he wrote *Oliver Twist* and in 1838–9 he wrote *The Life and Adventures of Nicholas Nickelby*, both of which were published in the monthly publication. People would stand on street corners and listen to the continuing adventures of *Oliver Twist*, read out by the educated to those who couldn't read. This was the origin of the modern soap opera. When Bill Sykes killed Nancy, the crowds ran through the streets and shouted for his arrest and hanging, such was the allure of the writings of Charles Dickens.

By 1840, Charles was wealthy enough to start his own publication called *Master Humphrey's Clock*. Issue one appeared in April 1840 and sold some 70,000 copies. In 1842 he went to America where his fame preceded him and he was treated like a king. However, that soon turned to anger when he returned to England six months later and wrote a series of articles called his 'American Notes', in which he severely criticised the American way of life. In early 1843 he again got itchy feet and travelled to Genoa in Italy, where he finished the novel *Martin Chuzzlewit*, which he had started writing in London. He also wrote *A Christmas Carol* before *The Chimes* in 1844. He then travelled around Italy and visited Switzerland before returning the London in 1845.

Shortly after arriving in London he took up the position of editor on *The Daily News*, but a fortnight later resigned and started travelling again. Returning to Italy he wrote *Dombey and Son*. Although he had resigned fairly quickly after being appointed the editor on *The Daily News*, he continued to send back letters of his travels which the paper printed under the title, 'Pictures of Italy.'

In 1849 he wrote *David Copperfield* and then in 1852 he wrote, what was probably his most prolific account of the age, *Bleak House*. This was a great time for Dickens, in the following years he wrote *Hard Times* (1854), *Little Dorrit* (1855–7), *A Tale of Two Cities* (1859), *Great Expectations* (1861) and *Our Mutual Friend* (1864). For the following five years Dickens wrote only three pieces, all Christmas works; 'All Year Round', 'A Holiday Romance' and 'George Silverman's Explanation'. After these he started to write *The Mystery of Edwin Drood*. He then started to do public readings of his many famous works, and was well-received by the people. In late 1867 he decided to return to America, where the people welcomed him and forgave him his previous criticism of their way of life. His public appearances in America were enormously successful, not only for his popularity, but for his bank account to which he was credited some £10,000 in fees. On his return to London, Dickens proceeded to complete the unfinished *Edwin Drood*, but died before he could finish it, on 9 June 1870. He said he didn't want an ostentatious funeral, but a dignified and cheap one in a private place without announcement. Although his executors did observe most of the great mans wishes, he was interred at Poets' Corner in Westminster Abbey on 14 June 1870, where his tomb can seen today among other great poets and writers, such as Chaucer and Byron.

William Penn, State Founder (1644–1718)

William Penn was born on 14 October 1644, near the Tower of London. The exact place is described as being on the east side of Tower Hill, within a court adjoining the London Wall. He was born to Admiral Sir William Penn and his wife Margaret née Van de Schure of Bristol. Margaret was a landowning widow of a rich Dutchman and daughter of John Jasper, a trader. William was baptised a Christian in the church of All Hallows by the Tower, Barking. Above the doorway you will find a small blue plaque commemorating his baptism, and quoting him as a Quaker and founder of the State of Pennsylvania, which contrary to common belief is not named after him. It was in fact named after his father, a friend, secret supporter and confidant of Charles I and Charles II. William inherited the lands which eventually formed the state from his father, who had them granted to him by Charles II in settlement of an old debt. In fact William Penn wanted to call the new territory New Wales or Sylvania. It was Charles II that persuaded him to name it after his father Penn, and the alternative Sylvania.

William Penn was born into a wealthy and influential family. His father served with the navy and was distinguished at many now-famous battles, mainly against the Dutch, who for many years were the sworn enemy of England. William junior grew up to be a rather free-thinking and radical young man, who felt a duty to his not-so-well-off fellow man. He excelled at school but was expelled from Oxford University for his radical views. He studied law at the Huguenot Academy at Saumur and at Lincolns Inn, London. In 1669 he went to hear the Quaker Thomas Loe preaching, and was immediately converted to the then radical religion. He was a wealthy man in his own right and also managed his father's vast Irish estate. Like his father, he was imprisoned in the Tower of London. William was incarcerated for unlawful, seditious and riotous behaviour, which was a hanging offence. The case was listed for the Old Bailey before the famous judge Sir Samuel Starling, who was also the Lord Mayor of London. The case caused such a furore and actually made legal history, bringing about a law that allowed juries to be independent of the case judge, which wasn't so when the trial started.

The whole affair came to a head when William turned up one day to preach at the Quaker Meeting House with his fellow preacher friend, William Mead. The entrance to the house was blocked by soldiers on the orders of the Aldermen of the City of London, who were determined to stamp out radical and dissident religions. In response to the blockade, William merely walked away and proceeded to preach in the street and this led to his arrest and incarceration in the Tower with Mead. When the case came up before Judge Starling, William caused a sensation by challenging the validity of the charges, and for the state to govern a man's right to follow his conscience. Having studied law, William probably knew what he was talking about. 'The question is not whether I am guilty but whether the indictment is legal,' were the words he uttered. The judge was furious and after a while he ordered the jury to retire and bring in a guilty verdict. As the jury discussed the case in the jury box, William shouted to them, 'You are Englishmen, mind your privilege! Don't give away your rights!'

The jury was swayed by his character and to the anger of the judge, gave a unanimous verdict of not guilty. Judge Starling was so angry at this disobedience that he ordered the jury to be locked up for contempt. William and Mead were returned to the Tower to await a retrial. However, his powerful friends were busy in another court and managed to get a writ of Habeas Corpus, and the rights of the jurors was upheld by Chief Justice Vaughan to bring in verdicts independent of judges. The two Williams were freed. The case was so famous in changing English law that a plaque was put on the wall of the entrance to the lobby of the Old Bailey to commemorate it.

In 1672 he married Gulielma Maria Springett and became deeply involved in the Quaker movement. In 1677 he wrote the famous document Concessions and Agreements Charter, which is revered by many historians as being the foundation of the much later Bill of Rights. The charter was devised by William after he met a group of Quakers in Holland that same year. The group was setting sail to start a Quaker colony in New Jersey. The charter provided for the right to trial by jury, freedom from imprisonment for debt, an edict against capital punishment and the right for all men to follow their conscience in matters of religion, without interference from the law. William Penn, although a wealthy man, lived beyond his means and ran up enormous debts in doing what he said was God's work.

In 1681, in order to raise some much-needed funds, he called on King Charles II and asked him to honour a debt owed to his late father. The king responded by granting to William a vast tract of land in the New World of 45,000 acres. The Pennsylvania Charter, which granted the lands and rights to govern them, was dated 4 March 1681. The next year he gained rights to land in Delaware from the king's brother, James the Duke of York, after whom Charles renamed New Amsterdam to New York. His plan was to sell of pieces of the land and raise funds to pay his growing debts. The land deals were very lucrative, but not as lucrative as he had hoped.

In 1682 he decided to travel to the New World to see his now vast estate. Although there is no written proof that it ever happened, it was while on this trip that William is said to have had his famous powwow with the Delaware Indians, the Leni Lenape, at Shackamaxon. All that exists is a Wampum belt allegedly given to him by the Indians as a token of trust. The first official written treaty is one dated 15 July 1682. The document records the obtaining of lands from Idquahan, who was among several other Leni Lenape chiefs who he dealt with. In the following twelve months he brokered many more land transactions. He presided over the governorship of the state and started building his mansion house. He was also involved in a border dispute with Lord Baltimore who controlled the territory South of Pennsylvania. In 1683 he returned to England to carry on his dispute with Lord Baltimore, gaining support from Prince James.

Charles II died in 1685 and James became the king. William openly supported James and courted favours from the him. It all went sour in 1688 when James had his son baptised in a Catholic ceremony, the rioting started by the Protestant zealots quickly turned into a civil war of sorts; the year is now known as the Year of the Glorious Revolution. William supported James in his right to choose and practice his own chosen religion; this was a bad judgement of error on William's part. James fled England and was replaced by his daughter Mary, now married to the Dutch King William. The agreement was that they would reign as equals. William was arrested and questioned on treason charges. He lost control of his colony for two years from 1692 to 1694.

Just as he got his lands back, he was devastated at the death of his wife, though he got over that quickly enough and in 1696 he was married to Hannah Callowhill. Meanwhile, back in Pennsylvania, George Keith had started a religious row in 1691, and the state of Pennsylvania was divided into two territories, Pennsylvania and Delaware. William Markham, William Penn's governor in Delaware chartered another Bill of Rights and when Penn returned in 1701, he revised the charter and set up a government, higher than the state governor which was now elected yearly. His mansion house was now completed and he lived there for only a few months; he called it Pennsbury. In 1702 he suffered a setback due to his lax way of keeping account fn the many papers he had to sign. His business manager, a Quaker named Philip Ford, embezzled a lot of money from the Penn estate. He then tricked Penn into signing over the whole of the State of Pennsylvania to him. Ford then demanded rents from Penn which were far in excess of his income. As luck would have it, Ford died weeks later, but his wife had Penn thrown in gaol for the debt.

Outrage ensued among his friends when the case was finally summoned to court in 1708. Bridget Ford was found to be a devious and contemptible person who was not fit to rule the estate. The Lord Chancellor ruled that the equity of redemption still remained in the hands of the Penn family; he declared that the deed of transfer from Penn to Ford must be a forgery or, at the least, a document of no substance as there was no remuneration attached to the document.

He was struck with apoplexy in 1712 which left him virtually disabled. Hannah took over the running of the family affairs while she continued to nurse William. William Penn died on 30 July 1718. In his lifetime he had created the first capital of the colonies, and through his beliefs and convictions he created a Utopia, where many war-weary nationals, Dutch, Irish, Scots, English, Italians and many more formed the original melting pot. The impact that this one man left in his lifetime was so great that it inspired Thomas Jefferson and many other great men to later write the Declaration of Independence in Liberty Hall, Philadelphia. William left his estate to Hannah. Upon her death in 1727; the entire estate was passed to his sons John, Thomas and Richard.

Richard Whittington, Lord Mayor (1357–1423)

The exact date of Richard Whittington's birth is not known though it is assumed to be around 1357. Little is know of the early life of the man who was to come to London from the town of Pauntley, Gloucestershire. He is a figure in English history that is so surrounded by legend that many people consider him to be as mysterious as the legendary King Arthur. At Christmas each year the theatres of Britain are full of people enjoying a traditional pantomime, and one of the most famous pantomimes is *Dick Whittington*, based on the life of Richard Whittington. It is from this pantomime that many of the fallacies of his life come from.

He was the son of the rich landowner William Whittington, who was also Lord of Pauntley. William was married to Joan, who was the daughter of William Mansell, the Sheriff of Gloucester. Joan was the widow of another rich merchant, Sir Thomas de Berkeley of Coberley. In 1360 William was arrested and charged with marrying without a licence, which was required in those days when a rich widow remarried. He was fined an enormous sum of money beyond his wealth, and went into hiding. William died in 1362 and his estate was inherited by Joan. When Joan died in 1365, her second eldest child, Robert, inherited the whole estate. Poor Richard got nothing and after much sibling rivalry, he was sent away to London to be apprenticed as a mercer (a trader in fine cloth). His new master was an old friend of the family, Lord Ivo Fitzwarin. Lord Ivo was a rich and influential man in the City of London. Formerly a soldier who made his money in France; he was a general at the Battle of Nantes and helped to sack the city after it fell. He was known in London as Lord John Fitzwarren and he had a beautiful daughter named Alice.

Richard was lucky to be apprenticed to Fitzwarren as the master treated the young Richard as one of the family. In true romantic style, Richard married the boss's daughter after he finished his apprenticeship, and John Fitzwarren set him up in his own business. With the connections attached to the Fitzwarren name, Richard soon made a small fortune of his own and started to come to the attention of many influential people in the City. In 1389 Richard sold two pieces of fine gold cloth to King Richard II for £11. He soon became a favourite of the king and spent many days at court advising the young king about fine cloth. King Richard bought a great deal from Whittington during his reign and became good friends with him. Between 1392 and 1394, the king bought over £3,500 worth of cloth from Whittington, making him the most successful mercer in London. In 1393 Whittington was elected an Alderman of the City and served for four years. He was also elected as sheriff from 1393–4. In 1395 Whittington was elected Master of the Company of Mercers for the first time.

In 1397 King Richard fell out with many of the City's leaders when the king ordered them to pay a fine of £100,000. They refused and he ordered them to resign their posts. The Lord Mayor Adam Bamme died before he could resign so the king replaced him with Whittington. Later that year, Whittington was officially elected Mayor and also an Alderman of the Lime Street Ward, a post he held until his death. Whittington enjoyed the favours of the royal court for a few more years. Then disaster struck on 30 September 1399 when King Richard II was deposed by his cousin, Henry Bolingbroke of Lancaster, who was then enthroned by parliament as Henry IV on 13 October. Whittington was owed a vast sum of money by King Richard, believed to be about £1,000, which was never recovered, and it set Whittington back for months. King Richard died, allegedly murdered on Henry's orders, in Pontefract Castle on 14 February 1400.

Richard Whittington feared that King Richard's demise would harm his position at court and in the City. To his grateful surprise it didn't, and the new King Henry and he became good friends; it seems that Whittington's reputation had preceded him. Henry IV was instrumental in the furthering of Whittington's career, both as a politician and businessman. He became an MP in 1416. Whittington was further elected Mayor of London in 1406 and 1419, making it four times in all and not thrice as the pantomime tells. He lent money to Henry IV as well as purchasing the cloth for all the royal weddings. In 1401 he gave a donation to Westminster Abbey to build a new nave. He also paid for a public water tap in the wall of St Giles, Cripplegate, and helped to renovate Newgate prison. He also rebuilt St Michael Paternoster church in the City, where he is buried. Richard Whittington died in March 1423 and was the most charismatic character to leave his mark on the city.

Whittington died a childless widower. He left his entire fortune of £5,000 to the city he loved; that is probably about the equivalent of £5–6 million today. Ironically, one of the trusts he started is still going today, and has provided aid to the poor for over six hundred years. Today it continues to do so, in the guise of providing housing and incomes to over sixty people each year in the county of West Sussex. The trust is still managed by the Mercers Company.

Mary Shelley, Author (1797–1851)

Mary Wollstonecraft Shelley (née Godwin) was born on 30 August 1797 to a very unusual union. Her father was William Godwin, a failed Calvinist minister, but successful historian. Mary's mother, Mary, was a famous feminist who had authored many books including *A vindication of the rights of Women* in 1792 and *The wrongs of Woman*, a novel about emancipation. William Godwin, though an obese spendthrift, was also a successful writer who was famous for writing a political piece called *An enquiry concerning Political Justice* in 1793. Mary Wollstonecraft died ten days after giving birth to Mary of puerperal fever.

Mary Shelley had a very tumultuous childhood; her father was an eccentric man and was usually drunk. Father William had a very learned circle of friends whom Mary used to educate herself. William did remarry, to Mary Jane Clairmont, although Mary and her sister Fanny never really got along with their stepmother, who preferred the company of her own two children. At the age of ten, Mary published her first poem and enjoyed the company of such great writers as Coleridge, Lamb and Hazlitt. In 1812 she met Percy Bysshe Shelley. Mary's father didn't like the friendship of his young daughter with Shelley and so he sent her away to Dundee. Mary continued her relationship with Percy and in 1816 she ran away to Switzerland with him. After a while they settled in France. They married at the end of 1816; Percy Shelley had been married before, but was now a widower. Their first child was born in 1819, but the baby girl died in Venice shortly afterwards. Mary had four children in all with Shelley. Alas only one, a son named Percy Florence, survived.

It is quite ironic that Mary should come up with such a fantastic storyline as *Frankenstein*, because Mary Shelley's life was interspersed with many tragic deaths. The story came at a time of wonderment and achievement in British industrial life. Priestley had just discovered the presence of oxygen in the atmosphere and the element's role in the breathing process. It was already a fact discovered by Galvani, that electricity was produced by the brain to move muscles and a vital element in the process of life itself. Shelley was fascinated with Galvanism after hearing about it at Eton; one of his teachers, James Lind, demonstrated the experiment made by Luigi Galvani on frog's legs. The subject was discussed many times at the Villa Diodati near Geneva, and it was there that on a stormy night in 1818 that Mary came up with the story of *Frankenstein* after a challenge to write a ghost story from Shelley, Lord Byron and step-sister Claire Clairmont.

Mary later wrote in 1831 that she got the idea for the story after a dream she had in which she claimed she saw a body come to life with the aid of a machine, though this version of the conception differed from earlier ones. The story was originally called *Frankenstein or the Modern Prometheus,* and it took her about eighteen months to complete. There have been many films made about the book, but few have really been true to the original story. Robert De Niro played the monster, created by Dr Frankenstein in one very well-made version; the monster ended up at the North Pole which is more like the story which starts with a series of letters written by Robert Walton to his sister. Walton was an Arctic explorer who meets Dr Frankenstein in the polar region. The doctor is in pursuit of the monster and while resting he meets Walton and tells him the story of how he created a man from dead tissue. The book was published in 1819 and was an instant success, probably because of the Victorian fascination with science.

Mary and Percy lived in London for some of their married life, at 24 Chester Square SW1. The house still stands today and is part of the estate owned by the Duke of Westminster. Ex-Prime Minister, Margaret Thatcher, now Baroness Thatcher, lives in a house on the opposite side of the square; some critics of the former P.M. find that coincidence very amusing. Mary had a very successful, though tragic life. Her mother Mary had an illegitimate child named Fanny by a soldier who deserted her and the child. Mary Shelley's father married Mary and took on the child as his own. Fanny was always a troubled child and took her own life with an overdose of laudanum, an extract of the opium plant. Mary never really got over the deaths of both her mother, who she only knew from her writings, and Fanny. As a child Mary was known to spend many hours at her mother's grave reading her books. Percy Bysshe Shelley died in a boating accident in 1822; he drowned just like his first wife. Her friend Lord Byron was killed fighting for the Greeks against the Turks in 1824.

Mary went on to use her influence in the literary world to champion the work of Percy, whom she loved very much. Mary wrote many other stories in her remaining years, but none ever had the impact of *Frankenstein.*

Mary wrote *The Last Man* in 1826, *Percy Warbeck* in 1830, *Lodore* in 1835 and *Falkner* in 1837. Mary also wrote many essays about her travels with her only surviving son Percy Florence and his many friends. She died in her sleep in 1851 at the age of fifty-four.

Dr Samuel Johnson, Writer (1709–84)

Samuel was born to Michael and Sarah (née Ford) Johnson on 18 September 1709 in Lichfield, Staffordshire. Samuel was the first born and later came his brother Nathaniel who died tragically at the age of twenty-five. The house he was born in was only a year old and is now The Samuel Johnson Birthplace Museum. Samuel was a sickly child and suffered with poor hearing and eyesight. He was educated in a local grammar school and later attended Pembroke College at Oxford. Michael Johnson was a bookseller and used part of the family house to run his business, which was not often successful and the family's fortunes waned more than they waxed. While at Oxford, Samuel got the news that finances were bad, and so he left without getting a degree.

After returning from Oxford, Samuel applied for many teaching jobs, but was always turned down. Johnson suffered many ailments in his adult life, symptoms left over from his sickly childhood including dark moods and twitching, thought to be the remnants of scrofula that he got as a youngster. In 1735 He met and married Elizabeth Porter, whom he called Tetty with great affection.

They started their own school in 1736, but a year later closed it owing to a lack of students. Samuel decided to try his luck back in London so he set off with one of his pupils, David Garrick, who later became a famous actor and had a theatre named after him. Soon after arriving in London, Samuel met Edward Cave, the editor of *The Gentleman's Magazine,* and tried his hand at journalism. He also wrote two published poems in 1738 and *The Life of Savage* in 1744. He was also very successful as a political satirist and wrote reports on parliament. In 1746 he was approached by a syndicate of printers to compile an English dictionary and rented 17 Gough Square with his advance after signing a contract. He employed six researchers and scribes for the work which was carried out in the garret. The house today is now the London Museum of Johnson, just off Fleet Street. Johnson was a great figure in the city and especially Fleet Street where he attended the taverns on a daily basis, mostly Ye Olde Cheshire Cheese, which was rebuilt after the great fire of 1666. The chair he sat in and told his stories to the willing listeners is still there in the pub in a glass case; you will notice it only has three legs.

He would tell his audience that he was a believer in exercise and relaxation, for exercise he would walk to the tavern (about 120 yards) and for relaxation he would be carried home. While working on his dictionary he continued to publish poems, and in 1749 he completed *The Vanity of Human Wishes*. In 1750 he published his famous *Rambler and Idler* essays, which he kept going for two years. In 1752 his beloved Tetty died and he took on a Jamaican servant named Francis Barber. Johnson was now the toast of London and entertained such dignitaries as Joshua Reynolds, Edmund Burke, Oliver Goldsmith and his old pupil, the now-famous David Garrick. The group were known as The Club and welcomed everywhere. In 1755 Samuel Johnson published *The English Dictionary* in two volumes and was awarded an honorary M.A. for his literary contributions to the English language by Oxford University.

He didn't publish the first English dictionary as many believe he did. Cawdrey's *Table Alphabeticall* was published in 1604 and had a list of some 3,000 words. Around twelve dictionaries were published by the time Johnson launched his version, with some 43,000 words and expressions. Nathaniel Bailey published his *Universal Etymological Dictionary* in 1721 and that one had thousands more words. The consistency of Johnson's dictionary was not too clever and had many miss-spelt words and contradictions. He described the highest room in a house as a garret and then went onto explain that a cockloft was the room above the garret.

Samuel continued to live the good life and often beyond his means. He was arrested in 1758 for debt over his mother's funeral bills, but quickly wrote his masterpiece *Rasselas* to redeem himself. In 1762 King George III gave him a pension of £300 for life and this secured him until his death. The Scottish lawyer James Boswell also came to know him well and wrote his autobiography which many claim to be the most prolific autobiography ever. In 1773, Johnson and his servant, Francis Barber, spent three months with Boswell touring Scotland, where Johnson insulted the Scots when he exclaimed one day that he 'knew of no reason why anyone would want to visit such a place.' He continued to write as his life ebbed away and in 1765 he wrote his *Annotated Shakespeare*, and *Lives of the Poets* between 1779 and 1781. He coined the phrase 'When a man is tired of London, he is tired of life; for there is in London all that life can afford.' He died peacefully at 7.15 p.m. on 13 December 1785 and Boswell published his book *Boswell's Life of Johnson* in 1791. Today in Gough Square between no.17 and the alleyway by Ye Olde Cheshire Cheese, there stands a bronze statue of his cat with some of his favourite food, oysters.

Sir Christopher Wren, Architect (1632–1723)

Christopher Wren's father, also named Christopher, was a well-educated man and a rector. Having been educated at St John's College, Oxford, he returned to his native Wiltshire and was appointed Rector of Fonthill in 1620. He met his wife, Mary Cox, when she attended church. They married just before he was appointed Rector of East Knoyle, also in Wiltshire, in 1623. Mary was the only heir to Squire Robert Cox of Fonthill, and when he died Mary inherited all his estates and they became extremely rich.

Christopher Wren junior was born on 20 October 1632 in East Knoyle; he already had three sisters, Catherine, Mary and Susan. His mother Mary had lost four children in childbirth. In 1634 Elizabeth was born. The birth was a difficult one and Mary Wren died weeks later, leaving the family without a mother. Wren senior was offered the position of Dean of Windsor which was then held by his own brother, Mathew, who was moving up to the position of Bishop of Hereford. He took up the deanship on 4 April 1635.

Young Christopher's eldest sister Mary brought him up with his father. Christopher Wren had two close friends as a child, his cousin Mathew Wren and Charles, The Prince of Wales, heir to the throne of Charles I. Wren had a private tutor till he was nine years old. Then he attended the Public School of Westminster attached to the abbey. This school is one of the oldest private schools in Europe. Started by the monks in the 1100s, originally called St Peter's college after the first church at Westminster, it was closed by Henry VIII under the Dissolution of the Monasteries in 1534–40. Henry took all the wealth from St Peter's and gave it to the new college of St Paul's; hence the expression, 'robbing Peter to pay Paul'. The school reopened in 1598 on the orders of Elizabeth I. It is still one of the best public schools in the UK.

The school was run at the time by the stern disciplinarian Dr Busby, and Wren was encouraged to pursue his interest in science and the arts as well as Latin. Some of the letters he wrote to his father in Latin survive today.

In 1642 the English Civil War broke out. There had been many civil wars before, but this one was considered the most prolific as the outcome changed the constitution, whereas previous civil wars simply changed the monarchy. The Wren family were staunch royalists and this made it very difficult for them. Christopher was taken out of school after his uncle Mathew Wren, a personal friend of Charles I, was arrested at Ely, the hometown of Oliver Cromwell. Mathew had become the Bishop of Ely by this time; he subsequently spent eighteen years in the Tower of London. The Parliamentary troops fighting against Charles I attacked the Deanery at Windsor, and so the Wren family fled to Bristol.

In 1643 Mary married William Holder who owned the rectory at Bletchingdon, Oxford, and the whole family moved to the safety of the house there. William Holder was a renowned mathematician and taught young Christopher mathematics and the science of astronomy which the young Wren took to like a duck to water. He later returned to Westminster school to finish his studies and left in 1646. He spent three years at Bletchingdon experimenting with sun dials, charting the stars and improving his artistic skills.

Wren found a new fascination when he went to consult Dr Charles Scarburgh, an anatomist, about his failing health. Scarburgh cured Wren and during the treatment he became interested in the study of anatomy. Wren drew illustrated charts to show how the muscles worked and helped Scarburgh on his lecture tours. He also worked and studied under William Oughtred the astrologer, for whom he translated *Oughtred's Mathematical Calculations on Sundials* into Latin.

Christopher Wren eventually went back to school. He entered Wadham College, Oxford, on 25 June 1649 and received a B.A. on 18 March 1651. He went onto Oxford where in 1653 he got his M.A. and was elected a Fellow of All Saints. In the next four years he carried out many experiments in the field of anatomy, and devised a way to transfuse blood. He successfully carried out a transfusion on two dogs and drew illustrated parts of the brain for Thomas Willis' book, *Cerebri Anatome*. He moved from one subject to another and during his few years at Oxford he worked on projects involving measuring devices, navigational instruments, weapons and pumps. It seems his hunger for knowledge knew no bounds. In 1657 he took up the post of Professor of Astronomy at Gresham College in London. He wrote a hypothesis on the planet Saturn and was about to publish it when Huygens published his theory about the rings of the planet. Wren was in awe of Huygens and never published his own paper.

He went back to Oxford in 1661 to take the post of Professor of Astronomy and then in 1662, the Royal Society, which Wren was a founder member, was officially recognised by Charles II who gave it a royal charter. It was in 1663 that Wren got the bug for architecture. He travelled to Rome and Paris and studied the works of the first century BC designer Vitruvius, who built the Theatre of Marcellus. In Paris he studied at the Sorbonne and Les Invalides. It was later said he got his ideas for the domes in his future buildings from Rome.

In 1664 he was asked by Charles II to refurbish St Paul's Cathedral; the building had fallen into decay during the English Civil War (1642–51).

Although the Puritans had won the war they didn't do anything to repair the hundreds of churches they used as garrisons during the nine-year conflict. St Paul's was used to station troops and horses, and after the war it was used to keep animals overnight before they were sold in the nearby Cheapside market. Everything was going well and Wren came up with some new extensions and elaborate masonry designs. Before he could get his plans approved however, fate intervened and decided for them, when the church burnt down during the fire of 1666. After the fire had died down, lots of wannabe architects put elaborate designs before the king to rebuild the city and its many public buildings and churches. Many of these designs were quite unique to the previous layout of Roman and Saxon London, with elaborate piazzas and squares.

Wren was only one of a few designers whose work was short-listed by Charles II. The king liked Wren very much, and commissioned him to design and oversee the building of many other buildings including the Monument, which Wren built as a memorial to the Great Fire. It is 202ft high, which is its distance from the baker's shop where it started. Wren had his first designs for St Paul's rejected for many reasons, mostly because it resembled a Catholic church too much, and also because of the huge cost. He eventually got the king to agree on a design and over the reigns of Charles II, James II, William and Mary, William III and Queen Anne, he eventually managed to build his original design.

Sir Christopher Wren died at the grand age of ninety-one on 25 February 1723 and is buried in St Paul's with a Latin inscription on his huge tomb which ends 'Lector Si Monumentum Circumspice', meaning 'reader if you seek a memorial to me, look around you.' He is accredited with many buildings and institutions both in the UK and America, most of which are still standing today, though some were destroyed during the blitz. Here is a list:

Chapels

Pembroke College Chapel, Cambridge, 1663–5.
Emmanuel College Chapel, Cambridge, 1668–73.
Catholic Chapel, Whitehall Palace, London, 1685–7.

Churches (All within London)

St Christopher-le-Stocks, Threadneedle Street, 1670–1.
St Dunstan in the East, 1670–1.

St Benet Fink, Threadneedle Street, 1670–3.

St Vedast, Foster Lane, 1670–3.

St Dionis Backchurch, Fenchurch Street, 1670–4.

St Michael, Wood Street, 1670–5.

St Mildred, Poultry, 1670–6.

St Olave, Old Jewry, 1670–6.

St Mary-at-Hill, Thames Street, 1670–6.

St Edmund King and Martyr, Lombard Street, 1670–9.

St Mary-le-Bow, Cheapside, 1671–3.

St George, Botoph Lane, 1671–4.

St Magnus Martyr, Lower Thames Street, 1671–6.

St Lawrence, Jewry, 1671–7.

St Bride, Fleet Street, 1671–8.

St Stephen, Walbrook, 1672–9.

St Mary, Aldermanbury, 1677

St Nicholas, Cole Abbey, 1671–7.

St Stephen, Coleman Street, 1674–6.

St Bartholomew, Exchange, 1674–9.

St Paul's Cathedral, 1675–1710.

St Peter Cornhill, 1675–81.

St Michael, Bassishaw, 1676–9.

St James, Garlick Hill, 1676–83.

St James's Church, Piccadilly, 1676–84.

St Michael, Queenhithe, 1676–87.

St Anne and St Agnes, Gresham Street, 1677–80.

St Antholin, Watling Street, 1677–82.

St Benet, Paul's Wharf, 1677–83.

All Hallows the Great, Lombard Street, 1677–83.

St Martin, Ludgate, 1677–84.

All Hallows, Bread Street, 1677–84.

St Swithin, Cannon Street, 1677–85.

Christ Church, Newgate Street, 1677–87.

St Clement Danes, Strand, 1680–2.

St Augustine, Watling Street, 1680–3.

St Mathew, Friday Street, 1681–5.

St Mary, Abchurch, 1681–6.

St Benet, Gracechurch Street, 1681–6.

St Mildred, Bread Street, 1681–7.

St Alban, Wood Street, 1682–5.
St Mary Magdelene, Old Fish Street, 1683–5.
St Clement, Eastcheap, 1683–7.
St Mary Pattens, 1684–7.
St Michael, Crooked Lane, 1684–8.
St Andrew, Holborn, 1684–90.
St Anne's Church, Dean Street, 1685.
St Andrew by the Wardrobe, Westminster, 1685–93.
St Margaret, Lothbury, 1686–90.
St Michael Paternoster Royal, College Hill, 1686–94.
All Hallows, Lombard Street, 1686–94.
St Mary Somerset, Thames Street, 1686–95.
Tower of St Mary Aldermary, Bow Lane, 1702–04.
St Michael, Cornhill, 1715–17.
The Protestant Church, Savoy Palace, 1689.

Court Rooms

The Court House, Windsor, 1688.

Gateways

Tom Tower, Christchurch, Cambridge, 1681–2.
Guard House, Windsor Castle, 1685.

College Halls of Residence

Garden Quadrangle, Trinity College, Oxford, 1668, 1682 and 1728.
Williamson Building, the Queens College, Oxford, 1671–4.

Government Buildings

The Custom House, London, 1669–71.
The Navy Office, Seething Lane, London, 1682–3.

Houses

Tring Manor House, Herts, 1680.
Thoresby House, Notts, 1685–7.
Bridgewater Square Development, London, 1688–93.
Winslow Hall, Bucks, 1699–1702.
Marlborough House, St James, London, 1709–11.

Hospitals

The Royal Hospital, Chelsea, London, 1682–92.
Royal Naval Hospital, Greenwich, London, 1696–1716.

Libraries

Lincoln Cathedral Library, Lincs, 1674–6.
Trinity College Library, Cambridge, 1676–84.

Monuments

The Monument, Fish Hill Street, London, 1671–6.

Observatories and Scientific Buildings

The Royal Observatory, Greenwich, London, 1675–6.
Repository, Royal Society, Crane Court, Fleet Street, London, 1711–12.

Palaces (Wren reconstructed only parts of each of these)

Winchester Palace, Winchester. 1683–85.
Whitehall Palace, London. 1685–87.
Hampton Court Palace, Kent. 1689–94.
Kensington Palace, London. 1689–96.

Schools and Colleges

Upper School, Eton College, Bucks, 1689–91.
Writing School, Christ's Hospital, London, 1692.

St John Moore's School, Appleby, Leics, 1693–7.
College of William and Mary, Williamsburg, Virginia, USA, 1695–6.

Theatres

The Sheldonian Theatre, Oxford, (used for ceremonies only), 1664–9.
Drury Lane Theatre, London, 1672–4.

Beatrix Potter, Author, Illustrator and Farmer (1866–1943)

Beatrix Potter was born on 28 July 1866 in a house on the Old Brompton Road in South Kensington, London; on her birth certificate it gave her name as Helen Beatrix Potter. Kensington was then, and still is, an area where the wealthier Londoners live. Born into a family that existed on two huge family trusts, Beatrix was educated at home and was a studious pupil. Her father, Rupert William Potter, was a barrister at law; his inherited wealth however, allowed him to live the life of an aristocrat and so he rarely practiced law. Instead he spent most of his time doing the rounds of the gentlemen's clubs, gambling and discussing the politics of the day. Her mother, Helen Potter née Leech, was also very privileged, and inherited her family fortune from her cotton mill-owner father. Helen spent her days entertaining visitors and holding meetings of her poetry society. Both parents were very strict and true Victorians. Beatrix spent a fairly isolated childhood in a city she longed to flee from. Her brother Bertram was born when Beatrix was six years old and she was so pleased to have an ally in the house although, sadly, he was usually away at boarding school, and the only time they spent together was on holiday.

She was quite an expert in mycology, the study of fungi; she became interested in fauna and fungi while the family were on their annual trips to the Lake District and Scotland. While in the Lake District on holidays in 1882, the family met and befriended Canon Hardewick Rawnsley who founded the National Trust in 1895. Hardewick and Beatrix became firm allies in their love of the Lake District and the nature that abounded there. It was here that she also got to improve on her other love; drawing. Hardewick Rawnsley became her mentor and would spend hours with Beatrix and Bertram at the village of Wray where they observed, studied and drew the wildlife of the Lake District. At home Beatrix would draw rabbits, squirrels and other wildlife onto hand-made Christmas cards for her friends.

In London Beatrix had a menagerie of animals to find solace in; her Spaniel Spot was her favourite, but she also had a newt, a bat, frogs, ferrets and two rabbits named Benjamin and Peter. Beatrix would spend hours drawing her pets and any plants she brought back from her holidays. She had no intention of becoming a writer, instead she wanted to become a member of the Royal Botanical Society at Kew Gardens. Her uncle, Sir Henry Enfield Roscoe, tried to get her in, but being a woman barred her from membership. She would spend many happy hours drawing at Kew Gardens. Her parents' disapproved of her studies into fungi and, in an effort to thwart her ambitions, they appointed her as the head of the household at the age of eighteen. This meant that most of her time would be taken up with the running of the house. Then, when she reached twenty-one, she would be married off to a wealthy husband. Well that was the plan anyway, but Beatrix was her own woman and had her own plans, which didn't include any of her parents' hopes for the future.

In 1890 she discovered a relationship between fungi and algae in that the algae produced food for the fungi through the transformation of light. Her paper and drawings on the subject of lichens, fungi and algae were presented to the Linnean Society by her uncle Henry. The society eventually recognised Beatrix as an authority on mycology, and she became a well-known figure in natural history circles, often lecturing at the London School of Economics.

On 4 September 1893 she sent a letter from her holiday cottage to the son of her last governess, Annie Moore. The sickly five-year-old Noel loved the story about rabbits living in a garden, and although Annie tried to encourage her to find a publisher, it wasn't until 1901 that Beatrix finally took the plunge. It was Canon Rawnsley who eventually persuaded her to go public with her book. She edited the original story and added black and white drawings to illustrate the story better; it was entitled *The Tale of Peter Rabbit and Mr McGregor's Garden*. It was turned down by six publishers who all commented that it lacked colour drawings, which were the fashion of the day. Not one to be downbeat, Beatrix privately printed 250 copies of the book and hawked them around the bookshops and schools. A fortnight later she printed another 200. In 1902 she went to see the Covent Garden-based publishers Frederick Warne & Co.; they were very impressed and so they signed her up to publish the book. Beatrix insisted however that she was involved in every aspect of the book, so she helped to pick the typeset, design the cover and pick the colours for every drawing. By September of 1902 the book had sold some 20,000 copies and another 30,000 by Christmas. This gave Beatrix a huge income and the independence to leave home. The company of Frederick Warne was started in 1865 by Warne, a former bookseller. He retired and left the company to be run by his three sons Harold, Fruing and Norman. Norman was the youngest and a bachelor when he was assigned as editor to Beatrix. They soon fell in love, but had to keep their relationship a secret from her parents, as they disapproved of people who worked 'in trade'. When they became engaged in 1905 only the Warne family helped them to celebrate the union, Beatrix's parents distanced themselves from the couple and refused to have anything to do with the wedding plans. Tragically, just four weeks later Norman died suddenly of pernicious anaemia, and Harold Warne took over as her editor. Beatrix was heartbroken and wrote a heart-rending letter to his sister Millie telling her of her great sadness, but she finished the letter saying that she would start afresh in 1906.

Now publishing on average two books a year, Beatrix was a wealthy woman in her own right and still single. In 1903 she had bought a field in Near Sawrey, Ambleside, where she would sit and draw while on holiday. In 1905 she bought the first of many farms that would form a huge estate for her. Hill Top farm became her home for the next eight years, and now reconciled with her parents again, she spent her days writing and drawing her books. The farm's day-to-day affairs were run by her farm manager John Cannon. He also advised Beatrix on the other farms, parcels of land and buildings that she bought with her ever-increasing royalties. Beatrix led a lonely existence while working at Hill Top; she never really got over the death of Norman. In 1909 the farm next to Hill Top came up for sale and Beatrix bought it to add to her property portfolio. She moved into Castle Farm House within a few months, and it was here that she created other characters such as Jemima Puddleduck, Samuel Whiskers and Tom Kitten. The gardens and fields were used as backdrops for the drawings.

While building up her property portfolio, Beatrix engaged the services of a Sawrey solicitor named William Heelis. They grew close and in 1913 at the age of forty-seven, Beatrix married him at a ceremony in London. Her parents objected again at her choice, as did the sisters of William, but her parents did attend the ceremony at St Mary Abbot's church, Kensington, on 15 October. The other two witnesses were an old friend of Beatrix, Gertrude M. Woodward, and William's cousin Lelio Stampa. By now Beatrix was a country girl and so they moved into Castle Cottage, a bigger house than the one at Castle Farm, and she continued to write her books. Frederick Warne & Co. continued as her publisher until 1983 when they were bought out by Penguin Books, who still print her books today. Beatrix and William soon became local dignitaries, and she started breeding Herdwick sheep, eventually becoming president of the Herdwick Sheep Breeders' Association.

In 1927 she started a writing relationship with the editor and owner of an American children's book magazine. In her few letters to Martha Mahony Miller she offered to sell autographed drawings to American tourists, the proceeds of which went to save a part of the Lake District. Beatrix also supported a local children's hospital. With William she became a regular figure at rural fairs and often acted as a judge at agricultural shows. However, getting old didn't agree with Beatrix and she upset a lot of people with her constant letters to newspapers, dignitaries and associations. She expressed her concerns about the destruction of the Lake District, the lack of research into sheep diseases and the Second World War. The local children in Sawrey used to call her 'Auld Mother Heelis' as she constantly chastised them.

With her inheritance she bought more land, and at her death on 22 December 1943 at Castle Cottage aged seventy-seven, she owned some 4,000 acres of land, the Sawrey post office, Castle Cottage and fifteen farms. In her will she bequeathed almost her entire estate, including fourteen of the farms, to the National Trust in honour of her friendship with its founder Canon Hardewick Rawnsley, who had encouraged her so much in her early career. Just four years later, in 1947, William died and left the last farm to the National Trust also. The Trust's headquarters are situated in Heelis House in honour of William and Helen Beatrix Heelis née Potter. Beatrix was cremated in Blackpool and her ashes were spread over fields in Sawrey.

From the age of fifteen to thirty, Beatrix kept a secret coded diary in which she recorded her thoughts and feelings. The diary recorded her childhood and adulthood living on the third floor of the family home. It revealed that she rarely saw her parents during the daytime, usually only at tea time and on special occasions and holidays. After brother Bertram was sent off to boarding school, Beatrix had her lessons from governesses and then played with her other 'friends', the animals she bought and smuggled into the house. In 1963 the diary was finally decoded and this part of her life was revealed; it is now kept by the National Trust. After her death some manuscripts were discovered of unpublished stories. Frederick Warne & Co. eventually published the books.

Beatrix Potter's books include:

The Tale of Peter Rabbit (1902)
The Tale of Squirrel Nutkin (1903)
The Tailor of Gloucester (1903)
The Tale of Benjamin Bunny (1904)
The Tale of Two Bad Mice (1904)
The Tale of Mrs Tiggy-Winkle (1905)
The Tale of the Pie and the Patty-Pan (1905)
The Tale of Mr Jeremy Fisher (1906)
The Story of A Fierce Bad Rabbit (1906)
The Story of Miss Moppet (1906)
The Tale of Tom Kitten (1907)
The Tale of Jemima Puddle-Duck (1908)
The Tale of Samuel Whiskers or, The Roly-Poly Pudding (1908)
The Tale of the Flopsy Bunnies (1909)
The Tale of Ginger and Pickles (1909)
The Tale of Mrs Tittlemouse (1910)
The Tale of Timmy Tiptoes (1911)
The Tale of Mr Tod (1912)
The Tale of Pigling Bland (1913)
Appley Dapply's Nursery Rhymes (1917)
The Tale of Johnny Town-Mouse (1918)
Cecily Parsley's Nursery Rhymes (1922)
The Fairy Caravan (1929)
The Tale of Little Pig Robinson (1930)

Samuel Pepys, Diarist and MP (1633–1703)

Samuel Pepys (pronounced Peeps) was born on 23 February 1633 to tailor John Pepys, and butcher's daughter Margaret née Kite, in the rooms above his father's shop in Salisbury Court off Fleet Street, London. The Pepys family were well connected with uncles in parliament and the clergy. Samuel was baptised in St Bride's church on 3 March; early baptisms were common in his day with child mortality rates high in London. He was the fifth child of eleven, but within a few years he was the eldest of only four surviving children. He attended some prestigious schools to obtain his education; these included Huntingdon Grammar School, then St Paul's School in London where he studied from 1646–50. Then he was given a

Mercer Company grant to attend Cambridge University. Here he studied for his degree which he was granted in 1654. After leaving Cambridge he went to live with one of his father's cousins, Sir Edward Montagu. Edward would later be granted the first Earldom of Sandwich for his part in the restoration of Charles II to the English throne in 1660.

While he was at St Paul's School he was a witness to one of England's most infamous events, the execution of Charles I at 2.00 p.m. on 30 January 1649. The fifteen-year-old Pepys later recorded in his now famous diary that 'the execution was met with such a groan as I have never heard before, and desire I shall ne'er hear again.' At noon on 13 October 1660 he also witnessed the execution of two men who formed the fifty-strong regicides who signed the king's death warrant. They were Major General Harrison and the Revd Hugh Peters; both men were hung, drawn and quartered at the junction of Whitehall and Hungerford Square (now Trafalgar Square) at the point where the Charing Cross once stood. He also later wrote in his diary that 'the general was looking as cheerful as any man could be in that condition.' It is statements such as these and other observations made during his life time, that help historians to get a real feel of what life in the past was really about.

While staying with the Montagu family, Pepys met, fell in love with and married Elisabeth Marchant de St Michel. Elisabeth was the daughter of French Huguenots, and so the ceremony was held on 10 October 1655 in secret as religious ceremonies were deemed illegal by the Puritan Commonwealth Government who ruled the country after the death of Charles I. They also married in a civil ceremony on 1 December that year at St Margaret's Church, Westminster. They used to always celebrate their anniversary in October.

In 1657, after trying to father children unsuccessfully, Pepys decided to get a permanent cure for his constant kidney stone problem. He had suffered from them from an early age and they often gave him so much pain that he found sex awkward. He sought the help of Thomas Hollier, a renowned surgeon. The operation took place in March 1658 at the house of his cousin, Jane Turner. The operation was not for the faint at heart and was a life-or-death decision for him. With no antiseptic or anaesthetic and with Pepys constrained to the bed with ropes, the doctor placed pincers into him through an incision made between his scrotum and anus, this was directed to the stone with the help of a probe which was pushed into his bladder through his penis. The operation, which was done while Pepys was heavily drunk with brandy, was a complete success, and the stone was said to have been the size of a real tennis ball. He recovered within two months, but was constantly bedridden thereafter when the wound would burst open and infect his bladder. He still produced kidney stones his whole life.

In June 1658 Pepys was introduced to George Downing who was a teller at the Exchequer. Downing was being primed to become an ambassador at The Hague in Holland, so he took Pepys on as a clerk and taught him the job. Later that year Downing was appointed to The Hague as a mediator, and to report on the exiled Charles II in France. Pepys earned £50 a year at the Exchequer and this allowed him to move into a house in Axe Yard off King Street, Westminster. Through the huge influence he had in government circles, mainly by way of Sir Edward Montagu who was a first cousin once removed, Pepys quickly moved through the ranks of prestigious government departments. On New Year's Day 1660 he started the diary that made him famous in history. On 23 March 1660 he was promoted to the post of secretary to Montagu and on the 30 March they set sail on a ship to Holland called *The Naseby* which was part of a fleet. The ship's name was changed on the return journey to *The Charles*; they were on their way to collect the exiled King Charles II and bring him back to England to be restored to the throne. Sir Edward Montagu trusted few men to complete the trip. For his loyalty Pepys was rewarded in June that year with a high-ranking job in the Admiralty.

He couldn't take the job straight away as there were a few problems with his lack of knowledge of naval procedures. General Monk and Thomas Barlow were particular in their objection to Pepys getting the job. Thomas Barlow was appointed as Clerk to the Acts in 1638 and was paid off by Pepys at the rate of 100s per year, but he died in February 1664 so Pepys only had to pay it for three years. General Monk was trying to procure the job for a Mr Turner in the navy office, but Montagu's influence overawed that of Monk and eventually Pepys took the office of Clerk to the Acts later that year. The position gave Pepys a ranking in the navy that equalled that of the navy commissioners, and a salary of £350 a year which gave him the means to live the high life.

The diary records that on 18 July 1660 he went to live in a naval department apartment in Seething Lane near Crutched Friars in the City of London. Here he learned with a private tutor the multiplication tables so he could do his job properly. On 24 July 1660, Pepys was sworn in as Sir Edward Montagu's (now the Earl of Sandwich) deputy for a Clerkship of the Privy Seal. This office, which he didn't think much of at first, brought him an extra salary of £3 a day. In June 1660, he was made a Master of Arts by proxy, and soon afterwards he was sworn in as a justice of the Peace for Middlesex, Essex, Kent and Hampshire, the counties in which the main naval dockyards were situated. He was now so highly regarded by Charles II that he even attended the coronation and the king's wedding to the Portuguese Princess Catherine of Braganza. In fact his influence at court went even further when Britain was given Tangier in Africa as a colony. The gift was presented to Charles II by Catherine's father, and Pepys was elected to a committee to oversee the colony's affairs.

The now famous diary was kept by Pepys only for nine years between 1660 and 1669. In it he recorded many historical events that he personally witnessed; the execution of Charles I, the restoration of Charles II, the second Dutch wars in 1664, the plague of 1665–6, the Great Fire of London in 1666. He also recorded his many affairs with other women, his work at the naval office, his love of music which he also wrote and many observations of life in the taverns and streets of London. The diary was, however, written not for publication, but rather for his own amusement. He wrote it in a shorthand method invented by Thomas Shelton and called tachygraphy. The diary remained hidden for many decades and after being discovered among his library collection, the Revd John Smith attempted to decode them in 1819. Three years later he was still at it and the translation was proving a difficult task. The key to the coded notes was found among his library collection and a second translation was published in 1875 by Mynors Bright over the next four years. Between 1893 and 1899 Henry B. Wheatley published another version; this in turn was revised in 1926. The latest edition is a complete works by Robert Latham and William Mathews and was done between the years 1970 and 1983.

One of the most puzzling questions asked about the diary is why he only wrote it over a nine-year period. It seems that he was losing his sight around 1669 and after that gave up writing; he now used clerks at the naval department to write from his dictation, and as the diary was a secret he could no longer carry it on without revealing its existence. His doctors recommended that he take a long holiday from his many offices, so he and Elisabeth went on a European tour. While in Holland, Elisabeth became ill. She died a month after their return. Pepys was devastated at the loss of his wife on 10 November at their apartment in Crutched Friars. He celebrated her life with a bust in the chapel of St Olav's Church in Hart Street in the City of London.

From 1669 to his death in 1703, Pepys went from favour to disfavour in his political and personal life. In 1669 Pepys made a speech to the House of Commons and it was so well-received that the Duke of York and many MPs persuaded him to stand for parliament. He was given the opportunity to stand for election when Sir Robert Brooke died, causing a by-election to take place, and so Pepys was put up to become the MP for Aldeburgh in Suffolk. However, the untimely death of Elisabeth made him forlorn and he lost the election to John Bruce. In November 1673 he was elected as the member for Castle Rising in Norfolk; however that victory was marred with an accusation of corruption by Mr Offely, his opponent in the election. The Committee of Privileges voided the return, the house discussed the matter a month later and they ran out of time, so no vote was taken and Pepys was returned to the seat. During the inquiry a search was taken of his London house, and it was alleged that a crucifix was found. In Protestant England this was a serious offence and he was accused of being a Papist. The allegation however was eventually dropped, but he was made aware that he had made some powerful enemies in parliament. He was made an Elder Brother of Trinity House at the same time as being promoted to the office of Secretary to the Admiralty Commission. In 1676 he became a Master of Trinity House.

In 1679 Pepys changed his election campaign to become the Member of Parliament for Harwich in Essex; he won the election jointly with a local Alderman named Sir Anthony Deane. The victory celebrations were short lived when both men were arrested in May for treason, and thrown into the Tower of London. Pepys' friendship with the Catholic sympathiser the Duke of York didn't help his cause. After a lengthy inquiry into the accusations of passing naval documents onto the French, the pair were released in July. They were eventually exonerated in June 1680. Later that year a former butler of Pepys confessed on his death bed that he had faked evidence of Pepys' Papist sympathies for one of his accusers, Sir William Harbord, MP for Thetford. At the next session of Parliament both Pepys and Deane were voted out of office and Pepys concentrated on his naval duties. He travelled to Tangier in 1683 to be part of the committee sent to oversee the evacuation and abandonment of the colony; he then spent six months travelling back through Spain and France.

In 1684 he was once again in favour and Charles II appointed him as the King's Secretary for the Affairs of the Admiralty. However, the king died in February 1685, but he retained the post under James II whom he was also a favourite of. He was also re-elected as a Member of Parliament for Harwich. He was elected at first as the MP for Sandwich in Kent, but he was again challenged and changed his allegiance to Harwich with the voters' approval. He served as a Member of Parliament for three years, then disaster struck again when James II fled England for France in the Year of the Glorious Revolution. James had angered the country when he had his son christened in a Catholic ceremony and was ousted from the throne. The Dutch King, William of Orange and his English queen, Mary the daughter of James II, were invited by Parliament to take the throne on the pretext of ensuring the state remained Protestant. Pepys was now out of favour again and decided to retire from public life.

Samuel Pepys isn't well known for his patronage of the arts, but he was as committed to the arts as to his public and governmental positions. When he retired he threw himself into writing more ballads, playing music and working on behalf of the Royal Society. During his lifetime he met and worked with many historic figures including Admiral Sir William Penn, the father of the founder of Pennsylvania and Sir Isaac Newton. During his early years with Elisabeth they both learned to play the flageolet and to dance, so he was always well-received at political and social events. He was imprisoned in the Tower of London once more in 1689 and 1690, accused of being a Jacobite supporter. His former friendship with the exiled James II constantly became a means of revenge for enemies of old. Samuel Pepys eventually moved out of London to the then village of Clapham; he lived as a permanent guest of an old ally named Will Hewer. He died on 26 May 1703 aged seventy, which was rare for anyone in those days. In letters written by witnesses to his death it is recorded that he suffered in agony for almost two days. The cause of the pain were the kidney stones which had blighted him all his life; seven conjoined stones weighing 4½oz were later removed from him. He is buried next to his beloved Elisabeth, even though he had an affair for many years after her death with another woman.

Pepys' will contained very specific details of his wishes; all his estate was bequeathed to his nephew John Jackson, on the condition that after his death the Pepys collection of books, drawings, documents and other important works be given to Magdalene College, Cambridge. Today the college still has the full library intact. It is regarded as one of the most important collections in English history.

Nell Gwyn, Actress and Royal Mistress (1650–87)

Eleanor 'Nell' Gwyn (sometimes spelt Gwynne) was born in Oxford. Her father, Thomas Gwyn, was a captain in the Royalist Army and came from Hereford. His father was Dr Edward Gwyn, a Canon at Christ Church, Oxford. Thomas's wife and Nell's mother was Eleanor Gwyn née Smith; they met at a bawdy house while he was serving in the army and was stationed in London. In 1644 Eleanor fell pregnant with their first child, Rose. The Civil War was going on and Thomas, being a Royalist soldier, was sent north; for protection he sent Eleanor and Rose to stay with his father in Oxford. Eleanor then fell pregnant again by Thomas, and on 2 September 1650 she gave birth to another girl who they named Eleanor. To stop any confusion with mother and child, everyone called young Eleanor 'Nell'. In 1651 Captain Thomas Gwyn retired from army life and the family moved to his home town of Hereford; he was ruined by the Civil War and took a job in a tavern in Pipewell Lane.

In 1655 Eleanor left Thomas and headed to the bright lights of London. Being a London-born girl she had a few contacts in the city. Thomas had become a drunken wife beater, who died in gaol of T.B. sometime around 1667. Eleanor and the girls lived in a slum in Coal Yard Alley near Covent Garden. At first, times were hard for them and Eleanor worked as a barmaid in the Rose Tavern in Covent Garden. Eleanor soon found better paid work looking after the girls in a nearby brothel; she became known locally as 'Old Madame Gwyn'. Nell and her sister helped out by serving drinks to the girls and customers. It is believed that at the age of twelve Nell became a child prostitute working the bawdy houses of sleazy Covent Garden. Eleanor Gwyn got drunk one night in July 1679 while visiting an old friend in Chelsea and on their way back from a tavern she fell into a pond and drowned.

It was in one of the Covent Garden houses of ill repute that the teenage Nell met a Guards Officer named Robert Duncan; she became his lover and for around two years he kept her. Duncan was married and kept her in a room at the Maypole Tavern in Maypole Alley. After dumping her in 1665 he got her a job working at The Theatre nearby. The theatre was owned by Thomas Killigrew who was granted a licence to form The King's Company and put on plays by Charles II. It was called The Theatre and was originally in Brydges Street. Today it is The Theatre Royal, Drury Lane. Killigrew had a mistress named Mary Meggs who was a former prostitute and friend of

Madame Gwyn. She was granted the rights to vend oranges, sweetmeats and fruit to theatregoers, and she in turn employed Nell and her sister Rose as a favour to Duncan and the girls' mother.

During the intervals in the plays the orange girls would also act as messengers for gentlemen who fancied ladies in the audience, and on the stage. Nell often pimped herself to men who bought her wares. She would often come into contact with high-ranking politicians and, indeed, the king himself. Charles II had thirteen mistresses during his reign and fathered many children, although his wife Catherine miscarried and never gave birth.

The job of selling her wares at the theatre enabled Nell to develop a repertoire, and this in turn made her a favourite of the theatregoers. It wasn't long before she was noticed by playwrights as a potential actress. Up until now only men were permitted to act on the stage with boys often dressed as women to play female parts. The restoration of Charles II encouraged women to become part of theatre life, and Nell was a natural. When she was fifteen, Nell was quite taken with an actor named Charles Hart. They became lovers and Hart taught her to act and memorise her lines; she was illiterate and never learned to read or write. An actor/choreographer named John Lacy taught Nell how to dance and, although it was rumoured by the theatregoing press, they were never lovers. Nell was never a great actress and just enjoyed the limelight; it was a sort of P.R. exercise to her. The first part she played went down well with the critics, she played the part of Cydaria, the daughter of Montezuma in the John Dryden play *The Indian Emperor*. Cydaria was the lover of Cortez who was played by her real life lover, Charles Hart.

With Charles Hart, Nell made a name for herself in comedies; the couple soon became the toast of London. Samuel Pepys even wrote about her calling her 'pretty, witty Nell' when he saw her perform in the comedy *The Gay Couple* alongside Hart. Later that year The King's Company of actors followed the royal household to Oxford; the plague had struck London again, and anyone who was important left the city for the safety of the countryside. The company often put on plays for the royals and it was here that she probably came close to Charles II. In 1667 Nell was once again performing in the comedy *The Gay Couple* when she caught the eye of Lord Buckhurst. Now a lovely, but still developing, young woman she moved uptown in her choice of lovers. She left Hart to stew in a post-fire London, while she went on holiday with Buckhurst to his estate in Epsom. Buckhurst's name was Charles Sackville and he was a very well-known aristocrat, with huge influence at court. Pepys recorded the affair and especially that Nell was now his kept mistress. However, the affair was short-lived and Nell was soon back in the arms of Hart and acting again.

Nell was doing well in her life as an actress, and was a firm favourite of Charles II. In 1668, Moll Davis, who was the king's principle mistress, was swept aside and Nell became his number one girl. She fell pregnant in 1669 and gave birth on 8 May 1670 to a son by Charles; they named him Charles Beauclerk. By now Nell was living off the king with a £4,000 a year annuity. She gave up the stage and the next year she moved into 79 Pall Mall. The house was just a stone's throw from St James' Palace; the official palace of the king. The house was on a lease and Nell complained to Charles that she had no security for her or their child.

On Christmas Day 1671 she gave birth to their second child, James Beauclerk. Nell complained again to Charles that Charles Jr had no title, as he should have. Only after she started calling him a bastard did the king relent and give him two titles, that of the Earl of Burford and Baron Hedington. James was also given a title as Lord Beauclerk. The king also finally conveyed the house as a freehold to Nell on 21 December 1676. The property passed to Charles who sold it in 1693; it is still the only property in Pall Mall that isn't owned by the royal estate. Nell continued to receive property deeds from Charles for years to come, mainly as a means of providing his children with an annuity. Other properties included Burford House which he had built specially for her within the grounds of the Home Park in Windsor. Nell stayed there when the king was at Windsor Castle; previously she stayed at a house in Church Street, Windsor. She also got the use of a house on the King's Cross Road. The house is long gone now, but a stone from the original was placed in the wall of the present building; it is a theatrical mask and represents Nell as an actress.

James Beauclerk was sent off to school in France when he was just six years old; he died in Paris of septicaemia after a gash on his leg turned septic in 1681, aged just ten years old. On 5 January 1684, King Charles II granted another title to Charles Beauclerk, his son and heir. He became The Earl of St Albans, the title came with an annuity of £1,000 a year. Other offices of Chief Ranger of Enfield Chase and Master of the Hawks also provided further income. The boy would never be king, but he could now live like one.

Nell had much respect in London, but she was forever in debt, and Charles would often settle these for her out of the secret service funds. However, Charles II died on 6 February 1685 and this left Nell heavily in debt. Without her royal protection she would end up in gaol or have to sell her properties to